Critical Issues in Curriculum
John Willinksy, Series Editor

Children's Minds, Talking Rabbits, and Clockwork Oranges:
Essays on Education
KIERAN EGAN

Feminist Teaching in Theory and Practice:
Situating Power and Knowledge in Poststructural Classrooms
BECKY ROPERS-HUILMAN

Gender In/forms Curriculum:
From Enrichment to Transformation
JANE GASKELL and JOHN WILLINSKY, Editors

Narrative in Teaching, Learning, and Research
HUNTER McEWAN and KIERAN EGAN, Editors

Sexuality and the Curriculum:
The Politics and Practices of Sexuality Education
JAMES T. SEARS, Editor

Understanding Curriculum as Phenomenological
and Deconstructed Text
WILLIAM F. PINAR and WILLIAM M. REYNOLDS, Editors

Reading and Writing the Self:
Autobiography in Education and the Curriculum
ROBERT J. GRAHAM

Children's Minds
Talking
Rabbits
&
Clockwork
Oranges

Essays on Education

Kieran Egan
Foreword by Elliot W. Eisner

Teachers College · Columbia University
New York and London

Published by Teachers College Press, 1234 Amsterdam Avenue, New York, NY 10027

Library of Congress Cataloging-in-Publication Data

Egan, Kieran.
    Children's minds, talking rabbits, and clockwork oranges :
essays on education / Kieran Egan.
        p. cm. — (Critical issues in curriculum)
    Includes bibliographical references (p.   ) and index.
    ISBN 0-8077-3808-5 (cloth : alk. paper)
    ISBN 0-8077-3807-7 (pbk. : alk. paper)
    1. Education—Aims and objectives. 2. Cognition in children.
3. Learning, Psychology of. 4. Curriculum planning. I. Title.
II. Series.
LB41.E382 1999
370.11—dc21   98-37458

ISBN 0-8077-3807-7 (paper)
ISBN 0-8077-3808-5 (cloth)

Printed on acid-free paper

Manufactured in the United States of America

05 04 03 02 01 00 99   8 7 6 5 4 3 2 1

Contents

Acknowledgments

John Willinsky, editor of the series in which this book appears, suggested this collection and made some recommendations for articles that might be included, so it seems only fair that he should shoulder some of the blame. I am most grateful for his help and good humor in nudging the project along.

It was with some trepidation that I approached Elliot Eisner for a Foreword to the book. I was only too aware of the time I was begging from a very active scholar. He was most gracious and kindly wrote the Foreword that I am proud to be able to include at the front of the book.

During the composition of the manuscript I have been the grateful recipient of a grant from the Social Sciences and Humanitites Council of Canada. The grant has enabled me to have the help of a number of graduate students in preparing the manuscript. Avril Chalmers, David Beckstead, and Jennifer Jenson, currently Ph.D. students at Simon Fraser University, have helped improve the book, and I am grateful for their hilarious help.

Foreword
Elliot W. Eisner

Kieran Egan's *Children's Minds, Talking Rabbits, and Clockwork Oranges: Essays on Education* is a collection of erudite essays that address a number of important themes bearing on educational theory and practice. Let me recite six of them here: First, schools, being an instrument of our culture, reflect a logocentric conception of mind. Second, theories of development have been predicated on a cultural conception of mind that renders those theories both inadequate and misleading with respect to the work of education. Third, the character of mind, what education has a responsibility to foster, is impacted by what might be regarded as the technologies of mind that are made available to the young. Fourth, assumptions that curriculum-planning practices should proceed from now to then, from here to there, misunderstand what children are able and like to do: The unfamiliar may be much more stimulating than what is immediately at hand. Fifth, imagination is the apotheosis of reason, not a diversion from the real business of thinking. Sixth, knowledge is not a thing, a "shippable" commodity, but a living process that occurs within the human mind. Books and other codified symbol systems are its prompts.

Forewords are not locations within which to provide a highly distilled abstract of the work that readers are to encounter, yet it seems appropriate to comment on the foregoing themes for they are central to the elegant analyses that Kieran Egan has provided in the body of the text.

Consider the first. We tend to think about theories, especially scientifically grounded theories, as being ideologically neutral descriptors of reality. After all, science is predicated on something called objectivity and theories are intended by their makers to describe the world the way it is. Yet increasingly, as Kieran Egan and others before him have pointed out, the very language one uses to conceptualize and theorize about the world not only establishes descriptive parameters but expresses values concerning what is important. One object of attention in Egan's book is the work of Jean Piaget. Piaget, by his own definition a genetic epistemologist, is interested in describing the unfolding of human intellectual capacity, marking its course, and, in effect, providing parameters to those in education who would seek to influence its development. Yet some of the assumptions that Piaget makes concerning differences in the cognitive stages that he identifies are, as Egan has shown, problematic at best. What we take to be as an ineluctable unfolding of the human capacity to know—a genetic epistemology—may be largely a function of how tasks used to evoke responses from the young have been couched, and how children use prior experience in conceptualizing the tasks put before them. These factors raise questions about the role of experience in influencing how Piaget's tasks are addressed. Furthermore, the hierarchy that Piaget provides in his work—from concrete operations to formal ones—conveys an inherent conviction that a scientific form of rationality represents the pinnacle of human cognitive achievement; we will have none of that artsy stuff in a Piagetian conception.

The implications—indeed the power—of Piaget's views concerning what counts as up in cognitive development can hardly be underestimated. Yet clearly there are many, many forms of thinking and acting that require complex forms of reasoning that are neither captured by Piaget's schema nor locatable in his stage theory of cognitive development. By calling attention to some of the logical difficulties in Piaget's theories, Kieran Egan helps us acknowledge other aspects of our cognitive selves that could be important candidates for educational development. In this sense, a more generous conception of mind offers educators a more generous array of educational goals to address. In an age in which so many people ring their hands about the inadequacies of schools, concerns that typically tend to result in constraining programs even further, attention to a more generous conception of mind is to be welcomed. Kieran Egan provides such a conception in his book.

Another theme that runs through the chapters of this book pertains to what might be regarded as "technologies of mind." One of the important contributions of culture to human cognition is that culture makes available to the young through acculturation and through an instrument called "the curriculum," an array of symbolic forms or forms of representation that students learn to use. These forms of representation become instruments through which thought processes are played out. Humans, clearly, have the capacity to visualize as well as to articulate. And humans have developed the technologies to depict as well as to describe. The technologies of mind that are available in the culture have epistemic functions. That is, each form of representation addresses the world in different ways and each has the capacity to disclose aspects of that world that are special to both the world and the forms used to describe it. The implications of such a view of cognition, that is, its dependency on the forms of representation an individual learns to use, which in turn are influenced by what is made available to him or her, are not without consequence. The curriculum, it can be said, is at base a mind-altering device and the ways in which mind is altered through the curriculum is through the provision of content that is appropriated and processed by children and adolescents: Children learn to think about aspects of the world that may have never dawned on them prior to being exposed to an array of ideas that come from elsewhere. The concepts of electrons and atoms, for example, are not likely to be invented by 12-year-olds.

But there is another way in which forms of representation influence the ways in which children think and that has to do with their relevance for the processes that will be employed. To think musically is to think with and through patterned sound having expressive properties. To think logically is to impose on the structure of thought a set of criteria that statements must meet. To think mathematically requires one to create visions in which quantitative relationships are displayed and managed. To think historically is to be able to put pieces and episodes together to form a narrative that can be retold and that reveals what is important to know about the past. Each form of representation not only reveals, it also conceals. And Kieran Egan is quick to point out that our theoretical conceptions of what matters regarding educational development is made manifest in the opportunities to learn that schools make possible.

A third theme addressed in the book challenges the widely held idea, particularly in the field of the social studies, that the way to proceed is through an expanding-horizons concept: first one starts with the self, then the family, then the neighborhood, then the state, then the nation, then the world. As intuitively appealing as this conception is, Egan points out that youngsters are interested in things that are very far from what they know firsthand: dinosaurs, Mars, "the torture instruments of the middle ages." In other words, it is faulty to assume that youngsters do not have the capacity to understand and find interest in ideas and practices that are not already in their midst. It is precisely the capacities of very young children to exercise their imagination that should be sustained rather than diminished in school. One of the great tragedies of many educational systems is their penchant for cultivating a logocentric conception of mind that diminishes the imaginative and romantic side of human nature. Egan calls for a resortation of attention to this aspect of the human condition. I couldn't agree more.

Imagination has been associated with the frivolous, with fantasy, with the less important, indeed with the process of play and, as we all "know," play is the opposite of work. In a society with deeply seeded Calvinist roots, play and imagination are at best questionable and at worst a distraction from what really matters.

When imagination is seen as reflecting reason functioning at its best moments, a fresh conception of what the development of mind entails is made visible. A culture whose inhabitants are afraid to imagine are unlikely to be much good at the creation of literature, at the making of art, at the doing of science, in fact, at doing virtually anything well. Herbert Read, the English poet, philosopher, and passivist, argues in his work that art is based on the principle of origination and the practice of perception. Read means that art depends on the individual's ability to conceptualize, that is, to imagine possibilities worth pursuing, and has a sensitivity to form that makes it possible for the contents of imagination to be realized through the forms the individual makes. This conception for Read is as applicable to fields like physics and mathematics as it is to painting and music. The aim of education, says Read, is the creation of artists, individuals who are able to make things well. I think that Kieran Egan would agree.

A final theme that I wish to comment on pertains to Egan's conception of knowledge. As I have already indicated, knowledge is not an object, it is a process. It is not a noun, it is a verb. It is not something that one discovers and ships to the four corners to the earth. Knowledge is something that leads a life of change in the context of the human mind. What we know we can forget, what we have learned we can change, what we come to understand we can share, but only insofar as the individuals to whom we speak or act or display what we have come to understand are able to participate and use in meaningful ways what we give them. As I said earlier, what we can do is to provide prompts. As John Dewey once pointed out, the best that we can do as teachers is to shape the environment in ways that increase the probability that the material and conditions the individual will address will have productive intellectual consequences.

In the end, what Kieran Egan's book is about is the promulgation of an expanded conception of human capability and a more diverse, multifaceted view of what it means to know. Educators in North America—and social scientists as well—will benefit from his observations. There is so much in our society that pushes us toward a narrowing view of the mission of schooling. Our blinkered vision of what counts and our anxiety about test performance reduce our aims, ironically, while we speak of becoming more rigorous, having higher standards, being tougher about the consequences of not doing well in school. Kieran Egan's view is a humane one. It is also one that is extremely challenging. Whether the values he embraces are achievable in a meritocratic society remains to be seen. In any case, the chapters on the pages that follow enumerate a generous and attractive vision. That itself is an important achievement.

Elliot W. Eisner
Stanford University

Introduction

I thought that selecting 10 or a dozen articles from the bundle I had written would be easy. I'd pick the best ones, put them in some more or less coherent order, and ship the manuscript off to the publisher. It hasn't proved so simple. My first assumption, that I had written about a hundred articles, while in some literal sense true, broke down as I realized that I had really written about 5 articles 20 times each, or perhaps 10 articles 10 times each. Even if this exaggerates a bit, it was interesting to discover the frequency of overlapping themes and topics. Such overlapping has made it difficult simply to select what seem to me the most interesting essays. It has been necessary to look also for pieces that are distinct from each other and then do a fair amount of trimming of repetition. Even so, there remain some overlaps where I thought it better to leave in some repetition in order to preserve the coherence of a piece.

Normally in an Introduction the author lays out the book's contents and themes. But this has been done so ably in Elliot Eisner's Foreword that I am saved from doing what would undoubtedly have been a less concise and clear job.

I should perhaps give some account of the book's rather odd title. When I began to think of the collection I started a file of notes about what articles might be selected. I scribbled "Children's Minds, Talking Middle-Class Rabbits, and Clockwork Oranges" on it, catching what at first blush seemed like the range of topics I would be dealing with. As time went by I found myself increasingly unable to think of it as anything else—though I excised the "Middle-Class" descriptor from the rabbits. And as no one in the process suggested that this is really an impossible title, here it is.

The "Children's Minds" part is fairly straightforward, and represents some kind of homage to Margaret Donaldson's book of that title—a book I have long admired and one that certainly influenced my thinking. Much of my work has been focused on children's thinking and how it is similar to and different from adults'. I want "children" here to refer also to adolescents—whose thinking I will also consider in what follows.

"Talking Rabbits" refers to features of children's thinking that seem to me to have been too much neglected in much previous theorizing and research. I have been interested in the nature and character of children's fantasy and their imaginative lives. It is the energy and creativity focused on characters and conditions unlike anything in their everyday environments that seem among the most engaging features of their thinking, and the ones least easily dealt with by the dominant conceptions of children's minds and their development that have influenced curricula.

"Clockwork Oranges" borrows Anthony Burgess's book title and refers to the confusion that inevitably follows when we treat organic things as though they are mechanical. I think there has been a fair amount of this in educational research, and the final section tries to indicate a few areas where education has suffered from this defect.

Children's Minds

CHAPTER 1

Literacy and the
Oral Foundations of Education

I wrote this essay in 1986 during a sabbatical in England. We lived on the top floor of the romantic-sounding Walnut Tree House in the village of Old Marston just outside Oxford. The splendid house was owned by the widow of the famous philosopher John Austin. Indeed, the essay was written at Austin's old desk, though I fear his precision and brilliance did not seep up adequately into my pages. The essay became, in revised form, a part of Primary Understanding *(New York: Routledge, 1988) which, happily for me, won the 1991 Grawemeyer Award in Education. It brought together work I had done, long, long ago, for my Ph.D. on the development of history from myth even longer ago in the eastern Mediterranean, with research I had been doing on literacy, and tried to show up the impoverished sense of children's thinking evident in much educational writing and curricula. I tried in this essay to provide a somewhat new kind of argument in favor of recognizing the greater complexity, abstractness, and general sophistication of children's thinking than seemed to be (and still seems to be) generally acknowledged. I wanted to emphasize particularly that children's thinking is not merely some embryonic and simple form of adults' thinking but has distinctive characteristics of its own—some of which are clearly superior to typical adults' thinking. Until this is recognized, I argue here and in other places in this book, our teaching and curricula for children will be far from ideal and in some ways dysfunctional. The essay was first published in the* Harvard Educational Review *in November 1987 (Vol. 57, No. 4), and I am grateful for permission to reprint it here.*

INTRODUCTION

We have inherited from the ancient Greeks a deeply etched distinction between rational and irrational thinking. The word they commonly used for "reason" was *logos*, which was also the term used for "word" or "speech." For the Greeks of the Platonic tradition, then, taking a rational view enabled one to give an articulate account of something: "We have a rational grasp of something when we can *articulate* it; that means, distinguish and lay out different features of the matter in perspicuous order"

(Taylor, 1982, p. 90). Rationality entails trying to perceive things as they are, despite our hopes, fears, or intentions regarding them. One may achieve such a view by *theoria* (sight, speculation, contemplation): Theoretical understanding results from taking a disengaged perspective. Only the knowledge that results from this kind of intellectual activity, Plato argued in *Timeus* and *The Republic,* is true knowledge. The manner in which Plato distinguished rational thinking and its product—true knowledge (*episteme*)—from irrational thinking and its various products—confusion, superficial plausibility, mere opinion (*doxa*)—involved setting up a number of enduring conceptual associations. Among these associated ideas, and of particular interest in this article, was that of adulthood with the attainment of *episteme* and childhood with *doxa*. This rational theoretic understanding, Plato and his pupil Aristotle argued, gives a superior view of reality. Those who violate the basic standards of the articulation of this theoretical understanding are, in this view, irrational, and they fail to articulate what is real and true.

With the "rediscovery" of classical Greece by 19th-century European scholars, and the growing sense of Greece's cultural superiority over the classical Roman models that had dominated European intellectual and artistic life during the previous century, the distinction between rational and irrational thinking began a new career. It proved a convenient tool for dismissing from serious comparison with Western science and rationality those forms of "primitive" thought that expanding colonial empires, early anthropological studies, and travelers' tales were bringing increasingly to the attention of Europeans and North Americans (Jenkyns, 1980; Turner, 1981).

When combined later in the century with the extensions of evolutionary theory, the distinction between "rational" and "irrational" thinking helped to generate theories about the development of human societies from irrational beginnings to the refined rationality of contemporary Western intellectual life. Frazer (1900), for example, argued that human thought always passes through a magical stage, to a religious stage, and finally to a rational-scientific stage. In the 20th century this distinction entered into everyday language, finding varied, more-or-less casual, use in terms of approval or disparagement. At the same time, in the scholarly world, the distinction has come increasingly into question. Anthropologists such as E. E. Evans-Pritchard (1937), for example, have argued the rationality of witchcraft in particular cultural settings, and classicists such as E. R. Dodds (1951) have pointed to the irrationality of significant features of Greek life and thought. Vexed and problematic though the distinction is, it remains deeply embedded in Western cultural history and habits of thought (Hollis & Lukes, 1982; Putnam, 1981; Wilson, 1970).

The mental life of children has commonly been represented in terms influenced by this rational/irrational distinction. Children are assumed to begin life in irrational confusion and ignorance, and education is regarded as the process of inculcating both rationality and knowledge. In his allegory of the cave in *The Republic*, Plato (trans. 1941) likens the process of education to unchaining prisoners in a dark cave; while chained, they can see on the cave wall only flickering shadows of what is happening in front of a fire further up the cave, and, when released, they are led up the cave to see the reality of which earlier they had seen only distorted shadows. Similarly, Christian ideas of education represented the child as beginning in sin and ignorance, able to progress only gradually and with great difficulty to virtue and knowledge.

Children and "savages" are often assumed to lack access to certain forms of thought that are considered the hallmarks of rational adulthood. Attempts have been made to capture the perceived differences between the thought forms of people in oral cultures and those of literate Westerners in distinctions such as primitive/developed, irrational or prerational/rational, mythic/historical, simple/complex, mythopoeic/logico-empirical, "cold"/"hot," traditional/modern, and so on (see Goody, 1977; Hollis & Lukes, 1982). Relatively recently, attempts have been made to break down these distinctions as applied wholesale to particular kinds of cultures. Jack Goody (1977), for example, has argued that any distinction that suggests "two different modes of thought, approaches to knowledge, or forms of science" is inadequate, not least because "both are present not only in the same societies but in the same individuals" (p. 148). That is, whenever we try to define precisely some distinctive feature of "our" thinking, we find examples of it in "their" cultures, and whenever we identify a distinctive feature of "their" thinking, we find cases in "our" culture. Robin Horton (1970, 1982) has shown that what have been regarded as distinctive features of scientific thinking are common in traditional cultures in Africa; and it has now, post-Freud, become a cliché that certain central features of mythic thinking are common in Western cultures (Blumenberg, 1985). (One wonders, for example, whether Bronislaw Malinowski's [1922] outrage at the wastefulness of piles of rotting yams in the Trobriand Islands would be equally directed at the "mountains" of dairy foods and grains and "lakes" of wine that have accumulated in support of the farming policies of the European Economic Community.) "We" and "they" constantly exhibit thinking that is both rational and irrational, complex and simple, logico-mathematical and mythopoeic. We are "them" and they are "us" (see Goody, 1977; Lévi-Strauss, 1966a).

What about the evident differences, then, between modes of thinking used in oral societies and those used in complex industrial ones? While we may indeed recognize common features in forms of thought that were in the past considered entirely dissimilar, we need to recognize also that modern science, history, and mathematics are hardly identical with anything found in oral cultures. One can scarcely claim that differences do not exist. How do we account for them if we reject explanations involving "primitiveness" or deficiencies of mind or of language? And how do we characterize the dramatic changes in forms of thought and methods of inquiry made during the Greek classical period—changes that involved the birth of philosophy, critical history, and modern science? Goody (1977), Havelock (1963), and Ong (1982) maintain that the evident differences are best accounted for by the technology of writing. Their arguments build on and extend a growing body of work that is seeking to clarify how literacy affects strategies of thinking. The economy of the mind inclines us towards using mental strategies in oral cultures—in which what one knows is what one remembers—and towards using some different mental strategies in literate cultures—in which various mental operations can be enormously enhanced by visual access to organized bodies of knowledge.

The path from orality to literacy is one that we want all children to take as they pass through our educational systems. Better understanding of what this movement entails might clarify some of our practical educational problems. It might, for example, help us find ways to reduce the rates of illiteracy in Western societies, and perhaps also to improve the quality and richness of literacy we can achieve. From the research that has so far drawn on our increasing knowledge of orality and of the transition to literacy, it is clear that any adequate conception of literacy must account for much more than simple encoding and decoding "skills" and must encompass significant features of rationality (Olson, 1977, 1986). That is to say, even though there is considerable difficulty in characterizing rationality with precision, it is increasingly clear that the acquisition of literacy can have cognitive effects that have traditionally been considered features of rational thought—particularly those associated with "abstract" thinking. Considering oral cultures, then, may help us to understand better what is entailed in the transition of Western children from orality to literacy.

This is not to posit some mysterious evolutionary recapitulation process in the lives of our schoolchildren. There is a trivial sense in which an education involves the individual's recapitulating the development of his or her culture; in a matter of years we learn knowledge, skills, and ways of making sense of the world that were developed over millennia. Recapitulation theorists in Europe and North America have gone further, however, and have argued that the classroom curriculum should be designed so that children learn the central content of their cultures largely in the sequence in which that content was invented or discovered. Recapitulation schemes in schools have been based on notions of biological recapitulation, logical sequences in the development of knowledge, and/or psychological predispositions (Gould, 1977). In what follows, however, I will be considering the recapitulation of specific techniques used in thinking. By making children literate, for example, we are recreating, in each individual's case, the internalization of a technology that can have quite profound and precise effects on cognitive processes and modes of communication. As Walter Ong has observed, "Technologies are not mere exterior aids but also interior transformations of consciousness" (1982, p. 82), and "Writing is a technology that restructures thought" (1986, p. 23). These general claims, of course, have been much disputed (cf. Olson & Torrance, 1991, for skeptical voices about the overall "literacy hypothesis"), and many have vigorously argued that "restructuring" effects on cognitive processes by literacy are certainly not automatic and may be rare (Heath, 1983; Scribner & Cole, 1981; Street, 1984).

Technology is a slightly aggressive term to use for writing, and "tools for thinking" is a handy but tendentious metaphor. One is led to assume that spades and computers have similar transforming powers over our manual and cognitive functions. That they have transforming powers is beyond doubt, but that these are the same as, or akin to, what internalizing literacy produces needs further evidence. I prefer to use a less aggressive term, coined, as far as I am aware, by Lévi-Strauss (1962). In discussing the structural categories underlying totemic classification, he debunked the notion that totemic species are chosen because of their economic or culinary value; he argued they are not so much *"bon à manger"* (good for eating) as *"bon à penser"* (good for thinking with). Literacy is a set of strategies that are not only utilitarian, but also *bon à penser*.

One purpose of this article is to explore oral practices that are also "good for thinking with." Orality, we shall see, is not a condition of deficit—to be defined simply as the lack of literacy. Regarding orality only in terms of literacy is (in Ong's [1982] neat simile) like regarding horses as automobiles without wheels (p. 12). Orality entails a set of powerful and effective mental strategies, some of which, to our cost, have become attenuated and undervalued in many aspects of Western cultures and educational systems. In the following pages I shall explore some of the effective strategies of thinking used in oral cultures, and then consider their relevance to education.

A word of caution is required. Any simplistic assumption that equates the thinking of adults in oral cultures with that of children in literate societies will be undermined in two ways. First, adults have the accumulated experience and cognitive development that children necessarily lack. Second, most children in Western cultures live in environments that presuppose literacy and its associated forms of thought: Constant adult interactions with young children assume conventions that depend on literacy, and preliterate children are constantly encouraged to adopt forms of thinking and expression that are more easily achieved as a product of literacy.

My purpose is to focus on forms of thought that are *bon à penser* if one is not literate. Consequently, I will be seeking comparisons between forms of thought used by members of oral cultures and those used by modern Western children. The basis of the comparison, however, is neither knowledge content nor psychological development, but techniques that are required by orality. Keeping this idea to the fore will, I hope, allow us to avoid the kind of deprecatory ethnocentrism criticized above.

I shall not try to establish an exhaustive inventory of the intellectual strategies common in oral cultures. Further, I do not consider that the purpose of education in Western cultures is to preserve and develop such strategies uncritically. We are not in the business of preparing children to live in an oral culture—though it may be worth reiterating that we are preparing them for a literate and oral culture. Indeed, we see fast developing around us features of what Ong (1982) has called "secondary orality." The electronic media are its most energetic promoters, but even newspapers and journals are explicitly, and somewhat paradoxically, relying less and less on strategies of communication that draw on the skills of "high literacy" and their associated forms of thought (Ong, 1977). Although orality is not the end of our educational development, we might consider whether it is a necessary constituent of it, and whether the study of orality might be *bon à penser*, as we attempt to construct both a richer primary-school curriculum and a fuller sense of how children might effectively learn its contents.

A central theme of this article might be summed up in Lévi-Strauss's (1978) observation:

> I think there are some things we have lost, and we should perhaps try to regain them, [but] I am not sure that in the kind of world in which we are living and with the kind of scientific thinking we are bound to follow, we can regain these things exactly as if they had never been lost; but we can try to become aware of their existence and their importance. (p. 5)

I shall begin with a brief account of some of the overlapping branches of research in classical studies and anthropology that have helped to clarify the kinds of thinking that have proven effective in cultures that do not have writing. Next, I shall discuss, in what may be a familiar story to some readers, some prominent features of orality—the poetics of memory, participation and conservation, and classification and explanation—that have proved *bon à penser*. I shall conclude by discussing the possible implications of these features of orality for early childhood education. Central to this discussion is a reconsideration of what the foundations of education are when literacy and rationality are conceived as growing out of, rather than displacing, the oral culture of early childhood.

THE REDISCOVERY OF ORALITY

The relatively recent rediscovery of orality by Western scholars is connected with some problems presented by Homer's epic poems. Thinkers could easily apply the influential late-Victorian evolutionary paradigm to the development of science, which was seen as a positive progression from myth to rationality to empirical science. When applied more generally to human cultures, however, this paradigm encountered the anomaly of Homer's literary achievements. Educated Victorians were more familiar with long-ago battles on the windy plains of Troy, the wooden horse, and the destruction of the topless towers of Ilium than with much of their own society. How, they asked, could such vividly powerful epics, with their richness of human insight, their technical sophistication and emotional force, and their overwhelming, engaging reality, be composed by and for what were in all other regards considered primitive people? "Primitive" mentality—supposedly a mess of irrationality and confusion—must, it would seem, have had the resources to create some great cultural achievements.

Two other complications arose. First, the story of the *Iliad*, long regarded as straightforward fiction, came to be seen as an account of events that actually occurred in the 13th century B.C. This historicity began to be established by Heinrich Schliemann's excavations at Troy and Mycaenae during the latter part of the 19th century and has gradually become fuller and clearer. (Recently, a persuasive picture of the period has been pieced together in Michael Wood's popular television series and book *In Search of the Trojan War* [1985]).

The second complication was the growing evidence that Homer and other poets in his tradition of wandering "singers of tales" were illiterate. As Berkley Peabody (1975) put it, "Despite the implications of its name, literature does not seem to have been the invention of literate people" (p. 1). The master poet Homer lived about 500 years after the events of which he sang, long after the kingdoms whose ships sailed for Troy had themselves been destroyed. Yet growing knowledge of the spread of literacy in Greece made it increasingly difficult for 19th-century scholars to imagine Homer—by tradition blind in any case—sitting at a table *writing* his poems.

But how could such technically complex poems, many thousands of lines long, be composed without writing? Surely no illiterate bard could make up such supple hexameters in a matter of hours while he sang, and then recall them word for word? Virgil, that other great epic poet of the ancient world, labored for years writing his *Aeneid* by hand. We know (Suetonius, *De Poetis*) that he revised it constantly and was so unsatisfied with it in comparison to Homer that on his deathbed asked that it be destroyed. Surely no illiterate bard could toss off a book an hour on the hoof, as it were, of a power, vividness, and quality that the great and highly literate Virgil struggled for years to match, and couldn't.

The story of the rediscovery of the Homeric methods of composition is itself an epic of scholarly ingenuity. In the 1920s, Milman Parry (1928), following a number of earlier scholars (Vico, 1744/1970; Wolf, 1795/1884), contended in his doctoral dissertation that the structure and distinctive stylistic features of the Homeric poems reflect directly the requirements of oral methods of composition (Burke, 1985; Griffin, 1980). Parry's analyses of the *Iliad* and the *Odyssey* showed that they were composed largely of verbal formulae—repeated morphemic clusters—whose form was dictated by the metrical requirements of the hexameter line. For example, Homer used a large number of adjectival epithets for most of the recurring nouns in the poems—for wine, the sea, ships, the major characters, and so on. The epithet chosen at any point is not necessarily the most apposite for the meaning of the line, but is dictated instead by its fit into the line's meter (Kirk, 1965, ch. 1). One-fifth of Homer's lines are repeated almost verbatim elsewhere in his poems; in about 28,000 lines there are about 25,000 repeated phrases (Parry, 1928).

The poet who performed orally did not memorize the poems, as we would have to do. Rather, the singer learned—through a long, *nonliterate* apprenticeship—the particular metrical form of his tradition, until it was absorbed like a somatic rhythm, which habitually accompanied and shaped his thought (Lord, 1964). The content of the song was held together first by the poet's clear grasp of the overall story, and the meter determined the pattern of sounds. As Albert B. Lord (1964) wrote, "Man without writing thinks in terms of sound groups and not in words" (p. 25). Traditional oral performance, then, does not involve repeated recitation of a memorized poem—the idea of a fixed text is a product of literacy. Rather, each performance is a new composition. It may be very like previous ones, and certain patterns will recur, but the singer is composing each time, not repeating something fixed in memory. It is, in Lord's words, "the preservation of tradition by the constant re-creation of it" (p. 29).

These metrically arranged units of sound, then, accumulated line by line in the Homeric poems to repeat the heroic story. The poet "stitched" together the formulae to fit the metrical line, and the episodes to fit the story. The Greeks called singers "rhapsodes"—literally, "song-stitchers." It seems likely that Homer, as one of the greatest epic poets, represented the culmination of this tradition, and that he recited his poems to trained scribes.

In the early 1930s, Parry supplemented his arguments by studying methods of oral composition being used by contemporary singers of heroic tales in Yugoslavia. After his death, his work was supported and extended by Lord's studies (1964) of comparable singers in the Balkans. Lord has described in some detail the conditions of their intensive, and almost invariably nonliterate, training, which cannot be very unlike Homer's (esp. ch. 2). This work has been further elaborated by Peabody's (1975) ingenious analysis of Hesiod's *Works and Days*. Peabody has shown in still greater depth how the oral poet uses the techniques developed over uncountable generations to realize for the audience a kind of alternate reality. That is, the techniques of oral poetry are designed to discourage critical reflection on the stories and their contents, and instead to "enchant" the hearers, drawing them into the world of the story. I will describe these techniques below.

This process of enthralling the audience, of impressing on them the reality of the story, is a central feature of education in oral cultures. Their social institutions are sustained in large part by sound, by what the spoken or sung word can do to commit individuals to particular beliefs, expectations, roles, and behaviors. Thus the techniques of fixing the crucial patterns of belief in the memory—rhyme, rhythm, formula, story, and so on—are vitally important. Education in oral cultures is largely a matter of constantly immersing the young in enchanting patterns of sound until their minds resonate to them, until they become in tune with the institutions of their culture.

The Homeric poems were called the educators of the pre-classical Greeks because they performed this social function. Poems were not listened to or learned solely because of their aesthetic value; that was incidental to their value as "a massive repository of useful knowledge, a sort of encyclopaedia of ethics, politics, history, and technology which the effective citizen was required to learn as the core of his educational equipment" (Havelock, 1963, p. 29). In the process of such an education a substantial amount of mental energy is spent memorizing the chief messages of the culture, because they can exist and survive only in people's memories.

According to Eric Havelock, little mental energy is left for reflection on those messages, or analysis of them, because such activities would interfere with the need to sink them unquestioningly into every mind. Perhaps talk of "energy" is inappropriate—rather it would seem that this kind of intellectual activity does not provide in any significant degree the cognitive "tools" that reflection and analysis require.

Havelock further extended Parry's and Lord's work. His *Preface to Plato* (1963), *Origins of Western Literacy* (1976), and *The Muse Learns to Write* (1986) help clarify the achievements of the early literate Greek philosophers by offering a better understanding of the oral poetic culture that preceded it. In particular, they highlight Plato's reasons for wishing to exclude poets from his ideal state. Havelock read Plato's *Republic* as a program for educating people to discard the residues of oral culture and to embrace forms of thinking made possible by full literacy. In Havelock's interpretation, Plato says that the mind need no longer be immersed in the oral tradition, memorizing and copying the paradigmatic structures and patterns of the Homeric poems, but can be freed to engage its proper objects—what we might call abstract concepts, and what he called Forms or Ideas. Plato characterized this mode of thinking as opposed to the Homeric tradition; the Platonic scheme of education, as he saw it, brought the mind to reality, while Homer's crippled the intellect through its seductive illusions and distortions of reality.

The new forms of thinking made possible by literacy, early in our educational discourse, were represented as enemies of the oral techniques that were *bon à penser*: "Plato's target was indeed an educational procedure and a whole way of life" (Havelock, 1963, p. 45). There are clear ambivalences in Plato's reflections on the oral tradition (see the *Phaedrus* and the probably authentic *Seventh Letter*) and on Homer, but in the end those earlier forms of thinking, education, and society had to be destroyed to make way for the new abstract forms of thought and whatever world they brought with them. Plato did not conceive his educational scheme as a structure built on the oral tradition, but as a replacement for it. His work, in Havelock's view, "announced the arrival of a completely new level of discourse which as it became perfected was to create in turn a new kind of experience of the world—the reflective, the scientific, the technological, the theological, the analytic. We can give it a dozen names" (p. 267). Plato's influence is so strong in Western thought that it is extremely difficult for us now to imagine the kind of consciousness created in the oral tradition, and the kind of experience created for listeners by a singer of tales or teller of myths.

Havelock's (1963) description of the techniques of oral recitation in the ancient world shows that audiences received poems rather differently from the way we read the same texts today. A youth in an oral culture, whether Greek or Australian aborigine, learned by listening constantly to these foundations of his or her cultural institutions. But the messages of the professional singers were also repeated everywhere by their listeners. Proverbs and maxims and riddles uttered at meals, on rising or going to sleep, in the market or the field, are constantly repeated pieces of the great myths or epic poems of oral cultures. African children, for example, traditionally learn the practices and mores of their ethnic groups through riddles asked by their grandparents. In religious schools throughout the Muslim world, young students commit to memory phenomenally long passages of Koranic literature and law. It is likely that biblical stories were first repeated and handed on by singers and storytellers, as are the tales of African *griots* in many places today.

Learning the sustaining messages of an oral culture differs from the effort at accumulation of knowledge with which we are familiar in literate cultures. In literate cultures memorization is usually an attempt to remember a text so that it is possible to repeat it verbatim on command; and our techniques are typically impoverished, involving largely repetition, some mnemonics perhaps, or saying words aloud with our eyes closed, and so on. In an oral culture, learning proceeds more somatically, with the whole body used to support the memorizing process. The Homeric singer, and singers throughout the world, usually use a simple stringed instrument, sometimes a drum, whose beat reinforces the rhythm of the telling and draws the hearer into the enchantment of the song. The audience does not so much listen to it, as we might listen to a play, as they are invited to live it. The acoustical rhythm created by the singer and his instrument is supported by the repetitive meter, rhythmic body movements, and the pattern of formulae and the story, to set up conditions of enchantment that impress the message on the minds of the hearers. The techniques of the skilled performer generate a relaxed, half-hypnotized pleasure in the audience. (For a full discussion, see Havelock, 1963, ch. 9, "The Psychology of Poetic Performance.")

This semi-hypnotized state is similar to that often described by anthropologists as the condition in which audiences receive the fundamental messages of their culture. Thus, Lévi-Strauss (1969), in his study of mythology, aimed "to show, not how men think in myths, but how myths operate in men's minds without their being aware of the fact" (p. 12). He preferred to compare this process to a musical performance rather than to linguistic forms or texts: "The myth and the musical work are like conductors of an orchestra, whose audience becomes the silent performers" (p. 17). While no Western educator would wish to replicate all aspects of this phenomenon in our schools, it seems important to understand the nature of this receptive state. Anyone familiar with children's rapt attention to television broadcasts may recognize Lévi-Strauss's descriptions.

Similarly, Edmund Leach (1967) argued that the structural patterns of myths and their underlying messages are communicated powerfully and unambiguously by oral performances, despite considerable variation in the surface stories settings:

> Whenever a corpus of mythology is recited in its religious setting, such structures are "felt" to be present, and convey meaning much as poetry conveys meaning. Even though the ordinary listener is not fully conscious of what has been communicated, the "message" is there in a quite objective sense. (p. 12)

According to Lévi-Bruhl (1910/1985), when a sacred myth is recited in the course of ritual settings or other situations characterized by heightened emotion, "what they [the participants] hear in it awakens a whole gamut of harmonics which do not exist for us" (p. 369). The written form of the myth that we can study "is but the inanimate corpse which remains after the vital spark has fled" (p. 369).

In his reexamination of orality, Goody (1977, 1986, 1987) has not only undermined traditional notions of the move from "primitive" to rational thought, and instead shown that the differences typically educed as evidence for such a shift are better understood as epiphenomena of the move from orality to literacy; he has also clarified some specific steps that accompanied the move from orality to literacy, and has detailed various consequences of literacy—for example, the development of Western scientific inquiry and abstract thought (Goody, 1986, 1987; Goody & Watt, 1968). (For surveys of this field, see Olson & Torrance, 1991, and Ong, 1982).

In the following discussion of several techniques of oral expression common in nonliterate cultures, my choice has been guided not by a desire to conduct a systematic survey, but primarily by educational relevance.

ORAL EXPRESSIONS: BONS À PENSER

In listing certain features of oral cultures I do not mean to imply that such cultures are all alike; nor do I imply that they all use precisely the same sets of techniques for preserving their institutions. Clearly, there are enormous differences among the cultures of preclassical Greeks and those of the early twentieth-century Trobriand Islanders, Australian aborigines, and the indigenous peoples of the Americas before extensive contacts with literate peoples. In particular, their myths, and the range of techniques used to transmit them, differ significantly. My focus, however, is on what we find common to so many oral cultures.

It is inevitably difficult for us to think of orality simply as a positive set of tactics that are *bon à penser*; the intellectual capacities and forms of communication that have been stimulated by literacy intrude upon our attempts to understand orally sustained forms of thought. But we need to see orality as an energetic and distinct set of ways of learning and communicating, not simply as an incomplete and imperfect use of the mind awaiting the invention of literacy. Orality is not at all the same as what we usually mean today by illiteracy in the Western cultural context. Illiteracy is perhaps best understood as a condition in which one has not acquired the positive capacities that either orality or literacy can provide.

Poetics of Memory

Let us begin considering orality by focusing on what seems to be the central reason it involves some different tactics of thinking from literacy: its need to rely on memory. If the preservation of the institutions of one's culture depends on the memories of its living members, then the techniques that most effectively impress the appropriate information on their minds and sustain it are vitally important. The Victorians, who judged members of oral cultures to be mentally "incapable" because of their supposed reluctance or inability to perform mental functions that are commonplace in literate Western cultures, often failed to recognize this fact at work in the intellectual "anomalies" of traditional societies they encountered. Lucien Lévi-Bruhl, writing in 1910, described various feats of memory that seemed to him prodigious, but to the oral peoples he studied, commonplace:

> This extraordinary development of memory, and a memory which faithfully reproduces the minutest details of sense-impressions in the correct order of their appearance, is shown moreover by the wealth of vocabulary and the grammatical complexity of the languages. Now the very men who speak these languages and possess this power of memory are (in Australia or Northern Brazil, for instance) incapable of counting beyond two and three. The slightest mental effort involving abstract reasoning, however rudimentary it may be, is so distasteful to them that they immediately declare themselves tired and give it up. (p. 115)

Lévi-Bruhl perceived there were no differences between his own capacities and those of his subjects on any simple scale of mental superiority or inferiority, but that the conditions of life in oral cultures stimulated different mental developments to deal with those conditions. The people he observed had a highly developed set of techniques for learning and remembering, and their apparent incapacity for "abstraction," as such, lay in the dissociation of the problems Lévi-Bruhl gave them from their lives. It may be helpful to remember this as we investigate the development of our children's capacities for abstract thinking (Egan, 1997; Hayek, 1970).

Goody's experience with the LoDogaa of Ghana (1977, pp. 12–13) makes this clear. When he asked some tribesmen to count for him, they responded with the—to them—obvious question, "Count what?" The LoDogaa have not only an abstract numerical system, but also several sophisticated forms of counting that are chosen according to what is being counted: Their methods for counting cows and for counting cowrie shells differ. "Abstract reasoning" is beyond no human mind, but abstraction that is very heavily dependent on writing is not available to people who do not write or read.

In describing the apparent anomaly of prodigious mental feats executed by the supposedly mentally deficient, Lévi-Bruhl (1910/1985) concluded that the uses of memory in oral cultures "are quite different because [memory's] contents are of a different character. It is both very accurate and very emotional" (p. 110).

Oral cultures engage the emotions of their members by making the culturally important messages event-laden, by presenting characters and their emotions in conflict in developing narratives—in short, by building the messages into stories. Lévi-Strauss (1962) pointed out that "all myths tell a story" (p. 26), and Lord (1964) concluded that the story provides the firm structure for the constant reconstruction of heroic songs. The various linguistic structures in the end "serve only one purpose, they provide a means for telling a story The tale's the thing" (p. 68). The story form is a cultural universal—everyone, everywhere, has told and enjoyed stories. They are one of the greatest cultural inventions for catching and fixing meaning. Perhaps "discovery" is a more appropriate term than "invention": Some enormously creative person or people discovered that messages shaped into the distinctive form of the story were those best remembered, and they carried a charge of emotional identification that greatly enhanced social cohesion and control.

Myth stories also, of course, have what we would consider aesthetic value. But whereas we distinguish aesthetic from utilitarian values, for members of oral cultures these are bound up together (Cassirer, 1946; Durkheim, 1965, ch. 4). The story form has been one of the most powerful and effective sustainers of cultures across the world. Its great power lies in its ability to fix affective responses to the messages it contains and to bind what is to be remembered with emotional associations. Our emotions, simply, are most effective at sustaining, and helping in the recall of, memories of events (Bartlett, 1932). This should not be a surprise if we reflect on the events of our lives that are most memorable. Almost invariably we find that they are accompanied by vivid emotional associations, and retain quite clearly a particular emotional tone. Most of the world's great religions have at their sacred core a story, and indeed we have difficulty keeping the facts of our history from being shaped constantly into stories. It is likely that the simplified histories sanctioned in the schools of most nation states (Ravitch, 1983) have at least as much in common with the origin myths of oral cultures as they do with the austere ideals of historiography. The story form also has important implications for schooling. Its survival among oral peoples as a technique for sustaining culture speaks to its appropriateness for education, despite our recent tendencies to neglect it. There are many ways in which we might use this most powerful of communicative media in education today, especially in the primary school (Egan, 1989)—I mean in addition to the uses of story that teachers have long and fruitfully deployed.

Rhyme, rhythm, meter, repetition of formulae, redundancy, the use of visual imagery—figures of speech used to create enchantment in oral cultures throughout the world—are also among the techniques used in Western poetry, and the state of mind they induce is close to what we describe as poetic. Like the singer of heroic tales or the reciter of myths, the literate poet shapes sound to create particular emotional effects and fix particular meanings. The shaping of sound finds one outlet in poetry and another in rhetoric. These two, along with music, are perhaps the most evident and direct manifestations of the oral tradition that have survived in the literate world.

Metaphor, metonymy, and synecdoche are important among the linguistic tools that are *bon à penser*. In oral cultures, thinking moves according to the complex logic of metaphor, more readily than it follows the systematic logic of rational inquiry. As Ernst Cassirer (1946) notes, "It is a familiar fact that all mythic thinking is governed and permeated by the principle [of metaphor]" (p. 92; see also Lévi-Strauss, 1966a, esp. ch. 7). Although the logic of mythic thinking, with its reliance on metaphor, has been difficult for some Westerners to make sense of, we should appreciate and find readily accessible this metaphoric power, as it suffuses all languages. It is one of the foundations of all our mental activity, on which our systematic logics of rational inquiry also rest, or—a better metaphor—the soil out of which they grow. Both myth and our everyday language, then, are permeated with metaphor; as Cassirer (1946) concluded, "The same form of mental conception is operative in both. It is the form which one may denote as *metaphorical thinking*" (p. 84, emphasis original). Or, as Lévi-Strauss (1962) observes, "metaphor . . . is not a later embellishment of language but is one of its fundamental modes—a primary form of discursive thought" (p. 102; see also Cooper, 1986).

The characteristics of oral literature that I have mentioned are generated by a people's need to memorize and be committed to their cultural institutions. We find these techniques to a greater or lesser degree in all oral cultures: "At different periods and in different cultures there are close links between the techniques for mental recall, the inner organization of the faculty (of memory), the place it occupies in the system of the ego, and the ways that men picture memory to themselves" (Vernant, 1983, p. 75; see also Finnegan, 1970, 1977).

We remain familiar with these tactics that are *bon à penser*, but usually in a much attenuated or altered form. Rhyme, for example, seems little more than fun for us now, a part of children's games, anachronistic and therefore ironic in modern poetry. We would hardly consider its systematic use a matter of vital social importance. We can write, so we do not need rhyme to sustain the memory of our institutions. These survivors of orality—rhyme, rhythm, meter, story, metaphor—serve largely (I am tempted to write "merely") aesthetic purposes for us. While metaphor and story may still seem to us culturally important in some imprecise way, we tend to think of rhyme and rhythm as only casual cultural survivors, anachronisms serving merely to entertain the literate—like the lords and ladies of a defeated civilization made into clowns and dancers. But art has a utilitarian purpose when it supports faith—in gods, in the validity of one's cultural institutions, in one's society, in one's sense of oneself. The origins of any of the tools of spoken language invented to create and sustain memory lie in the remarkable human ambition "to liberate the soul from time and open up a path to immortality" (Vernant, 1983, p. 95). All the world's amazing cultural and technological achievements since the development of literacy have been built on the efficacy of these oral tools of communication and the intellectual space they once did, and can still, generate. We would do well, therefore, to consider carefully their actual and potential roles in early childhood education.

Participation and Conservation

An Ojibwa Indian observed: "The white man writes everything down in a book so that it will not be forgotten; but our ancestors married the animals, learned their ways, and passed on the knowledge from one generation to another" (Jenness, in Lévi-Strauss, 1966a, p. 37). This sense of participation in the natural world, of having knowledge that is different from the kinds of propositions generated by rational inquiries, reflects a mental condition anthropologists have often tried to describe as a kind of oneness with nature. By comparison, our normal "literate" relationship with the natural world seems alienated. "The mainspring of the acts, thoughts, and feelings of early man was the conviction that the divine was immanent in nature, and nature intimately connected with society" (Frankfort, Wilson, & Jacobsen, 1949, p. 237). All the attempts to pinpoint the causes and character of this sense of participation in nature display a conviction that, despite their inadequacies when it comes to pragmatic control over the world, myth and consciousness in oral cultures somehow enable people to feel that they are comfortable participants in their life world. But it is not a simple condition, obviously, nor one we can feel unequivocally regretful of having largely lost. Ong (1977) describes it this way:

> The psyche of a culture innocent of writing knows by a kind of empathetic identification of knower and known, in which the object of knowledge and the total being of the knower enter into a kind of fusion, in a way which literate cultures would typically find unsatisfyingly vague and garbled and somehow too intense and participatory. (p. 18)

One of the cornerstones of Western rationality is knowing, as it were, where we end and the world begins; distinguishing the world from our feelings, hopes, fears, and so on. This form of thinking seems to be very largely a product of literacy. As Ong (1982) puts it, "Writing fosters abstractions that disengage knowledge from the arena where human beings struggle with one another" (pp. 43–44), or, in Peabody's (1975) words: "The shift in medium from utterance to record affects the way such an institution works and tends to change what was an immediate, living, active agent into an increasingly distant, timeless, passive, authority" (pp. 1–2). In an oral culture the ear is most highly attuned to picking up cultural messages, supplemented by the eye. In our "literate" case it is usually the other way around.

Sound is alive and participatory. It is effective only within a short physical range. The hearer must be in the presence of the speaker—there are no carefully crafted memos from the president or manager. "The living word," as Socrates put it in Plato's *Phaedrus*, "has a soul . . . of which the written word is properly no more than an image" (trans., 1892, p. 279). The living word is the word in the arena of human interactions and conflicts. It is not the distanced and "cooled" word of the written text. Language use in an oral culture tends to be, in Ong's (1977) phrase, "agonistically toned" (p. 113); it is charged with the direct energy of the speaker's body, and thus with the speaker's hopes, fears, wants, needs, and intentions. Oral heroic tales are full of bragging, elaborate abuse of adversaries, and exuberant praise of leaders or those from whom the speaker wants a favor. The tensions of daily struggles are felt face-to-face in an oral culture. These facts of oral life lead to a verbally highly polarized world, of good and evil, friends and enemies, fear and security. Ong (1977) points out that the mental life of oral cultures "is sure to carry a heavy load of praise and vituperation" (p. 112), because "if one does not think formulary, mnemonically structured thoughts, how can one really know them, that is, be able to retrieve them, if the thoughts are even of moderate complexity?" (p. 104). Thus, because oral cultures "necessarily store knowledge largely in narrative concerned with interacting human or quasi-human figures" (p. 112), there is a powerful pressure to polarize. The African Batomba, for instance, have two typically polarized paraphrastic names for white foreigners: "The white man, honored by all, companion of our chiefs" or, as occasion may demand, the pointed expression "You do not touch the poisonous caterpillar" (p. 112). In such societies the forms of verbal play also tend to be "agonistically toned"—riddles, tricks, and jokes are often characterized by a playful competitiveness or even aggressiveness.

In an oral culture "the meaning of each word is ratified in a succession of concrete situations, accompanied by vocal inflections and physical gestures, all of which combine to particularize both its specific denotation and its accepted connotative uses" (Goody & Watt, 1968, p. 306). As a result, words typically are not themselves objects of reflection, and thus oral cultures have no epistemology as we might define it. When words are closely tied into their context of reference, philosophical problems do not arise. People in oral cultures do not dissociate words from things to the point where they might wonder how short the legs of a small table have to be for it to be considered a tray. This feature of their thinking has nothing to do with "defects" or "inadequacies" of the mind, but is rather a function of the uselessness of many of our forms and techniques of thought in the conditions of most oral cultures.

In nearly all oral cultures, for example, time is reckoned in terms of the significant daily activities of the social group. An "abstract" or dissociated system for measuring time, such as we employ, is useful only when it is necessary to coordinate a large number of quite diverse kinds of activities. Such diversity does not exist in most oral cultures, where time measurement reflects the sequence of activities that constitute the rhythms of daily life. In Madagascar, a villager told a photographer that the distance to the next village was "three pots of rice"—that is, walking, the time it takes to cook three pots of rice (David Beckstead, comment on this ms.).

In his studies of nonliterate peasants in remote areas of the Soviet Union, Alexander Luria (1976) posed to them apparently simple problems, such as "In the far north, where there is snow, all bears are white. Novaya

Zemlya is in the far north and there is always snow there. What colors are the bears around Novaya Zemlya?" His subjects, no doubt politely wishing to play their part in the conversation, would reply that they had never been to Novaya Zemlya and so didn't know, or that they had seen a black bear but never a white one, and so on. The rules and underlying forms of thought of the kind of conversation in which Luria tried to engage these nonliterate people are familiar to us, but appeared bizarre to them. The point is a concern not with mental capacity, but with social utility, and the influence of the latter over cognition. Pragmatic thought in oral cultures participates more intimately in the life world; it does not treat the world and experience as objects distanced from people's emotional, aesthetic, and utilitarian needs. As such, it makes "no clear-cut distinction between subjective states and the properties of the cosmos" (Lévi-Strauss, 1969, p. 240).

Oral cultures have been described as being intellectually inclined toward homeostasis, conservatism, and stability in ways that our modern literate cultures are not (see Geertz, 1973, esp. ch. 5). Such cultures, of course, undergo changes of many kinds—migration, disaster, invasion, merging with other groups—but the mental forms dominant in oral cultures strive to maintain verbal accounts of the culture's life that assert continuity and stability.

One striking difference between oral and literate cultures is in their different attitudes toward the past. Literate peoples have, and value, accurate historical accounts. Oral societies cultivate what J. A. Barnes has called "structural amnesia"—systematic procedures for "forgetting," or wiping out from the oral records of the culture's past (in Goody & Watt, 1968, p. 309). Although oral cultures often preserve the memory of particular historical events in stories or in memorized genealogies of leading families, it usually turns out that the record kept does not reflect past reality with complete accuracy. Rather, it is faithful to present social conditions and statuses. As conditions change, so do the accounts or genealogy. Malinowski (1954) showed this process at work among the Trobriand Islanders. As changes occurred in the structure and power relationships of their society, the myths of origin changed to reflect the current social structure; that is, historical changes were gradually effaced. Malinowski concluded that "myths serve to cover certain inconsistencies created by historical events" (p. 125). The oral record, then, ensures that "the individual has little perception of the past except in terms of the present" (Goody & Watt, 1968, p. 310). (The growing Western consciousness that "we" are "them" also, of course, encourages reflection on the ways in which "our" scientific history is clearly not some simple opposite of oral cultural history; "we" too engage in our own forms of structural amnesia.)

We find it hard to think of this structural amnesia as anything other than an unawareness of history, another difficulty resulting from the lack of literacy. It seems merely a way of making the best of things, or the only strategy manageable if the society cannot keep written records. But the positive value of such structural amnesia is that it tends to preserve a sense of stability and clarity. The social structure and its prevailing institutions are constantly supported by whatever sanction is contained in the myths, whether of sacred ancestors or gods, and are constantly renewed: "Time is recorded only biologically without being allowed to become 'history'— that is, without its corrosive action being able to exert itself upon consciousness by revealing the irreversibility of events" (Eliade, 1959, pp. 74–75). One technique constantly used to achieve this end is the assertion of continual rebirth—rebeginning as the first beginning. We preserve a vague shadow of this sense of birth in our New Year festivals. Even if we, like Malinowski (1954), discount other functions of myth, we ought not to disregard the sense of intellectual security conferred by sloughing off the memory of events that are no longer relevant or useful to present life. This is indeed another way in which orality is *bon à penser*.

This emphasis on the preservation of stability through selective memory of events relevant to present social conditions leads to what is often characterized as a conservative frame of mind. It is indeed conservative, but in a radical sense. The pressure to preserve in memory the institutions of one's culture does not invite innovation or experimentation. Although some oral cultures are undoubtedly more resilient in this regard than others, on the whole anthropologists attest to the powerful sanctions against change. "The most apparently trifling innovation may lead to danger, liberate hostile forces, and finally bring about the ruin of its instigator and all dependent upon him" (Lévi-Bruhl, 1910/1985, p. 42). The cultural institutions support a limited stock of archetypal forms of appropriate behavior for each member of the society, and the repetition of these alone is sanctioned and validated by the myths. These are believed to be the behaviors of sacred ancestors or gods, which it is the human task to imitate: "The inhibition against new invention, to avoid placing any possible strain on the memory, continually encourage[s] contemporary decisions to be framed as though they were the acts and words of the ancestors" (Havelock, 1963, p. 121). As Mircea Eliade (1959) wrote, the individual in oral cultures "acknowledges no act which has not been previously posited and lived by someone else, some other being who was not a man. What he does has been done before. His life is a ceaseless repetition of gestures initiated by others" (p. 15). In such a culture, "only the changeless is ultimately significant" (Frankfort, 1961, p. viii).

Although these generalizations may be somewhat less appropriate for some oral cultures than for others, they do point to further common ways in which their orality is, in their cultural context, *bon à penser*. The pressures against change and innovation serve stability, order, and intellectual security. One's familiar territory is intellectually mapped out, categorized, and under secure control. The resources of orality considered in this section help to provide intellectual security and a sense of persisting order in society despite historical changes. They also help to preserve a sense of participation in nature that users of literate forms of thought find somewhat alien. Not entirely alien, of course; attempts to recapture this sense of participation in nature find their most common literate expression in poetry. It is in the work of poets such as Wordsworth that the sense of participation in nature is most plausibly recaptured, and, significantly for my general argument about the cognitive effects of orality, it is in preliterate childhood that he most vividly locates it:

> Blest the infant Babe . . .
> No outcast he, bewildered and depressed.
> Along his infant veins are interfused
> The gravitation and the filial bond
> Of nature that connect him with the world.
> *(The Prelude*, Bk. II, 241–244)

Classification and Explanation

Members of oral cultures often have remarkably detailed knowledge of the flora and fauna of their environments, but their systems for classifying this knowledge tend to be very different from ours. Many anthropologists have commented on members of traditional societies who could give remarkably precise inventories of kinds of plants, trees, or weather conditions but had no words for "plant," "tree," or "weather." This phenomenon further supported their conclusions about such people's inability to "abstract." Yet, indeed, some purely oral languages use abstractions where speakers of English would prefer concrete terms (see Boas, 1911). For example, the proposition "The bad man killed the poor child" is rendered in Chinook: "The man's badness killed the child's poverty" (Lévi-Strauss, 1966a, p. 1). A major difference between oral cultures and our own lies not in their incapacity for abstraction, but in our dissociation from the life world. This kind of dissociation is a product of the techniques of writing, not some property that some human minds possess and others lack: "Writing, and more especially alphabetic literacy, made it possible to scrutinise discourse in a different kind of way . . . this scrutiny favoured the increase in scope of critical activity, and hence of rationality, scepticism, and logic" (Goody, 1977, p. 37).

Among the common basic techniques of classification in oral cultures is the use of what Lévi-Strauss (1966a) called "binary opposites": "All classification," he wrote, "proceeds by pairs of contrasts" (p. 139). These are not necessarily opposites in any precise logical or empirical sense, but become used as such by serving as the basis for further discriminations: "The substance of contradictions is much less important than the fact that they exist" (p. 95).

Lévi-Strauss (1969) began his four-volume analysis of myths by identifying sets of binary opposites on which each myth was built. Although many of his critics have regarded this as a rather arbitrary procedure, he presents a strong argument by demonstrating the prevalence of such oppositions giving structure to the contents of the corpus of myths he studied.

Attempts at classification are fundamental to rational thought. It makes little sense to consider people who develop sophisticated taxonomic schemes "irrational" (Lévi-Strauss, 1966a, p. 15). The differences between classificatory schemes in oral cultures and those in our scientific culture commonly rest on the qualities of phenomena used as the basis for classification. Lévi-Strauss's study of myth is, as he puts it, an attempt "to prove that there is a kind of logic in [the] tangible qualities of the concrete phenomena of everyday life—of the raw and the cooked, honey and ashes, and so on" (1969, p. 1). While our children's constant classifications of their universe seem unsophisticated, an understanding of the logic they use in forming them may help us understand their development of literacy.

The kinds of explanations offered in oral cultures about natural and cosmological phenomena often seemed to Victorian intellectuals perverse or crazy, and were taken as clear evidence of oral peoples' infirmities of mind. Unfamiliar medical practices were considered bizarre (although today a growing body of anthropology and medical literature elucidates the physical or psychological efficacy of many traditional practices). Lévi-Strauss (1966a), however, pointed out that the mistake of earlier interpreters of such explanations "was to think that natural phenomena are *what* myths seek to explain, when they are rather the *medium through which* myths try to explain facts which are themselves not of a natural but a logical order" (p. 95). We must, he said, attend to the form as well as the content of such explanations if we are to understand them (as we must if we are to appreciate poetry).

For us, explanation is a central part of our efforts both to understand and to control nature, to have practical effects. But its main purpose in oral cultures "is not a practical one. It meets intellectual requirements rather than or instead of satisfying needs" (Lévi-Strauss, 1966a, p. 9). In serving such intellectual purposes it does not, like our logic, tie itself to the ways the world in fact works; indeed the "savage" mind "does not bind itself down, as our thought does, to avoiding contradictions" (Lévi-Bruhl, 1910/1985, p. 78). Certainly in the myths and medical lore of oral cultures, the literate, rationalistic concern with noncontradiction is not a prominent structuring feature. Underlying the surface of explanations that may seem bizarre to Western observers, however, is a quest for order in diversity whose motive should be familiar to us from the similar motive that drives our science (see Horton, 1970, pp. 131–171).

The mode of thought that directs the approaches of various oral cultures to classification and explanation is closely linked with the modes of expression discussed earlier. Malinowski (1954) observed of the Trobriand Islanders: "They never explain in any sense of the word; they always state a precedent which constitutes an ideal and a warrant for its continuance, and sometimes practical directions for the procedure" (p. 110). What seem like explanations in oral cultures do not focus only on the relevant relationships among content features, but they mix in the whole equipment of the psyche—the explanation, that is, is cast in the form of a narrative in which characters, events, motives, and emotions carry the ideas forward— leading to what Goody (1977) calls the "personalization of theory" (p. 42).

IMPLICATIONS FOR EARLY CHILDHOOD EDUCATION

The research on orality sketched above has a number of implications for early childhood education. Here I will consider just two. The first concerns the early childhood curriculum; the second concerns methods of teaching.

The implications turn on the validity of the connections that can be established between characteristics of orality and the thinking of young children in modern literate cultures. I started by noting the need for caution in making such connections. First, psychological developmental connections seem particularly inappropriate. For example, the fact that adults in oral cultures commonly cannot perform intellectual tasks such as properly concluding "disembedded" syllogisms or successfully achieving Piagetian conservations (Ashton, 1975; Buck-Morss, 1982) does not mean that they are psychologically or developmentally equivalent to children in Western literate cultures, nor does the fact that adults in Western literate cultures can commonly perform such tasks make them psychologically superior or intellectually more fully developed. It means only that Western adults have adapted to a cultural environment shaped by centuries of elaboration of the thinking techniques made possible by literacy. Second, it is inappropriate to seek connections in the *content* of thoughts between adults in oral cultures and children in Western cultures; the concern here is, rather, what they think *with*. The connections I am focusing on are in certain formal characteristics of thought, in the strategies and resources the human mind has available and has developed over countless centuries in oral cultures. As young children in Western literate cultures themselves inhabit an oral culture, they have access to the intellectual resources of early orality until such a time as literacy is internalized.

The body of this essay has outlined a variety of formal characteristics of thought inferred from observations in oral cultures. One obvious source of equivalent material about modern Western children is in ethnographic studies of their lore and language. Fortunately, there are a number of quite substantial studies of children's oral cultures, notably those made by the Opies (1959, 1969, 1985) in Britain, and the Knapps (1976) and Sutton-Smith (1981) in the United States.

Those techniques used in oral cultures to shape sound into more memorable forms we find also to be prominent in children's oral cultures. Rhyme, rhythm, meter, and the story form are ubiquitous. The prominence of rhyme in everyday speech will in all English-speaking countries elicit the response "You're a poet and didn't know it" (Opie & Opie, 1959, p. 73). The strength of rhythm and meter is such that many children's songs are made up of parodies of well-known, usually solemn or sacred, songs carried on echoes of the same rhythms and meters. The Opies (1959) report variants of this practice all over Britain (p. 108). A children's taunting rhyme recalls the lively competitiveness and moral core of many verbal games observed in oral cultures:

> Liar, liar, pants on fire! Nose as long as a telephone wire. (Knapp & Knapp, 1976, p. 11)

Children's easy use of metaphoric thinking is evident in their ability to understand the kinds of metaphors that fill all languages—"It's bitter cold," "He feels bouncy today"—and their easy perception of the distinction between literal and metaphoric usage—"Mom killed that plan!" In what might be expected to be the constraining circumstances of constructed tasks, Gardner, Kircher, Winner, & Perkins (1975) report that nursery school children are much more likely than older children to use a metaphor to complete a sentence of the form "He looks as gigantic as ———." This ready grasp of metaphor and punning is prerequisite to an understanding of the jokes that are common in children's oral culture: "What did the quarter say when it got stuck in the slot?" "Money's very tight these days";

"Why does Fred work in the bakery?" "I guess he kneads the dough"; and so endlessly on.

Children's sense of the story form seems to exist very early in life; it is clearly evident in the language of many children by age two (Applebee, 1978; Pitcher & Prelinger, 1963). Themes framed as binary opposites, too, are evident as the most prominent structuring elements in the classic folktales (Bettelheim, 1976) and in children's invented stories (Paley, 1981). The stories are particularized versions of the struggles between such moral concepts as good and evil, bravery and cowardice, fear and security, hope and despair, and so on.

Rhyme, metaphor, and stories are, of course, found in modern culture as well. This in no way undermines their identification as prominent features of orality. In literate Western cultures we do not move from orality to literacy, but rather from orality to a combination of literacy and orality. The techniques that are *bon à penser* for oral peoples do not disappear with the acquisition of literacy; they may be attenuated, but even the most highly literate people are also dependent in many circumstances of their lives on some aspects of orality. In addition, literate adults use techniques of thinking encouraged specifically by literacy; the Western forms of rational inquiry and the standard written forms for reporting their results have developed in part by their exclusion of the techniques of orality. Attempts were made in the past to reach accommodation between the two in the field of rhetoric (see Ong, 1971; Todorov, 1982, ch. 3), but their clear separation, institutionalized by the dominance of positivistic science, is evident in the commonly dismissive use of the phrase "mere rhetoric." Previously, mingling the features of orality and literacy was not considered odd. Orality tends to survive, however, only in the daily lives of literate peoples; it is attenuated to the point of near invisibility in the cultures of positivistic science and technology, and in the realms of the most refinedly "literate" scholarship.

It is possible to take each of the characteristics of orality indicated in the body of this chapter and find clear analogies in the oral culture of modern Western children (Egan, 1988, 1997). That such empirical connections are unlikely to be merely coincidental is suggested by the analysis of orality and what it implies for linguistic forms and techniques of thinking—an analysis owed largely to the main authorities cited above. Let us provisionally assume that this kind of study of oral cultures throughout the world can yield a better understanding of orality and that an understanding of orality can help us better understand young children's minds in literate cultures.

Too often, I think, our perception of young children is clouded when we consider them illiterate and lacking in the skills of Western rationality. It is far better, I would argue, to regard them as oral in a positive sense; they have a distinctive culture of their own. While the image of young children as *tabulae rasae* or as empty vessels to be filled with knowledge is no longer prominent in educational discourse, we persist in characterizing young children in terms of the absence of the development and knowledge that constitute the mature condition. Theories such as Piaget's, for example, represent the developmental process as the gradual accumulation of increasingly sophisticated capacities and their hierarchical integration (Inhelder & Piaget, 1969). Such theories, when used to reflect on education, focus attention on the sequence of capacities to be developed, helping further to define young children in terms of what they lack. In Piaget's scheme, for example, they are *pre*-operational. Developmental schemes focused on the acquisition of the forms of thought characteristic of literate cultures, such as Piaget's focus on logico-mathematical structures, show a gradually rising scale of achievements to adulthood. If we were to focus instead on the thinking techniques of oral peoples, we would surely produce a quite different "developmental" profile. If the techniques of orality are, as I suggested earlier, conducive to formation of the imagination, we might be sensible to give them as much attention in designing educational programs as has been given to theories more concerned with logico-mathematical thinking.

Perhaps we need a *New Science* of childhood based on the insight that led Vico (1744/1970) toward a better understanding of the "irrational" thinking of early peoples: He argued that notions of irrationality were beside the point; rather, these people were "poets who spoke in poetic characters. This discovery, which is the master key of this Science, has cost us the persistent research of almost all our literary life because with our civilized natures we cannot at all imagine and can understand only by great toil the poetic nature of these first men" (p. 5).

Vico's (1744/1970) thesis was that literacy and rational prose, and the forms of thought associated with them, which Westerners consider so fundamental to their "civilized natures," were late achievements in human thinking. He contended that they grew from, and on, our "poetic nature." If, instead of viewing children's transition from orality to literacy as unqualified progress, we were to view it as a trade-off made for obvious functional advantages in a literate culture, then we might gain a different view of what is entailed in early education. This might make us more wary of displacing orality with literacy, and more sensitive to how we might preserve some of the more valuable characteristics of orality. We cannot hope to preserve orality in children just as it existed before the achievement of literacy, with all its cultural consequences. But we can hope to preserve or regain some things we have been in danger of losing, or have lost, in the dominant conceptions of early childhood education. These conceptions, I would argue, focus primarily upon the absence of literacy and the skills of Western rationality, and fail to recognize the presence of positive orality.

What are these valuable characteristics of orality, then, and how can we hope to preserve or regain them? They are the characteristics Vico (1744/1970) summed up by calling people in oral cultures "poets"—in the sense of people whose culture relied on, and whose cultural environment stimulated the development of, the features of orality sketched above. (The poet in Western cultures is, of course, the person who most forcefully retains and deploys the resources of orality—the sensitivity to the sounds of words and their emotional effects, the precise use of metaphor, the arrangement of sound in metrical patterns, the use of rhyme, and so on.) The young child, as a "maker" of imaginative worlds, is a kind of poet, and is in command of some considerable intellectual resources developed and exercised by such imaginative work. It is worth remembering that in our attempts to create artificial intelligence in computers, the most refined mathematical and logical operations have proven the easiest to simulate, while we still have no idea how to simulate these sophisticated and complex "poetic" operations.

The need to remember led, in oral cultures, to the invention of particular techniques to convey and make memorable ideas and information. We saw as prominent among these techniques the story-shaping of narratives—myths—made up of vivid characters and events that carried those ideas and information. What we generally call the imagination is a mental capacity that is evoked, stimulated, and developed by the needs of orality. Its value for literate culture persists, yet we have been in danger of depreciating it. We would be wise to preserve it as fully as possible. Valuable too is the fluent and flexible use of metaphor, as it is fundamental to language and thought, and is, along with the systematic logic of Western rationality, one of the tools of effective thinking (Cooper, 1986). In the education of modern children into literacy, then, we will want to ensure that fluency of metaphoric thinking is maintained and, if possible, increased. Similarly, the sense in which members of oral cultures see themselves as participants in nature, rather than as set off against it and "conquering" it, seems a valuable characteristic that we should try to preserve in children and regain for literate Western cultures. The development of this sensibility in some form may save us from destroying the natural world that sustains us.

What kinds of curricula will stimulate the development of young children's orality? Two main concerns will have to guide development of such programs. First, they must ensure the fullest possible development of the techniques of orality. This follows the recognition that associating literate/oral with the polarities of rational/irrational is inappropriate. Oral and literate are not opposites; rather, the development of orality is the necessary foundation for the later development of literacy. Second, it must be remembered that our school curricula are preparing children not for an oral culture, but for a literate one, with distinctive forms of thought and understanding. They must prepare children for particular kinds of scientific understanding, logic, and historical consciousness, among other things. During the early school years, children will also be learning to read and write with increasing sophistication. Stimulating orality is not incompatible with the early stages of acquiring the skills of literacy—indeed a sensitive program of instruction will use the child's oral cultural capacities to make reading and writing engaging and meaningful. I think one can plausibly argue that Western schools' relatively poor achievement in teaching literacy is due in significant part to the failure to recognize and stimulate the development of a rich orality in the first place, and then to use the capacities of orality to teach literacy. Following Ong (1982), I think the "transforming" effects of literacy do not begin to have significant impact on children's oral culture until literacy is fluently mastered, used for pleasure, and "internalized," a process that occurs around age 7 or 8 in most Western cultures. (For a more extensive account of an "oral" curriculum, see Egan, 1997.)

A useful guiding question for the curriculum developer considering how best to initiate children into science, logic and philosophy, or history would be, "What is the oral foundation of science, or of logic and philosophy, or of history?" Throughout, our focus has been not on knowledge content or psychological development, but on the *techniques* that are *bon à penser*. The question about oral foundations is not, therefore, about curriculum content; it does not lead us to magic, astrology, or myth, but to the forms of thought that undergird them. In history, for example, our aim is not to teach children myths, but to provide them with the foundations of historical understanding that underlie myth. This involves the sense of intellectual security that comes from knowing one's place in a wider context of human experience—even if that "place" may increasingly be a shifting and ironic location (Egan, 1997, ch. 5).

We might, for example, construct an early childhood history curriculum that tells the story of Western culture as a struggle for freedom against tyranny, for peace against arbitrary violence, for knowledge against ignorance, for power against powerlessness, and so on. In the first year the overall story of Western culture, for example, might be taught as one such struggle of binary forces. In each of the next 2 or 3 years the overall story could be taught again using different binary organizers to illuminate further dimensions of the culture's history. In my view, such a curriculum would be more engaging, meaningful, and educationally valuable than the typical content of the social studies curriculum (as I argue in detail in Chapter 9 of this book). Such a presentation of historical content need not falsify history, though, like all historiography, it must simplify it. And its problems of ideological bias are no different in kind from those of any historiography.

What are the oral foundations of science? Among the characteristics of orality noted above are a sense of participation in nature and a sense of inquiry about it. In oral cultures those inquiries might lead to magic, witchcraft, and forms of classification that seem strange to Western science. Yet if our elementary curriculum is concerned with providing foundations that will remain constituents of scientific understanding, we might consider how to encourage respect and appreciation for the natural world and our place in it.

One part of our elementary science curriculum, then, might involve children in close and systematic observation of some particular natural object or process—a tree, rain, a spider's web, a patch of grass. Each child would have his or her own object. It might become usual, for example, to see young children observing that object at length—say, for 20-minute intervals three times a week. They might break off other activities to observe how a tree moves in winds of different intensities, how the leaves hang in the sun, or how rainwater drips down. This would not be a matter of "training in observation skills," with checklists and reports. Rather, the activity would have no end beyond itself; the child would be encouraged to share the life of the tree, let his or her imagination flow into it, feel its branches and stretch with it toward the light, let stories form about it, converse or commune with it. This brief example may indicate how our conception of the range of human characteristics that are appropriately addressed by the curriculum is changed by a focus on the oral foundations of education. Such efforts might reinforce the sense of participation in nature that scholars have seen as characteristic of oral cultures.

Another capacity that tends to be very largely ignored in present curricula is sense of humor. The early stimulation and development of the sense of humor, and even the sense of the absurd, seem to me to be ways of setting in place the foundations of logic and philosophy. Recognition of the categories deployed in arguing and thinking, and fluency in analyzing them, are integral to those disciplines. One of the arenas of oral culture in which fluency in manipulating categories occurs is the joke. Lewis Carroll was one logician who seemed keenly aware of this, and used such category-manipulating jokes extensively. His *Alice* adventures, which grew from stories invented aloud for children, contain many examples of the kinds of jokes that stimulate flexibility in the use of categories, and that high-light the limits of the grasp our categories have on reality. The beginnings of logic and philosophy, then, might involve encouraging each child to "see" jokes and become jokesters. (Not that much encouragement will be needed.) From there we could move on to more sophisticated jokes, like Zeno's paradoxes, and later to consideration of paradoxes in the nature of knowledge, morality, art, and so on.

What implications follow for teaching? I will focus briefly on some that seem to follow from the prominence of the story form in oral cultures. We might think of teaching the curriculum as telling young children the great stories of their culture. In the case of Western culture these involve the stories of their history, mathematics, logic, arts, and sciences. They *are* terrific stories. At present, teachers are encouraged to plan by organizing the curriculum into sets of objectives to be attained. If we were to think of lessons and units as good stories to be told rather than (or in addition to) objectives to be attained, we might be able to organize our content in ways that make it more accessible and engaging to young children (a topic considered at more length in Chapter 2).

If we consider just a few features of the story form, we should be able to develop a technique for the planning and teaching of lessons and units that would offer an alternative to the now dominant objectives-content-methods-evaluation schemes derived from Ralph Tyler's model (1949). The selection of content for the class or unit to be planned would be determined by identifying what binary opposites best catch and expose its most important themes. A unit on heat, for example, might be planned around the dichotomy of heat-as-helper/heat-as-destroyer. A class on the Vikings might use survival/destruction as a central story theme. We might re-create the terror induced by a Viking raid on a monastic community. We would not have to *explain* the value of manuscripts or sacred vessels, but instead would *show* their value through the horror felt by the monks at their destruction. Then we could select the remaining content according to the related criteria provided by the central binary conflict, to elaborate and develop the story. The conclusion of the lesson, or unit, would come with the resolution or mediation of the binary opposites whose conflict set the story in motion. Mediation might be sought, for example, by indicating the value of the constructive energy of the Vikings in the overall story of Western culture. Evaluation of such lessons or units might focus on children's understanding of the content in the context of the overall story, and on their coherent use of the content in stories of their own.

I recognize that the prominence of binary opposites here will seem a little odd to many people. Their use need not lead to extreme reduction-ism. My argument, made at greater length in Chapter 4 and mentioned in other chapters, is simply based on the prominence and utility of initially grasping the world in binary terms. Some (for example, Lévi-Strauss, 1966a) argue that the use of binary opposites is simply a function of the structure of the human mind. I think one need not go so far in order to recognize their ubiquitousness in the forms of thought common in oral cultures and in the ways young children spontaneously make sense of the world and experience.

Some of the teaching and curriculum practices sketched above are, of course, already evident in some classrooms. If my description of orality is accurate and relevant to the education of young children, it would be surprising if many teachers had not shaped their lessons and teaching methods, in their own ways, to draw on some of the same observations about children—even though those observations might be articulated in different terms. I do not claim originality for these ideas on educational implications of orality; rather, I am concerned to establish a set of principles that might help us more systematically and routinely achieve the kinds of successes that good teachers manage daily.

The most general implication of this brief exploration is that we should consider children when they come to school as already in possession of some features of orality that are *bon à penser*. Their ability to think and learn is, in general, sophisticated, but structured according to norms significantly different from those of literate adults. Two corollaries follow. First, clear understanding of children's orality is essential if we are to make what we want to teach engaging and meaningful; second, orality entails valuable forms of thought that need to be developed as the foundation for a sophisticated literacy and Western rationality. If we see the educational task as simply to put literacy in place, we risk undermining the very foundations on which a rich literacy must rest. Stimulating children's imaginations, metaphoric fluency, and narrative sophistication can become a more prominent aim of early education. Such a view might help to resolve what is often seen as a conflict in early education between the need to establish the "skills" of literacy and rational thought and the wish to encourage more varied experience and imaginative development. This brief exploration should have shown that these are not competitors; rather, the fullest achievement of literacy requires the fullest achievement of oral capacities as well.

CHAPTER 2

Narrative and Learning:
A Voyage of Implications

I wrote this essay originally for a symposium that Hunter McEwan, University of Hawaii—poor guy—and I organized for the 1993 American Educational Research Association conference. Papers from that symposium, augmented by some others we solicited, appeared in book form in our co-edited Narrative in Teaching, Learning, and Research *(New York: Teachers College Press, 1995). After the conference I was asked to submit the essay to the journal* Linguistics and Education *(Vol. 5, No. 2, 1993), where it appeared as a "target" article with responses from Howard Gardner, Ann Berthoff, Deborah Hicks, Jenny Cook-Gumperz, and others. I am grateful to the editor and publisher for permission to reprint the article. I have placed it here because it picks up the general theme of the preceding essay, and, I'm afraid, repeats a bit of its argument. But this is much more concise and uses the argument for rather different purposes.*

INTRODUCTION

Jerome Bruner's *Actual Minds, Possible Worlds* (1986) has helped popularize within educational research a conception of the mind that gives renewed prominence to the role of narrative in our ways of making sense of the world and of experience. The conception of the mind as, in whatever degree, "a narrative concern" (Sutton-Smith, 1988, p. 22) is supported by a wealth of modern research, from Bartlett's celebrated studies on memory (1932), to Bransford and associates' (1972, 1975) and Rumelhart's (1975) work in the 1970s, to the recent and current large-scale focus on scripts, schemata, and stories. This research has established, to use Gardner's (1985) summing up, "that human subjects do not come to tasks as empty slates: they have expectations and well-structured schemata within which they approach diverse material" (p. 126). While this may seem only to echo a point that *Gestalt* psychologists earlier in the century took for granted, the additional result of this research has been to give us a more elaborate and detailed understanding of how such scripts, schemata, and stories are deployed in our sense-making.

My aim here is not to explore this research, nor to assess its findings, but rather to assume the validity of its most general conclusion and explore some implications for our concepts, theories, and principles of learning. That is, I will consider how focusing on the mind as a narrative concern might affect our ideas about learning in general and about some of the learning principles we use to guide teaching practice and even curriculum structure. (This is not, of course, to presume that the mind is *only* a narrative concern.)

The general conceptions we may hold about the mind obviously influence in profound ways our ideas about learning. Often it seems that significant changes in general conceptions of mind take some time to percolate through the range of mental attributes on which research goes forward. The "narrative mind" has had limited percolation onto conceptions of learning. Or, at least, there seems some lag between acceptance of a significant narrative component in our mental lives and elaboration of ideas about learning that clearly reflect that narrative component.

What I want to do here, then, is briefly examine just one kind of narrative that seems universally engaging to young children—the classic fairy tale. I will try to show that an analysis of a few simple observations we can make about these narratives raises quite dramatic challenges to the concepts of learning derived from traditional kinds of research based on non-narrative tasks. Straightforward inferences from these observations also challenge some of the more prominent learning principles that one finds underlying teaching practices and curriculum structuring. This is intended as a very general exploration of how wide and deep through education might run the implications of taking the narrative mind to heart.

OBSERVATION I: THE STRUCTURE OF FAIRY TALES

The classic fairy tales, such as "Jack and the Beanstalk," "Hansel and Gretel," "Cinderella," "Little Red Riding Hood," and so on, have a considerable power to engage young children in Western cultural settings, and children learn and remember their contents quite readily. One of the most obvious structural features of these stories is that they are based on powerful conflicts between security and danger, courage and cowardice, cleverness and stupidity, hope and despair, and good and evil. This feature of these stories has been observed often, and is commonly taken as a reflection of the "manner in which the child can bring order into [his or her] world . . . by dividing everything into opposites" (Bettelheim, 1976, p. 74).

The stories are made up of characters and events that give a concrete form to the underlying abstract binary concepts. The narrative brings the underlying security/danger, courage/cowardice, cleverness/stupidity, and so on, into conflict, then elaborates the conflict and finally brings it to some resolution. Two features of these underlying concepts are noteworthy. First, they are abstract, and, second, they are affective.

For the classic fairy stories to make sense, children must in some sense be familiar with security/danger, courage/cowardice, hope/despair, and so on. Children need not, of course, be able to articulate, or define, such terms to be able to deploy them. It seems uncontentious to observe that these abstract, binary concepts are constantly deployed by children in making sense of the world and their experience. We can see such concepts structuring children's own invented narratives constantly (Paley, 1981, 1984, 1990). The ubiquity of abstract binary concepts undergirding classic fairy stories and children's invented narratives suggests that their presence is hardly an incidental or casual matter. Also, Lévi-Strauss's (1969) observation of their vital role in structuring myths suggests that we might sensibly give them more attention.

IMPLICATION I: ABSTRACTIONS
IN YOUNG CHILDREN'S THINKING

We are familiar with claims that young children's thinking is in some sense "concrete," and that if we want to make material accessible to them we need to present it in concrete terms. But the implication of the above observation is that young children's thinking is also "abstract," or at least that abstractions are clearly important and necessary ingredients in children's ability to make sense of the kinds of stories they find readily engaging. And it seems to be the abstractions, especially when organized in terms of binary opposites, that provide access to and engagement with the "concrete" content. The wanderings of Hansel and Gretel through a medieval forest would not engage interest without the underlying conflict between anxiety and security. Far from young children being unable to deal with abstractions, in such narratives they deploy easily and readily the most abstract ideas we ever learn.

This implication yields the hypothesis that to make content most accessible and engaging to young children, it should be organized in terms of abstract binary concepts. That is, it is the combination of concrete content with powerful abstractions that enables young children to understand material most readily. (And we can organize mathematics and science content on such concepts as easily as we can construct fictional fairy stories on them, as I have tried to demonstrate with examples in a number of books.)

IMPLICATION 2: RELEVANCE TO ABSTRACT CONCEPTS

It is commonly claimed—indeed, it seems to be generally accepted as a truism—that children will learn more effectively if what is taught is made relevant to their experience. This has most commonly been interpreted as the learning principle that new knowledge can be made "relevant" by connecting it with what Dewey (1916/1966) called the "material of ordinary acquaintance" (p. 258). This in turn is most commonly interpreted as requiring some association between what is to be taught and students' everyday experience, environment, or interests. The earlier observation implies that any content can be made relevant to children's experience if we can identify within that content, or can organize it in terms of, the abstract binary concepts children deploy so readily. That is, "relevance" moves from a principle of content associations to one of finding the appropriate binary abstractions to embody the content.

This implication also challenges a prominent principle used in curriculum design. It is a principle that finds expression in "expanding-horizons" curricula. The elementary social studies curriculum has for generations been structured on the assumption that what is most relevant, and so meaningful, to young children is content to do with themselves, their homes and families, their neighborhoods, and so on. The curriculum is designed to expand gradually outward from these to other communities, the nation, other nations, and so on, building on the concepts familiar from everyday experience.

It is worth noting how common this assumption is. Nearly all social studies textbooks justify the structure of the curriculum by reference to this principle as though it is entirely unproblematic: "Thus, kindergarten and first-grade students spend a lot of social studies time studying self-awareness and families because these two topics have a sense of relevance and immediacy to young children" (Ellis, 1986, p. 9). The set of expanding-horizons topics is justified because "the social studies program should be built on what the child already knows," (Jarolimek, 1982, p. 12). But consider also the following use of the principle: "The sort of familiarity which a child demands in a story is often a social one, a doing of things which the child expects to have done. Thus *Peter Rabbit* is a manageable story for Carol at two years eight months because of its familiar family setting" (Applebee, 1978, p. 75). But if it is familiarity from the child's experience that makes the story accessible or manageable, one must wonder why Peter is a rabbit. Also, one might wonder about the wild wood, which is safe, and the cultivated garden, which is dangerous, and the closeness of death, and so on. Clearly something other than familiarity with everyday experience makes narratives and their content engaging to children. The one element observed above implies a principle quite at variance with what shapes the social studies curriculum and claims such as Applebee's. Similarly, Jarolimek's claim that the curriculum should be built on what the child knows fails to notice that children also "know" love/hate, anxiety/ security, courage/cowardice, and so on, and that through these profound, affective concepts any content can be made accessible and "relevant." The key to what children can learn is not simply content associations with what they already know. We can observe medieval forests, galaxies long ago and far away, witches, giants, and space warriors all becoming immediately and vividly "relevant" to children's interests by their embodying abstract binary opposite concepts.

OBSERVATION 2: MEDIATION OF BINARY CONCEPTS

How can we account for the fact that young children are so commonly engaged by a story about a rabbit who wears a nice blue coat and is given cups of camomile tea by his mother? The idea that children's grasp of the world proceeds from the familiar gradually outward cannot account for one of the most obvious features we may observe in children's narrative intellectual lives—the engagement by the fantastic, by talking middle-class rabbits and endless things outside of their or anyone's experience.

It is difficult to gain evidence of some features of children's conceptual development, because some developments can be reliably traced only by longitudinal studies requiring constant monitoring. For example, it is not clear how children master sets of concepts related to such phenomena as time, space, temperature, and other phenomenal continua (see the discussion in Siegler, 1991). Not only are adequate data hard to come by, but, as Flavell (1984) has noted, it is even harder to know how to characterize the mechanisms of development that the data give hints of (p. 189). But we may observe some common procedures, and build simple models that are, while in this case not empirically uncontentious, at least consistent with what data we have. The other support for the model I will describe comes again from studies of the thinking of people in oral cultures, and how myths encode information (see Chapter 1). There is also an element of logical necessity in the process. Further, the following observation merits attention because it seems to offer an explanation of what no other theory seems to account for adequately.

If we consider how young children accumulate concepts concerning, say, the temperature continuum, it seems that they first learn the concepts "hot" and "cold." This would seem to verge on logical necessity, given that initial discriminations of temperature would be "hotter than my body temperature" and "colder than my body temperature." Also, any discrimination is built on such a binary logic, which most simply distinguishes X from all other things that are not X. Following Lévi-Strauss's observations (1966a, 1966b, 1967), it would seem that it is common then for a mediating concept, such as "warm," to be grasped. Then the child may mediate between "warm" and "cold," gathering the meaning of a concept like "cool," and by a similar process of mediating between binary terms a set of concepts is discriminated for dealing with the temperature continuum.

Now this might be dismissed as possibly interesting but no more than an unsupported speculation. It is an awkward speculation, because on the one hand it would be very hard to design experiments to either support or falsify it, and on the other hand it has a nagging plausibility for anyone who has spent much time observing young children's narratives—in which this binary opposition and mediation process appears irritatingly ubiquitous once one has had the model suggested.

Another reason for not casually dismissing this model of conceptual development is its potential for explaining the appeal of Peter Rabbit. If this binary discrimination and mediation process is common in children's conceptual development, helping them to gain an efficient and effective conceptual grasp on a whole range of phenomenal continua in the world, what happens when it is applied to phenomena that are made up of discrete opposites? Any continuum allows one to form binary oppositions, set at each end of the continuum, and then form a concept that mediates between the two extremes. The new concept, such as "cool" between "hot" and "cold," might be seen as a coalescence of the two extremes. But what if the binary terms are "life" and "death," or "human" and "animal," or "nature" and "culture"? How does one mediate between these?

Indeed, discrimination between things that are alive and things that are dead is typically learned very early in our experience, and is certainly presupposed in the most basic stories. It is precisely the fear of death that makes Peter Rabbit's exertions in Mr. McGregor's garden meaningful, and gives tension to Hansel and Gretel's adventures. What happens when we mediate between life and death, or when we coalesce these concepts? Well, we get things like ghosts. A ghost is both alive and dead, as cool is both hot and cold. And when we mediate between human and animal? We get things like yetis and sasquatches—creatures that are both human and animal as ghosts are alive and dead, and cool is both hot and cold. And what do we generate when we mediate between things that are natural and things that are cultural? We get creatures like Peter Rabbit. Peter is a rabbit—a natural creature—but he is also human in his use of language, his clothes, and his emotions. That is, the fantasy stories of children are in significant degree made up of mediational categories between the most basic discriminations we make between empirically discrete categories. (This would seem to be a much more economical explanation of the fantasy worlds of young children than those offered in various psychoanalytic theories.)

IMPLICATION 3: LEARNING AND CURRICULUM

From reflecting on the curious content of children's fantasy narratives— and we find similar characteristics in both the classic fairy tales and in children's own narratives (Paley, 1981, 1984, 1990)—we are inclined in the direction of a hypothesis about children's learning that is powerful and plausible, and that merits research attention. Whatever the conclusion of research about the prevalence of the binary discrimination and mediation procedure in children's learning, the observation about the exotic content raises a further challenge to the expanding-horizons model of curriculum organization. It may be that the hypothesized explanation of the mediational categories that fill children's fantasy is the wrong explanation, but the fact of the peculiar categories, such as talking middle-class rabbits, fairy godmothers, hobbits, and so on, carries its own implications.

The expanding-horizons model assumes that children's understanding moves most effectively from local and familiar content and experience gradually outward, by means of threads of content association. It is a linear model (even if the line is supposed to "spiral" outward). An interesting feature of the binary discrimination/mediation model is its ability easily to account for children's engagement with both fantasy and exotic real-life content. Such content forms a prominent part of children's thinking. The linear learning principle embedded in expanding horizons would seem to be quite incapable of accounting for this very prominent feature of children's thinking. Indeed, children's own narratives (Paley, 1981, 1984, 1990) jump around to fantasy and the exotic very readily. Any attempt to trace expanding horizons–like connections would seem entirely futile. What is also evident in the binary opposites/mediation model is that the generation of the mediating category is commonly made by a metaphorical leap rather than by a content association. Given the abstractness of the most powerful binary opposites, this is hardly surprising, of course.

The degree to which we impose an expanding-horizons style of curriculum on children, and the degree to which we incorporate its associationist learning principle in teaching, reflects the degree to which we contravene or ignore something important in children's learning. Obviously children can learn content organized in this fashion, but accepting it as a general truth about children's learning is to adopt an unnecessarily restrictive principle for both curriculum and teaching.

CONCLUSION

The simple observation that young children have no difficulty being engaged by the weirdest creatures in the most exotic locales plainly denies the general validity of expanding-horizons principles, and those taken for granted even by so sensitive an interpreter of children's stories as Applebee (1978). It might be objected that what is true of being engaged by fantasy worlds does not translate to learning about the real world—that fantasy concepts are not equivalent to realistic concepts. This is a reasonable defensive position for those who wish to defend learning theories derived from non-narrative tasks, but the onus is on them to explain why that should be the case. If our concern is some mechanisms of children's thinking brought into focus by reflecting on children's narratives, it seems that we can see at work some forms of thinking that challenge current learning theories, and learning principles applied in teaching and curricula.

A few qualifiers before closing: Calling the mind a "narrative concern" does not imply that it is not also a logico-mathematical, aesthetic, and moral concern; focusing on the few characteristics of learning that are addressed above does not imply that these are all there are; suggesting that children use binary opposites and mediating does not imply that children *only* use binary opposites and mediation in learning; suggesting the value of the story in shaping the curriculum does not imply that *all* curriculum content must be story-shaped, all the time; and focusing on the discourse form of the fairy tale does not imply that children do not grasp and use in learning a wide variety of other discourse forms.

CHAPTER 3

Teaching the Romantic Mind

A colleague pointed out to me that the English Journal *was inviting articles for a special section to be titled "The Visionary Gleam," which appeared in Vol. 83, No. 4, in April 1994. They had used a brief discussion of my book* Romantic Understanding *(New York: Routledge, 1990) to frame their invitation for articles that explored what Romanticism as an intellectual movement could contribute to our understanding of how to teach adolescents today. They wanted to follow up the connections among Romanticism, imagination, and adolescents' thinking. I can't remember now how I contacted the editors—perhaps I brazenly phoned—but I was invited to contribute a piece. Anyway, I put this essay here because it follows the theme of the previous one—of observing common features in students' everyday imaginative engagements and exploring their educational implications. In this case, though, I look at adolescents' imaginative lives. While I use an example from English—to show how one might imaginatively teach punctuation—the principles of what engages students' imaginations apply across the curriculum. I was relieved, on rereading it, to see that Peter Rabbit makes an appearance yet again, if only very briefly. I am grateful for the editor's and publisher's permission to reprint the essay here (pp. 16–25 of the April 1994 issue of the* English Journal*).*

INTRODUCTION

"Romanticism" is one of those labels for enormously complex histori-cal events, like "Renaissance" and "Reformation," that have been found useful in highlighting some features of a period, but that historians con-stantly warn us not to take too seriously. *Romanticism* is a term that was first used in the late 19th century to point up a set of characteristics that seemed especially prominent in the works of some writers and artists of the late 18th and early 19th centuries. People like Coleridge, Wordsworth, and Keats would probably have been puzzled to hear themselves called "romantics," as a romance to them was a kind of gothic narrative inhab-ited by peculiar characters like Sir Galahad. But the term was chosen to highlight a set of characteristics found in their writings, some of which can be quite easily listed: delight in the exotic, emphasis on individualism, revolt against conventional forms, stress on the importance of imagination, intense inquiry about the self, resistence to order and reason, glorification of transcendent human qualities, and so on.

Consider for a moment your favorite group of adolescents in terms of these characteristics. Or consider the modern pop-singing idols or the comic-book heroes. While the list above is in language used by literary critics, some of the characteristics apply quite well to the typical adolescent today, or to the appeal of a performer like a comic-book hero such as Wolverine or to the Myst computer game, or to *The X-Files* television show. Is this similarity a result of simply straining meanings? Or a coincidence? Or is there perhaps—as I will argue—something profoundly important for education here, something largely neglected by current educational research?

Perhaps the central distinctive feature of Romanticism was the recognition and assertion of the importance of the imagination in our intellectual makeup. We are creatures defined and marked off from other animals by our reason, as prominent thinkers of the Enlightenment had argued, but we are also at least equally defined by our imagination: "The primary imagination I hold to be the living power and prime agent of all human perception and a repetition in the finite mind of the eternal act of creation in the infinite I AM" (Coleridge, 1817, p. 185).

The importance of Romanticism for education today seems manifold, and is largely unexplored. One of the greatest educational thinkers in the Western tradition is surely William Wordsworth, but because he wrote in verse rather than in dull prose his ideas have been largely ignored by educationalists. Let me move into my main theme through two of Wordsworth's educational ideas.

First is his conception of development, elaborated in his long autobiographical poem *The Prelude* and vividly sketched in his "Intimations of Immortality" ode. Imagination plays a significant role in Wordsworth's conception of development; consequently, the profile of development that he draws is quite unlike that commonly articulated in modern theories of psychological development. In these latter, the developmental process is represented as inevitably progressive, leading by gradually improving stages to completion in adulthood. Such theories, like Piaget's and those of his successors, are "hierarchical integrative" schemes, and they focus on a relatively narrow thread of logico-mathematical thinking among the broad band of human cognition. Once one considers imagination, and the metaphoric fluency that provides one index of it, it becomes clear that the typical developmental profile in our culture cannot adequately be represented by the usual ascending stages. A conception of educational development enlightened by a concern with imagination presents us with a view of our

task that is more risky; education becomes not just a process of maximiz-
ing gains, but also one of minimizing losses. It becomes a process in which
literacy, for example, cannot be viewed as a simple gain, but one in which
conventionally and dully taught literacy can lead to the suppression of
important imaginative capacities.

Second is Wordsworth's recognition that the conflict between reason
and imagination is unreal, that the dichotomizing of the two leads to an
improper conception of how human beings make sense of their world and
experience. It is hard for us to conceive of education without the ancient
quarrel between reason and imagination, and the curriculum divided
among subjects that are supposed to exercise and develop one or the other.
But Wordsworth argues for just such a curriculum, showing how we should
transcend the split between the two ancient antagonists, and recognize
that "Imagination is . . . Reason in her most exalted mood" (*The Prelude*,
XIV, line 192).

Following Wordsworth's lead, then, I want to focus on characteristics
of students' thinking in which reason and imagination work together. The
kinds of categories or descriptions of thinking that result are rather unlike
those we are familiar with from typical developmental theories and theories of learning, which have focused very largely on logico-mathematical
skills. In the following sections I will briefly consider a set of characteristics derived in part from a study of Romanticism and in part from a study
of modern adolescents' thinking when they are imaginatively engaged with
favorite games, films, pastimes, stories, hobbies, and so on. This comes
without the usual appurtenances of empirical research, because dominant
methods of research have had considerable difficulty dealing with the
imagination, except in very restricted ways (Egan, 1992). What it does offer
is a range of empirical observations that seem not to need documentation
for the most part because they are uncontentious.

So I will begin by characterizing some features of adolescents' imaginative thinking. I will note briefly a principle for teaching that seems to
follow from each feature, and I will construct from the principles a planning framework that could be used to teach in a way that should be imaginatively engaging to adolescent students. Finally I will give a brief example
of how the framework might be used to plan a set of lessons on what might
seem like the intractible topic of punctuation.

But how is there a connection between Romanticism and adolescents'
thinking today? This is not something I can show in any detail here (but
see Egan, 1990, 1997). In general my claim (echoing that of many people
before me) is that the "technologies" we use in our thinking—like language and literacy—influence the kinds of understanding we construct
of the world and of our experience. Print-based alphabetic literacy as it

has developed in the West stimulates a particular kind of understanding. In cultural history one result of this "technology" is Romanticism. As adolescents today internalize this technology, a related result is what I call "romantic understanding," some characteristics of which I will discuss below. What I hope will be evident from the following sections are some surprising parallels between the historical cultural movement and adolescents' engagements today, and that my general claim will seem at least plausible.

THE LIMITS OF REALITY AND
THE EXTREMES OF EXPERIENCE

If you tell a typical 5-year-old the story of Cinderella, you are not likely to be asked "What means of locomotion does the Fairy Godmother use?" But if you tell a typical 10-year-old the equally fantastic story of Superman, you will need to explain his supernatural powers by reference to his birth on the planet Krypton and to the different molecular structure of our Sun from that of his home star, and so on. (Alas, I've forgotten the details and, lamentably, none of the reference books I have to hand is able to help.) For the younger audience, magic is entirely unobjectionable as long as it moves the story along. Peter Rabbit's world does not make the kind of accommodations with reality that are necessary for the rabbits Hazel and Bigwig in the world of Richard Adams's *Watership Down*; Hazel could not bring Bigwig a nice cup of camomile tea, for instance—his paws wouldn't be able to hold it.

One way to simplify what we see happening between 5 and 10 through such an example is to say that with literacy we begin to focus on what we come to call reality. It has been a part of the folklore of teaching that if you want to teach students about reality you must begin with what they already know, with what is familiar in their everyday environment, with "where they are at." This is a principle that derives from a focus on students' logicomathematical thinking. But if we also consider their imaginative lives, we see something quite different from what this principle leads us to expect.

Consider for a moment, if you want to engage students' imaginations on a Friday afternoon, whether a unit on "the structure of your neighborhood" or one on "torture instruments through the ages" would do the job better. This is not a curriculum recommendation (!), but it exposes something that seems profoundly at odds with the recommendation that we begin with what the student already knows. The resolution, of course, is that the students do already know about pain and horror and cruelty. That is, if we consider their affective lives and their imaginative lives in what they "know," we can save the principle.

But we should reformulate that principle if it is to offer clearer guidance to teaching. The most casual observation of what engages adolescents' imaginations shows that materials that deal with the limits of reality and the extremes of experience are most engaging: the most courageous or cruelest acts, the most bizarre and strange natural phenomena, the most wonderful and terrible events. *The Guinness Book of Records* exploits this characteristic, most profitably for its publishers, as do TV shows, comics, films, books, and so on, that focus on the bizarre, the amazing, the extreme, the exotic.

Let us, then, discard the logical principle that students' understanding moves along associations from the known to the unknown; clearly they can directly engage new knowledge that is affectively engaging and deals with some extreme or limit. In place of the logical principle we can try the reformulated one that we should bring out some exotic or extreme feature of any topic. This does not mean that every class must become an eye-popping extravaganza of the bizarre, but it does require the teacher to locate in the material something that is strange, wonderful, or extreme.

This principle is not intended to lead to empty sensationalism, but is designed rather to put students in touch with the boundaries, the limits, the context of the material they are dealing with. After all, attention to the limits and extremes is a perfectly sensible strategy for exploring the world being exposed by expanding literacy. We begin sensibly by locating the limits, setting clearly in place the context of our world. The principle of "starting where the student is" need not be mischievous as long as we remember that the student has an imagination, and "where the student's imagination is" can be in the valleys of the moon as well as in their local neighborhood. We make sense of our neighborhood no less in terms of our imagination of the valleys of the moon than we make sense of the valleys of the moon in terms of our understanding of our neighborhoods. There is, that is, constant dialectical play between what we know and what we imagine. If our beginning principle focuses only on what we know in some simplistic sense, ignoring how that is enlightened by what we imagine, we will unnecessarily constrict our teaching, our curricula, and students' learning, and we will incidentally likely bore them mindless.

TRANSCENDENCE WITHIN REALITY—THE HEROIC

Adolescents are relatively powerless but grow increasingly aware that the society that hems them in and constrains them is one of which they are becoming a part. A common imaginative response to the constraints on their lives, such as the rules of parents, of schools, of authorities of all kinds, is to associate with those who seem best able to transcend, to overcome, the constraints that most irk the student. So a pop singer or a basket-ball star might form the object of a "romantic association" because he or she might seem to embody the reckless disregard of conventions or the independence and power the students lack or cannot express in their lives. Teen-exploitation movies, such as *Ferris Bueller's Day Off*, or novels such as *Anne of Green Gables* and its down-market kin, feature characters who are at one level subject to constraints similar as those of the student read-ers or viewers, but the characters transcend the constraints and triumph over those who contrained them, whether parents, teachers, conventional behavior, or adult society in general. The student associates with the con-fidence, self-reliance, persistence, ingenuity, strength, or whatever, of the heroic character and so shares the transcendence.

But it is not so much the heroic character with which the student as-sociates, but rather the transcendent quality the character embodies. So it is not so much that we need to find heroic characters all the time, Sir Galahads, Florence Nightingales, or Marie Curies; we can locate transcen-dent qualities, such as courage, compassion, persistence, energy, power, ingenuity, and so on, in almost anything in the world. It could be the tenacity of a weed on a rock face, the serene patience of a cat, or the en-durance of standing stones in a gale; almost any feature of the world can be imbued with a transcendent quality if we conceive of it romantically. Associating with the transcendent involves the student in imaginatively inhabiting the object in some degree.

A principle that follows from this common observation is that we might plan to encourage students to see some transcendent quality in the mate-rial being studied with which he or she could romantically associate. The trick is to see how one can easily "heroize" anything: That discarded styro-foam cup, instead of being conceived simply as environmentally destruc-tive litter, can be conceived, if only for a moment, as the product of immense ingenuity and the patient work of chemists over centuries; we can hold our fingers within millimeters of scalding liquids and not be burned or even discomforted. For a moment we can see the cup as an object of wonder. This capacity to highlight anything and hold it in a transcendent light is something we can "turn on" at any time. It isn't exactly Wordsworth's "visionary gleam," but is perhaps a little sibling of it that the teacher can call upon to stimulate imaginative engagement with any material.

IMAGE AND CONCEPT

Bringing the imagination to the fore in thinking about education raises the question of the role of affective images in teaching. We have inherited ideas and practices of education that give pride of place to the dis-embedded concept and seem to have neglected or forgotten what all the most powerful communicative media in our cultural history make plain to us—that the affective image is crucial in communicating meaning and significance.

Certainly affective images are not necessary to all imaginative activity. We can define imagination as the capacity to think of things as other than they are, or of things as possibly being so (White, 1990) or even as "the subjunctive mood" (Sutton-Smith, 1988). But however we define it, it is clear that somehow significant to imaginative activity is thinking and feeling using mental images.

The images that seem to have most power are those we generate ourselves from words. Films, for example, rarely capture the emotional vividness and force of literature. This is to emphasize that I am not suggesting that we need more visual illustration of materials, but rather that the teacher be more hospitable to the mental images evoked by any topic. In planning teaching, to draw a principle from this observation, we should not just dwell on the concepts that are important, but give at least equal time to reflecting on the images that are a part of the topic. It is the images that can vividly carry the concepts most richly to the students' understanding. The image can carry the imagination to inhabit in some sense the object of our study and inquiry. By such means mathematics and physics, history and auto-mechanics, are not conceived as external things that the student learns facts about but become a part of the the student; students thus learn that they are mathematical, historical, mechanical creatures.

So, for example, in teaching poetry this principle will lead us to attend to images not only as things to be observed in the mind's eye and understood in the overall structure of the poem, but also as things the student can inhabit or get inside of, so to speak. Poetry, then, is not something we make or read, but something we are. Perhaps this principle is more urgent for the science or the mathematics teacher, where the image is more commonly neglected, but, even though images might be the focus of much poetry teaching, the affective power that can come from inhabiting them could probably be more frequently drawn upon. If teaching William Blake's *The Tiger*, one can encourage the students to evoke as vividly as they can "the forests of the night" and then the "Tiger! Tiger! burning bright" within them. What are the students' forests of the night—the dread places of their imaginations? On a re-reading, ask them to be the burning tiger, being violently constructed piece by piece; to feel the distant deeps that become the fire in their eyes, their massive pounding heart, the deadly terrors of their brain. On a further re-reading, ask them to build an image of the maker of this deadly terror—twisting sinews in the awful factory with its inconceivable hammer, chains, furnace, and anvil; then after constructing this demonic horror perhaps turning to compose the Lamb. The images will probably not be precise quasi-pictures so much as intimations of power, terror, immensity in the fragmented, flashing images Blake uses to express a very particular kind of awe and wonder.

IDEALISM AND REVOLT

Increasingly during adolescence, students recognize that the world that constrains them is also their inheritance. It is a period of adjustments, from powerlessness to growing independence and power. Inevitably students will sometimes feel that the adult world is not according them appropriate independence and power; parents are unjustly restrictive, schools are excessively restraining, society at large treats them too inconsiderately. Typically, students respond with revolt, even if only in the muted form of sulking reluctance to conform or quiet resistance. More visibly it takes the forms of flaunting styles of hair, clothing, music, and dancing that confront adult conventions and values.

It is the world's failure to live up to some ideal that justifies the revolt, in the student's eyes. The sense of the ideal world typically shifts unstably during these years, as do students' views of their ideal selves. We see them trying on roles, much as was common during the Romantic period: the confident hero (adopted for real life by Byron from Walter Scott's novels [Butler, 1981]), the serene lady, the rebel, the fashion plate or dandy, the hoyden, the macho, the tease, the socialite, the cool dude, the iceberg, the friendly innocent, and so on. These are reflections of roles played out more fantasically in the imagination—the waster of cities, the silent, unseen benefactor, the film-star beloved of millions, the swashbuckling savior of nations, the preserver of the planet from polluters, and so on.

We routinely observe, and no doubt remember, and perhaps still experience, this characteristic of adolescence. But how do we extract from it a principle for more imaginative teaching? It is a cliché that adolescents develop varied forms of revolt and begin to fashion ideals, and that these two are connected. At the simplest level, material to be learned can be given a heightened "romantic" power of engagement by being shown in a context of revolt against unjust or inadequate and constraining conventions. Even if it is just punctuation and paragraphing that we want to teach, we might see how it can be made more meaningful and engaging if we see these as revolts against constraining conventions in early manuscripts. So we might consider their introduction by revolutionary figures like Hugh of St. Victor (Illich, 1993) whose daring new ideas made texts easier to decipher and read. What this suggests in general is the desirability of re-embedding knowledge we want students to learn in the emotional and imaginatively reconstructed reality of people's lives from which typical textbooks usually rip it.

DETAILS, DETAILS

The imaginative engagement with the extremes of reality represents one strategy for exploring the world. It is reflected at the other end of the scale by another strategy that we see at work in students' collections or obsessive hobbies. By discovering everything about something, one can gain further intellectual security. The typical profile of a hobby or collection is that it gets seriously underway at about the time literacy becomes internalized, about 8 in our culture, peaks at about 11 or 12, and begins to lose energy at about 15.

Students may collect almost anything: ornamental spoons, memorabilia of a favorite pop singer—records *and* tapes *and* CDs, tour T-shirts, pictures, and so forth—hockey cards, dolls in national dresses, comic sets, beer bottle caps, the books of some author in a uniform edition, stones or shells, leaves, illustrations of costumes through the ages, or whatever. The object of the collecting instinct or the hobby seems arbitrary; what matters is the intellectual control of some feature of reality and the intellectual security it can provide.

This urge to master something in exhaustive detail is perhaps the most powerful learning drive that one sees in the typical adolescent. It is a drive exploited more by commercial interests than by educators, however, and seems largely ignored by educational research. But how can this observation lead to a principle for more imaginatively engaging teaching and learning? Obviously any material dealt with in schools can become a focus for detailed work. The trick here seems to be twofold. First, one of the other principles has to be deployed to engage students with a particular topic and, second, the teacher has to focus on material within the topic that is *exhaustible*. Simply indicating material that might be studied in greater detail does not meet either of these two criteria. What is needed to meet the second criterion is material about which the student can learn *everything*, or at least learn securely what the scale of the topic is. Even if the students cannot learn everything, they can learn what would have to be known to exhaust the topic—as the collector of hockey cards may not have all of a set but knows which further cards comprise the whole set.

HUMANIZING KNOWLEDGE

As any journalist knows, information can be made more engaging if given a "human interest" angle. That is, knowledge seen through, or by means of, human emotions, intentions, hopes, fears, and so on, is not only more directly comprehensible but is also more meaningful and engaging than knowledge presented disembedded from its human source. Every teacher knows how the illustrative anecdote, particularly if it involves extremes of human endurance or foresight or ingenuity or compassion or suffering, grabs students' attention. Can we generalize from this widely recognized practice, seeing why it is so engaging of students' imaginations, and develop a more widely applicable principle?

The structure of typical textbooks with neatly organized and segmented knowledge tends to support the belief that the textbook or the encyclopedia exhibits the ideal form of knowledge. This bizarre idea is no doubt one of the more peculiar consequences of literacy. In the face of this seemingly unconscious assumption, it is necessary to emphasize constantly in education that books do not contain knowledge. Books contain symbolic codes that serve as external mnemonics for knowledge. Knowledge exists only in human minds, and in minds its meaning derives from how it connects with our hopes, fears, and intentions, and with our imaginative lives.

In emphasizing the difference between inert symbolic codes in books and living knowledge in human minds, attention is drawn to something significant, and often neglected, about teaching. The point is not to get the symbolic codes as they exist in books into the students' minds. We can of course do that—training students to be rather ineffective "copies" of books. Rather, the teaching task is to reconstitute the inert symbolic code into living human knowledge. The point that knowledge is *living* seems crucial. Knowledge in our minds is a function of the organization of our living organism; it is not some interchangeable code we can pick up, like computer data.

The educational task, then, involves the resuscitation of knowledge from its suspended animation in symbolic codes. The task is to convert, to reanimate, to transmute the symbolic codes into living human knowledge in students' minds. This is the challenge whether the knowledge is about earthworms or is a literary text. The codes do not carry guarantees of meaning. The instrument best able to ensure the transformation from codes to living knowledge is the imagination. Students can most easily resuscitate knowledge if they learn it in the human context in which it was first generated or discovered.

THE NARRATIVE MIND

Focus on the imagination brings to the fore, as has been noted already, the emotions. The emotions in turn are not subject to neat categorization, but seem to be expressable only in narratives. The main narrative we have for clearly conveying emotional meaning is the story: "Man is in his actions and practice, as well as in his fictions, essentially a story-telling animal" (MacIntyre, 1981, p. 201). Any event or behavior or information "becomes intelligible by finding its place in a narrative" (p. 196). As Barbara Hardy (1968) famously put it: "We dream in narrative, daydream in narrative, remember, anticipate, hope, despair, believe, doubt, plan, revise, criticize, construct, gossip, learn, hate and live by narrative" (p. 5). We might begin to think of teaching as storytelling (Egan, 1989), and teachers as connected with an ancient tradition rather than as conveyers of skills required by local economic conditions—as many seem to view them.

This observation leads us to a principle concerning how we might most generally construct our lessons and units. If we plan them as imaginative narratives rather than as rationally ordered conceptual structures, we might stand a better chance of engaging our students' imaginations in the material being taught. But this way of putting it falls into the dichotomy Wordsworth warned us about. We do not face an either/or here, of course. Rather, what I am arguing is that we can devise ways of incorporating both into our planning. How? Well, let me try to construct a framework for planning teaching that pulls together the set of principles indicated above.

A "ROMANTIC" PLANNING FRAMEWORK

I will construct the framework as questions under a set of headings, such that answering the questions should produce a lesson or unit plan. This may be seen as an alternative or supplement to the more common Objectives-Content-Methods-Evaluation schemes, derived primarily from Ralph Tyler's work (1949). In this case the framework is derived from a focus on students' imaginative lives:

1. *Identifying transcendent qualities*
   What transcendent qualities can be identified—felt—as central to the topic?
   What affective images do they evoke? What within the topic can best evoke wonder?

2. *Organizing the material into a narrative structure*
   2.1 *Initial access*
   > What features of the material, distinct from students' everyday experience, best embodies the transcendent qualities most central to the material? Does this expose some extreme of experience or limit of reality?
   2.2 *Composing the body of the lesson or unit*
   > What material best articulates the topic into a clear narrative structure? Sketch the main narrative line.
   2.3 *Humanizing the material*
   > How can the material be shown in terms of human hopes, fears, intentions, or other emotions? What aspect of the content can best stimulate a sense of wonder? What ideals and/or revolt against conventions are evident in the material?
   2.4 *Pursuing details*
   > What parts of the material best allow students to pursue some aspect in exhaustive detail?
3. *Concluding*
   > How can one best bring the topic to satisfactory closure? How can the students *feel* this satisfaction?
4. *Evaluation*
   > How can one know whether the material has been understood and has engaged and stimulated students' imaginations?

I will try to provide a compact example of how one might plan a unit on punctuation using this framework. While space does not allow an extensively worked-out example, I hope what follows at least indicates that the framework, and the principles underlying it, can be useful in directing us to think of ways of teaching that focus on engaging students imaginatively.

First we are directed to identify transcendent qualities, affective images, something wonderful, something "heroic" in punctuation. We might consider its purposes and how it developed. In early texts there was no punctuation, just letters one after another filling all the space on a page or tablet or stone. Reading was difficult and, to make sense of a text, one would most commonly read aloud. Punctuation is made up of a set of simple, elegant, and ingenious inventions that have been added to texts to make them easier to read. Our transcendent quality, the quality we can "heroize," then, can be this simple, elegant, ingenious, inventiveness.

We need to organize our material into a narrative. As a newspaper editor might say, we also must ask: "What's the story here?" Our story is the revolution that has had an immense impact on our civilization and even on our very sense of ourselves. It is the story of the profound shift from the reliance on the ear for access to knowledge to reliance on the eye. It is a part of the story of moving in the West from an oral to a literate culture, with all that that has entailed (see, e.g., Havelock, 1963, 1986; Ong, 1982). In this story, punctuation plays a decisive role in transforming text so that it can be easily read and its meaning can easily be grasped. It is an important part, also, of the story of democracy, as reading texts became increasingly less a task for a skilled elite and more accessible to all. Spaces between words, paragraphs, subheadings, capitals and lower-case letters, commas, periods, quotation marks, exclamations points, and the rest, all help to divide up the text into meaning chunks that elegantly permit us to engage in this curious silent communication.

INITIALACCESSMIGHTBEPROVIDEDBYGIVINGTHESTUDENTS
APIECEOFTEXTWITHOUTANYPUNCTUATIONSIMPLYALLTHE
WORDSFLOWINGTOGETHERWITHNOBREAKSCOMMASPERIOD
SORANYOTHEROFTHEELEGANTANDECONOMICALCUESTHAT
MAKETEXTSEASILYACCESSIBLETOTHEEYEJUSTSEEINGHOW
MUCHMOREDIFFICULTTOREADWILLGIVESOMEIMMEDIATE
SENSEOFAVALUEOFPUNCTUATIONHAVETHESTUDENTSREAD
THETEXTALOUDTOHEARRATHERTHANSEEHOWMUCHEASIER
ITISTOUNDERSTANDCHOSESOMETHINGWITHLOTSOFQUOTA
TIONSSUBHEADINGSANDSOONGRAPHICILLISTRATIONEH

In composing the body of the unit, we are directed to detail the particular content we want to deal with. Given our narrative line, we may decide to take the items either in the sequence of their historical development or, which turns out to be much the same, in the degree of their impact on making the page hospitable to the eye. This narrative line, incidentally, brings into the topic some items not normally considered matters of punctuation, such as the separation of words by spaces. We could begin with just that, seeing how dramatic an improvement it led to. Then we could add the use of capitals and lower-case letters, the comma and period, and so on. Each item can be introduced in terms of its contribution to the move from ear to eye, and each may be presented in terms of the simple elegance and ingenuity by which it achieved its dramatic impact. One might begin, for each example of punctuation, with a text in which it is absent, contrasted with a text in which its presence can be seen as particularly dramatic.

We can humanize the material by reference to the hopes of those who introduced the various innovations. We can see the struggles they were involved in and the interests of those who resisted the innovations. This could be done in the abstract, seeing the particular effects of each innovation as exemplifying the transcendent quality, or a little research could discover some of the particular heroes of this story. Useful resources include the book on Hugh of St. Victor, mentioned earlier (Illich, 1993), or the rich set of examples in David Olson's (1994) *World on Paper*. We can use such cases to show how huge social and psychological changes were brought about in the revolution involved in making texts easily readable. The truly revolutionary nature of punctuation can be emphasized here; its inventors transformed the world and lives much more than did Caesar, Napoleon, or all the celebrated military and political figures who loom large in our history books.

Each student can be given some aspect of the topic to explore exhaustively. One group might explore the history of the comma, another the variety of rules given for its use, and so on. Similar inquiries could focus on all other punctuation marks, and all the innovations studied in the unit.

One might conclude such a unit by considering the arbitrariness of our forms of punctuation. Examples of 18th-century writers who favored the dash over commas and periods might be considered. Students might be given a page of unpunctuated text and be asked, in the process of punctuating it, to invent at least one new punctuation technique, at the expense of current conventions if they wish. The emphasis would be on acknowledging the simple elegance and ingenuity of our techniques of punctuation, but recognizing that they are only conventions, useful as long as they are useful, to be changed and discarded when not. But their uses and values will probably have become clear as students have dealt with texts that lack them.

Evaluation could follow any of the traditional forms, to which teachers might add a means of observing the degree to which students recognize that punctuation is not merely a utilitarian convention, but is a product of much ingenuity; those taken-for-granted squiggles and marks on a page have a romantic quality of their own as revolutionaries in a great adventure. One will probably not find a means of getting a clear index of this sense of romance but, if the teacher is sensitive to its importance, some alertness to it can lead at least to an informal qualitative assessment.

CONCLUSION

I have considered a few characteristics of students' imaginative lives that form distinctive echoes from prominent features of Romanticism. Each item yields a principle that can influence teaching, and the set can be combined into a practical planning framework. Even if the moves from Romanticism-influenced observations to principles to framework may seem stark and unlike the inferences from particular empirical studies, this is an approach to teaching that comes from contemplation of the rich cultural stuff with which education is wrapped up. Such an approach need not be pursued in a way that excludes more traditional kinds of research, but I hope that even so brief an exploration suggests that looking to our cultural history on the one hand and at students' imaginative lives on the other can lead to practical benefits to teaching.

CHAPTER 4

Conceptions of Development
in Education

This is the most recently written article in this collection. I wrote it after publication of my book The Educated Mind: How Cognitive Tools Shape our Understanding *(Chicago: University of Chicago Press, 1997), in part to try to situate the theory in that book within a wider range of conceptions of children's intellectual development. Its first outing was as a paper delivered to the Philosophy of Education conference in Boston in March 1998, and it is reprinted here with the kind permission of the editors of the proceedings of that conference, which appeared as* Philosophy of Education, 1998.

INTRODUCTION

Charles Darwin provided a somewhat new way to think about, and account for, gradual change. In his major theory, *evolution*—which had derived from the Latin for "rolling out," as of a written scroll—took on a new precision and layer of meaning. His attempt to account for the differentiation of species and changes in the fossil record has led, by metaphoric extension, to the use of the term for processes quite unlike those that absorbed him: for example, "the team's evolution from a bunch of layabouts into a well-oiled machine." The related word, *development*, went through a similar process during the same period. From its original meaning, of unfolding something, it came to mean processes in which the mature final form is attained by the gradual unfolding of elements that are initially present in rudimentary or embryonic forms. The two words developed or evolved side by side, influencing each other. One can see the influences and close relationship in late-19th-century biological theories that proposed that the human fetus went through stages of development in the womb that recapitulated the evolutionary changes the species went through. Development also gathered some of its more precise and changed sense from its use in biology to refer to the theory that the embryo already possesses in rudimentary form all the parts of the mature organism—the process of development is the process of growth of those rudimentary forms to maturity.

This sense of development—even though abandoned by biologists long ago—has been profoundly influential on education, and on conceptions of the young child as a learner. Childhood, seen through this sense of development, is a stage in which humans possess in embryonic or rudimentary form the intellectual capacities that gradually elaborate and expand until they achieve their mature forms in adulthood. Theories of development in education have thus been what are called "hierarchical integrative"—that is, each later stage integrates the attainments of the earlier stage(s) in a higher, more sophisticated form.

The dominant ideas about development during this century have been derived from this 19th-century background, and have been psychological and have drawn heavily on biology (Morss, 1990). They seemed, earlier in the century, to hold great promise for education, but it is not clear that the promise has been fulfilled. (See, for example, the attempts to evaluate the results of using Piaget's developmental theory in schools in Brainerd, 1978, pp. 293ff.) This dominance of particular psychological conceptions of development has tended to hide other conceptions. What I want to do here is look at some other conceptions of development and see how they may complement or conflict with what has been the dominant conception, and consider their various values to educational thinking about development of the mind. I will suggest a somewhat novel way of integrating features from some of them, while suggesting reasons for discounting what has been long assumed the best way of characterizing intellectual development.

TWO COMPETING CONCEPTIONS OF DEVELOPMENT

The first Western conception of what I will, for now, somewhat anachronistically call development in education was Plato's. To Plato (trans. 1941) the mind is, in significant degree, an epistemological organ. Its development is measured, in significant degree, in terms of the knowledge it learns. That adolescents may begin to use abstractions, for example, is accounted for by the fact that after a certain amount of particular knowledge is taught to a particular degree of complexity, abstract concepts emerge. Certain forms of knowledge are more suited to this elaboration and Plato describes, for example, how mathematics can be used to draw the mind from the world of change to that of reality (*Republic*, vii. 521–524). That is, his account does not suggest that the mind is the kind of psychological organ we are accustomed to thinking of it as, which reaches a stage at which it becomes "ready" to think abstractly. Rather, abstraction is a characteristic of elaborated knowledge, and learning such knowledge actively and directly develops the learner's mind. He proposes that the everyday world disclosed by our perceptions and conventional beliefs can somehow be better understood by a rational grasp of some transcendent world of abstract theoretic ideas, which are accessible only after decades of refined scholarly activity guided by a kind of spiritual commitment. It hasn't proven everyone's cup of tea.

The process of mental development, then, is the process of mastering the various forms of knowledge that will carry the mind from its initial confusions and unclarity to a recognition of the truth about reality. He lays out for us (*Republic*, vi. 509–511) the steps of this process, from *eikasia* to *pistis* to *dianoia* to *noesis*. In Plato's conception, then, the mind *is* what it learns, so the construction of a curriculum that will allow the vehicle of increasingly elaborated forms of knowledge to carry the mind onward to *noesis* is the crucial educational task.

The second major Western conception of development in education was Rousseau's (1762/1911). His central and continuous theme was that if you want students to understand what you teach, then you must make your methods of teaching conform with the nature of students' learning: "The internal development of our faculties and organs is the education of nature. The use we learn to make of this development is the education of men" (p. 11). Thus, in order to educate properly, we must first understand that internal development process. The most important area of educational study, then, is the nature of students' development, learning, motivation, and so on. The more we know about these, the more efficient and humane we can make their education. The key is that underlying natural development: "Fix your eye on nature, follow the path traced by her" (p. 14).

The mind, in this conception, goes through an autonomous process, rather like the body. The human body is programmed so that, given appropriate environmental supports, it will pass through a series of changes that will carry it from embryo to adult. It doesn't greatly matter whether the body eats beans or peas; it will still develop arms and legs and ears and so on. That is, in Rousseau's (1762/1911) conception of development, the knowledge a student learns, the "aliments" (to choose a term used by that most Rousseauian of psychologists, Jean Piaget) of the mind, do not profoundly effect its development. Eating lots of broccoli does not make us look more like a broccoli, and so learning mathematics rather than science or history or anything else will have little general influence on the mind's development. In Plato's conception of the mind's development, of course, consuming broccoli, as it were, makes it broccoli-like.

Once one conceives of the mind as having its own distinct process of development, then education tends to be seen in terms of furthering and fulfilling that process. A difficulty for such a conception of education is knowing securely just what that internal developmental process involves. Rousseau's scheme was rather general and offered only imprecise guidance. The task of the developmental psychologist ever since has been to clarify that process.

These two conceptions of development in education have been the most influential ideas that have shaped educational practice. The trouble is that they are mutually incompatible. If we are guided by Plato, then educating the mind becomes a matter of selecting the forms of knowledge, in appropriate breadth and depth, that will shape it to grasp the truth about reality. If we are guided by Rousseau, then educating the mind becomes a matter of supporting and facilitating the fullest elaboration of its spontaneous, internal, autonomous growth. It is hard to look for a balance between these two, because they pull away from each other; the more we try to do one, the harder it is to do the other.

Some have suggested that we can square this particular circle by accepting Plato as providing the conception that enables us to select material for our curriculum, and Rousseau as providing the conception that allows us to discern how best to teach it. That compromise, leaving Plato's descendants with the content and aims of education and Rousseau's with the methods, appeals to many as a neat division of labor. So the educational philosophers can deal with content and aims, drawing on the knowledge generated by the educational psychologists about learning and development. It seems so obvious that facts about students' psychological development can blend with philosophers' research into the nature and structure of knowledge to yield a more easily understood math or history curriculum. It seems so obvious that such collaboration should be common that one would expect the absence of it to compel reassessment of what looks, but clearly isn't, obvious. Why hasn't, say, Paul Hirst's work been coordinated with, say, Jean Piaget's to give us a forms of knowledge curriculum organized according to Piagetian principles? Or, more generally, why can't traditionalists and progressivists work out some such neat compromise?

Well, Rousseau and his modern followers are not simply making methodological or procedural recommendations, which might allow us to do the Platonic academic job more efficiently. They are actually recommending a different job. Rousseau's idea is not one that yields us an easy accommodation with Plato's. These ideas conflict—most profoundly in identifying the cause and dynamic of the educational process. In the Platonic view, knowledge drives development; in the Rousseauian view, development drives knowledge—it determines what knowledge is learnable, meaningful, and relevant. In the Platonic view, education is a time-related, epistemological process; in the Rousseauian view, it is an age-related, psychological process.

The conflict between these two ideas has been the basis of the continuing struggles between "traditionalists" and "progressivists" during this century. One sees them at odds in almost every media account of educational issues; where the Platonic forces argue for "basics" and a solid academic curriculum, the Rousseauians argue for "relevance" and space for students' exploration and discovery. A key battleground as I write this is the elementary social studies curriculum in North America. The traditionalist forces are pressuring for a revision that will reintroduce history and geography in place of the progressivists' preferred "relevant" focus on families, neighborhoods, communities, interactions among communities, and so on; the progressivist forces argue that history and geography require abstract concepts and are not "developmentally appropriate" for young children and the traditionalists argue that any content can be made comprehensible if presented in a sequence of logically organized prerequisite structures. Those who favor a psychological order tend to prefer to begin with self, families, neighborhoods, "expanding" outward on the vehicle of known—because experienced—understandings, and those who favor a logical order tend to prefer beginning with cosmogony, the birth of stars and planets, the history of life on earth, "contracting" from the general to particular features of the world that may thus be understood in a meaningful context.

One can manage compromises only by undermining the distinctive virtues of either idea—which is a fair description of the average school's approach today.

TWO ALTERNATIVES BRIEFLY NOTED

I will consider just two alternative conceptions of development, because I want to take features of both of them to suggest a further kind.

One alternative that was popular in the late 19th century was recapitulation. In this view the human mind was preprogrammed to develop through a sequence of stages that were a recapitulation of the stages that "the race" had passed through. Herbert Spencer (1861) compactly expressed the basis for a cultural recapitulation theory of education in the claim:

> If there be an order in which the human race has mastered its various kinds of knowledge, there will arise in every child an aptitude to acquire those kinds of knowledge in the same order. . . . Education should be a repetition of civilization in little. (p. 76)

This might be called the "folk-recapitulation" position. To become more scientific, a recapitulation theory had to show some precise causal connection between past cultural development and present educational development. The challenge was to show exactly *what* was recapitulated and *why* there should arise in every child the aptitude Spencer claimed. If one could do that, then, in the words of another enthusiast, recapitulation "when explored and utilized to its full extent will reveal pedagogic possibilities now undreamed of" (Hall, 1904, p. 222).

Recapitulation curricula came into conflict with the urgent social needs of the new mass schools of America and Europe to prepare the immigrants and indigenous working classes for new kinds of work in rapidly changing economies. A system that brought the child slowly through the cultural history of the race, reaching the modern world only at the end of the process, was not one that appealed to those who were paying the pipers of the new progressive curricula. Also, in *Democracy and Education*, we find what have become the standard reasons for rejecting recapitulation. Dewey (1916/1966) argues that acceptance of recapitulation leads to an influence on the curriculum such that it "tends to make the . . . present a more or less futile imitation of the past" (p. 75).

Another alternative appeared in the work of Lev Vygotsky (1978). He was born in the same year as Piaget (it is always mildly surprising to realize) (1896), and was critical of Piaget's theories of development because, in his view, they failed to recognize the degree to which the mind's development incorporated the social environment in which the child grew up. Vygotsky argued that the mind, unlike the body, takes on in significant degree the shape of what it "eats." In Vygotsky's view, the kind of sense we make of the world is in significant part due to the particular cognitive tools we learn to use as we grow up in a particular sociocultural milieu.

"Vygotsky defined development in terms of the emergence or transformation of forms of mediation" (Wertsch, 1985, p. 15). That is, Vygotsky argued that intellectual development could not be adequately understood in terms of the accumulation of knowledge nor in terms of a sequence of psychological stages like Piaget's, but it requires an understanding of the role played by the cognitive tools, the forms of mediation, available in the culture into which a person is born. It is these tools that determine the kind of understanding that develops. He focused particularly on the development of oral language as a distinctive sign system, concluding that the *"system of signs restructures the whole psychological process"* (Vygotsky, 1978, p. 35; emphasis in the original). The contribution of Vygotsky's that I want particularly to draw on is his recognition that the mind is, in its operations from the beginning, not only an epistemological and psychological organ, but also a social organ, and it only reaches any realization of its capacities, beyond basic perception, in social contexts, and these social contexts are crucial not just in providing some "environment" within which the mind's supposed spontaneous process will unfold, but for becoming integral ingredients of whatever processes *can* unfold.

PROBLEMS AND A DIRECTION TOWARD SOLUTIONS

I have sketched what seem to be the main ideas about development that have influenced, and continue in varying degrees to influence, educational thinking. The problems with Plato's conception are well rehearsed. The kind of *episteme* or *noesis* that forms the aim and apex of his scheme is generally thought to be impossible to achieve; it is taken to be based on, of all things, an epistemological error.

The biology-derived psychological theories, most notable of which has been Piaget's, are being increasingly persuasively shown to "deemphasize uniquely human features of the acquisition of knowledge" (Morss, 1990, p. 5). Their 19th-century biological assumption of a uniform and inevitable schedule of stages of growth from embryo to adult seems to encourage them to ignore some of the more distinctive features of young humans' development. In particular, psychological theories have not been good at accommodating intellectual things that young children do better than adults. They ignore the peculiarity of human development that equips us with forms of cognitive activity early in life that are required for learning a language and for the representation of beliefs about society and the cosmos. To manage these tasks, young humans develop rapidly a set of cognitive tools—like metaphor generation and recognition, story-shaping, use of binary structuring and mediation, generation of mental images from words, and so forth—that typically go into decline later in childhood, and are typically much less evident in adulthood. Hierarchical integrative theories, that is, have difficulty dealing with capacities that seem to reach a peak in childhood and decline thereafter. Such capacities are not "integrated" in some developing hierarchy; they tend rather to atrophy. Certain kinds of intellectual gains also seem to entail other intellectual losses— literacy, for example, seems to entail some greater or lesser loss of our sense of participatory immediacy in the natural world (Donald, 1991)—and hierarchical theories have not represented development as a business of gains and losses, only one of gains.

Piaget's and neo-Piagetian accounts of development have not proven compelling to all psychologists or educators. Indeed, even as his theory comes in for increasingly severe criticism, it still makes sense to ask just what the theory describes (Egan, 1982). Perhaps more scholars than at any time during the 20th century now concur with Jerry Fodor's (1985) reflection: "Deep down, I'm inclined to doubt that there is such a thing as cognitive development in the sense that developmental cognitive psychologists have in mind" (p. 35). Of course, developmental cognitive psychologists don't have one mind about this issue, and it is perhaps an exaggeration to claim, as Fodor does elsewhere, that "Piaget taught that infants start out as sensori-motor reflex machines and develop into formal intelligence, but practically nobody outside Geneva believes that any more" (1996, pp. 22–23).

Even so, the two major ideas about intellectual development that we have inherited seem each to have problems, and tend to undermine one another when we try to apply them both to education. That leaves us with the two more recent ideas. Let us consider the developmental idea—recapitulation—that has been generally decisively rejected. It has long been obvious that students in the process of their education recapitulate in some way the inventions and discoveries that constitute their evolution and cultural history. The young child learning to talk is recapitulating an evolutionary achievement; the child learning to write and read recapitulates techniques invented a few thousand years ago; the student learning history recapitulates a way of making sense of experience whose development in the ancient eastern Mediterranean we can trace in some detail. That educational development is connected with our evolution and cultural history is as obvious as it has proven difficult to specify just how. One problem Spencer (1861) and his fellow 19th- and early 20th-century enthusiasts for recapitulation had was in specifying just what was to be recapitulated. Was it the content itself? But that answer became strained and often silly; does one teach first that the sun travels round the earth and later that the earth travels round the sun, recapitulating the process of cultural understanding? Was it a psychological process from savagery to civilized rationality we were to recapitulate? But we keep a wary distance from this idea when we look back on the racism it supported. That some hidden psychological process is at work becomes implausible when it cannot be identified.

What seems fair to conclude is that recapitulation has failed to sustain significant influence on education for ideological reasons on the one hand—it conflicted with the socializing needs of early 20th-century industrialized societies—and because its proponents could give no plausible account of just *what* from cultural history was to be recapitulated in the process of education and *how* the mechanism worked. As Phillips and Kelly (1975) stated a quarter of a century ago: "The notion of recapitulation which links [the process of development of the individual child and of evolutionary development of the human species] is an empirical hypothesis, and it must be supported in some way by evidence" (p. 354).

A CONCLUDING SUGGESTION

I think it is possible to suggest how one might make a recapitulation scheme at least plausible. The connection to be sought between evolution and history and the modern student concerns the development of a set of cognitive tools that profoundly influence how their users understand the world and make sense of experience. The answer to *what*, then, is sets of cognitive tools or "mediators" created in cultural history and learned as a child grows into a society and its cultural life. I mean such things as an oral language—which Vygotsky (1978) has explored so intensively—and literacy, and abstract theoretic thinking, and irony. If Vygotsky is right, these somewhat distinctive layers of complexity in our major system of signs should have detectable implications for the kind of understanding experienced by their users, whether those users lived long ago or whether they are students today.

So the answer to *what* is recapitulated and *how* the recapitulationary mechanism works is not like either of the two classic answers given; education is not a process of acquiring privileged knowledge accumulated in our cultural history, nor is it the process of fulfilling to the limits of our potential some putative psychological process. Rather, education as recapitulation requires us to learn to use as fully as possible the cognitive tools that we have inherited from our evolutionary and cultural history. (Knowledge accumulation and psychological development will incidentally be required in this process, but will not be its focus.) In the case of oral language, this will entail elaborating and developing various of the subset of tools or mediators that it brings along with it—such as narrative forms of causality, rhyme, rhythm, and meter, story-shaping of events, binary structuring, mental images formed from words, cognitive orientation to a society and a cosmology, and so on. These shape the kind of sense we make and can make of the world we grow into and they are products of our evolutionary and cultural history. So we might make a priority of our early curriculum to teach children about the cosmos, and shape our lessons into story-structures—this doesn't mean telling them fictions or myths, but rather implies shaping the knowledge into forms in which young children are predisposed by oral language, without literacy, to learn it. By analyzing the major cognitive tools that we have inherited, one can construct both a curriculum and methods of teaching that can support their elaboration and development (see Egan, 1997). Literacy, for example, will incorporate some of the tools of oral language, but also will tend to suppress some of them, and will bring with it a further set of tools that shape the kind of understanding we can form of the world.

Even without any further description of such tools, it might be recognized that the focus on major cognitive tools provides us with a plausible candidate for what can be recapitulated in education, and what might make a better candidate for an account of cognitive development than the knowledge and psychological processes that have preceded it. Certainly these tools were developed in our evolution and cultural history and certainly we develop them more or less adequately in our education. What has not been considered before, that I am aware of, is that their historical and contemporary development yield particular, describable kinds of understanding, which will be in significant degree common to whoever develops them in whatever social or historical conditions.

Such a recapitulationary conception of education also frees us from expecting some precise sequence that is reflected from cultural history to modern classrooms. Whenever such tools are learned and used, a particular kind of understanding will result. So we need not look for some sequence determined by a hidden psychological mechanism or by some arbitrary historical accumulation of knowledge. The sequence is determined by tangible and describable cognitive tools, like oral language, literacy, theoretic abstractions, irony, and their subset of smaller-scale cognitive tools.

But what about the evidence Phillips and Kelly (1975) pointed out was lacking from earlier recapitulationary schemes? The main evidence required for this scheme is to support the claim that whenever the cognitive tools are developed they will yield the particular kinds of understanding. Evidence will be provided if we can see that the development of oral language in whatever circumstances entails certain kinds of understanding. I think, in general terms, it may again be seen as plausible that this is so. The set of characteristics I indicated above as subtools of oral language development are prominent both in children and in oral cultures around the world. This doesn't mean both use these tools for the same purposes, but simply that the cognitive tools shape understanding in particular ways. I think that one can similarly show some precise cognitive effects of literacy, both among newly literate people in the ancient eastern Mediterranean and among early adolescent students today. This doesn't mean that the average student shares Herodotus's genius, but it does mean that the kind of understanding evident in Herodotus's *Histories*—with its heroic underlying story of freedom-loving Athens defeating the tyrannous might of the Persian Empire, its emphasis on the extremes of experience and the greatest achievements, its personalized causality, its fascination with the exotic, and so forth—finds precise parallels in the newly literate student today, whose *Guinness Book of Records* enthusiasms are weirdly echoed in Herodotus's work. I think it is at least plausible that this is a kind of evidence that we could seek with some hope of success and that it would provide appropriate support for a new kind of recapitulation scheme. The research that would deliver this support would be, on the one hand, historical and analytical, and on the other, looking for consequences of learning to use cognitive tools among students today, it might deploy more traditional empirical methods.

Curriculum Issues

CHAPTER 5

Letting Our Presuppositions Think for Us

I began teaching a course on the curriculum in the mid-1970s—or was it the 1870s? One of the things that struck me while reading around the topic was how ineffectually people typically engaged others' arguments. It seemed more like a marketplace in which people shouted their wares than an arena where clearly agreed questions were debated. Part of the trouble seemed to be how little most writers seemed aware of their own presuppositions. At first I tried to get students to see the problem by exposing presuppositions, particularly in cases where people were arguing for or against some particular curriculum innovation. I wanted to show that the overt arguments rarely engaged each other, and each side's had no impact at all on the other's, because they were failing to recognize the real source of their disagreements. I then prepared some notes on the role of presuppositions, elaborated them for the next time I taught the course, worked the notes into a lecture, and the lecture into this essay. It appeared in the Journal of Curriculum Studies *(vol. 10, no. 2, pp. 123–33, 1978), under the title "Some Presuppositions That Determine Curriculum Decisions." I have probably had more favorable feedback from colleagues on the usefulness of this piece in teaching than anything else I have written. It is a "slight" piece, overly simple perhaps, but does, I think, get at something important and still neglected.*

INTRODUCTION

If I argue that the store on the corner sells paint, I presuppose that there is a store on the corner. For my claim that the store on the corner sells paint to be true, or even meaningful, my presupposition must be true. If you believe that there is no store on the corner, you would be engaging in a weird strategy if you were to argue only that it does not sell paint. You would clearly be more sensible to argue, and present evidence if need be, that there is no store on the corner. If I argue on behalf of child-centered education, it is not altogether clear what set of presuppositions I am working from. For claims on behalf of child-centered education to be true, or even meaningful, the presuppositions on which they are based must be true. It would be an absurd strategy to deal only with the claims and

71

ignore the presuppositions, because it may well be that our disagreements are at the level of presupposition.

I will try to show that disagreements about presuppositions are usually the case when it comes to arguments or decision making about curriculum, and I will then go on to discuss the implications of this for the proper strategy we should pursue in dealing with decisions or arguments about curriculum.

My purpose in this chapter is to excavate just a few presuppositions that have a determining force over a range of curriculum issues. I do not attempt anything like an exhaustive mapping of such presuppositions; I deal with the set chosen in no particular order; they are not a coherent set of presuppositions—they overlap, some are more influential than others, they are at different levels of generality. I will deal with them in a very general way, simply noting their most significant features and roughly the range and kind of decisions they determine.

HUMAN NATURE: GOOD/BAD?

(A few words first about this and the following subheadings: I use the most simple, not to say crude, terms to indicate the presuppositions I want to characterize. Clearly, few people hold the simplistic notion that human nature is either absolutely good or bad, or even try to make a rational assessment of the trustworthiness of human nature in general. But I use these bald terms to suggest a continuum along which a range of presuppositions about human nature can be located.)

One of the most powerful influences on our curriculum decisions is our subtly and subconsciously formed presupposition about how good, reliable, trustworthy—or the opposite—human nature is. The presupposition that human nature is typically good leads to the belief that people will incline to do good if unconstrained—"good" being used here for whatever one approves of, pro-human behavior generally or learning physics in particular. Thus people who hold this presupposition tend to blame environmental conditions, formal constraints, or institutions for anything "bad" that occurs—whether it be antihuman behavior, or not learning physics or how to read, or whatever. With regard to curriculum, this presupposition leads to the range of positions that favor lack of constraints on children, and trust in their instincts: If children will move naturally toward the good, and if learning physics and how to read are good, then, if not prevented by some external condition, they will choose to learn those things of most value to them.

Holding this presupposition leads to feeling no sense of risk or danger in removing constraints and providing greater freedom. Indeed, quite the reverse—change and innovation are favored, almost regardless of their nature, not just because they may involve the removal of constraints, but because they provide moments when the freedom for "good" human nature to express itself is at a maximum. Even innovations designed to provide greater freedom tend to become formalized and rigid, so it is the freedom involved between the breaking up of one structure and the closing in of another that is valued—with the result that more or less constant change tends to be preferred. Rigid classroom formats, "traditional" teaching methods, structures and formalities of all kinds, are thus seen as barriers preventing natural goodness from being exercised. "Free schools" and "child-centeredness" will tend to be supported, and supported with confidence that education will naturally improve because of the reduction of constraints involved. Student-initiated inquiry and "open-ended" project work will be preferred to teacher domination and prescribed "closed-ended" tasks.

The person who presupposes that human nature is bad is led to see traditional forms, institutions, and constraints as carefully built defenses against the exercise of a naturally destructive, ignorance-preferring human nature. Consequently, periods of change and innovation are seen as times of high risk at which it is only too easy to lose far more than may be gained. With regard to curriculum, this presupposition leads to the desire to defend all institutions and forms that achieve however small a degree of success in teaching and controlling children. This sense of the importance of institutional constraints leads to a particularly strong feeling that quite severe constraints and pressures are justified, and required, to ensure that children master those skills society needs for its continuance. It is obvious that these general feelings will lead to more or less the opposite kind of programs to those favored by persons believing in the goodness of human nature.

It may help to clarify this continuum if I sketch more radical positions at either end, and then the middle position. The radical "left" presupposes that human nature is so good that all constraints and institutions should be immediately removed. Nothing can be lost in throwing out curriculum guides, classroom structures, formal courses and disciplines, because only in the absence of these constraints will the natural goodness of the child flower. And if this freedom fails to produce the basic skills necessary for the continuance of society, so much the worse for society: This only shows what an artificial, inhuman, and stifling set of institutions it is. The "rightmost" radical position is led to see humans as untrustworthy animals, whose civilization is an incredibly frail structure holding in control the human bestiality that threatens to overwhelm civilized life at every turn. All change is resisted because no possible change could be worth what is put at risk. ("When it is not necessary to change, it is necessary not to change," as Viscount Falkland put it in a 1641 speech about the episcopacy).

The person in the middle of this continuum presupposes that human nature is neither good nor bad, or perhaps that human nature is in some circumstances likely to produce good, in others, bad. This leads to the desire to provide some structural defenses against the latter, but to leave sufficient flexibility so that the good might have room for exercise. If at the far right no change is acceptable, and at the far left any change is desirable, in the middle readiness to accept changes will be qualified by the requirement that either evidence or good reasons be given that the changes will lead to improvements.

Well, these are very broad brushstrokes, and of course there are other continua of presuppositions about human nature that lead to equally diverse positions. People have, for example, differing presuppositions about the plasticity or flexibility of human nature, which leads to different positions on the extent to which teaching may be effective. This range of presuppositions underlies the nature/nurture or environmentalist/geneticist disputes. Let the above suffice, however, as an indication of how different presuppositions about human nature lead to different positions on some curriculum issues. I will consider a few more such presuppositions before dealing with the implications for curriculum decision making.

CULTURE: WITHIN/WITHOUT?

This second set of presuppositions is nearer the surface of typical conscious reflection than the first. Overt arguments about curriculum rarely try to locate where the arguers think culture lies. This location is important, however, because presuppositions about where it is determine people's views of what culture is, and consequently what role it has in the curriculum.

If one presupposes that culture is "without," one conceives of it as somehow contained in, or composed of, objects—the products of "great minds," books, pictures, theatrical performances, music—and associated feelings and attitudes. These cultural objects and the appropriate feelings and attitudes about them exist in a publicly determined hierarchy of value. Education thus becomes the process of making children familiar with the hierarchy of cultural objects and internalizing public standards of evaluation and appreciation of them. This leads to seeing the curriculum as largely a curriculum of content, and education as a process of acculturation "up" the various hierarchies. The cultural objects are seen as being of permanent value and meaning, unaffected by any current situation. Indeed their value cannot change, because they are the fixed standards of value against which present experience, products, and events may be measured.

This presupposition leads to a curriculum in which authority is important—both the authority of "culture" itself, which the child has to absorb to become, as it were, fully human, and of the teacher as the representative or, better, the embodiment of the public standards that must be learned. The curriculum will be highly structured to ensure the child's proper development up the various hierarchies. As access to the best cultural products requires mastery of a considerable range of knowledge and skills, the curriculum will involve pressure for "achievement," and will frequently contain tests to ensure that each step has been taken successfully. The value that will result from this mastery will be more important than any discomfort, distress, or even suffering that may result from pressure in the process.

(Authoritarian attitudes tend to follow from the presupposition that culture is without, but they need not. Similarly this presupposition tends to be associated with the presupposition that human nature is "bad," but, again, it need not. It is, for example, possible for someone who presupposes that human nature is "good" to presuppose that culture is "without"—in which case that person would be led to believe that, if children are left largely to their own devices, they will naturally come to internalize the public hierarchy of values, and appropriately appreciate the "best" cultural objects. The more common combination, however, is for the person who presupposes human nature to be "good" to presuppose culture to be "within.")

The person who presupposes that culture is within is led to see it as a set of experiences, not objects. The quality of a book, for example, is measured not in terms of any public standard, but simply by its effect on the individual reader. The hierarchy of cultural values is thus composed by each individual for himself or herself, and each person's hierarchy is considered autonomous. Shakespeare, then, might move one person profoundly but be no part of the culture of someone else; and no value comparisons can be made between these cultures, and there can be no sense in which one should work to get from some object the same general kind of experience someone else gets. Public standards or claims about the cultural value of objects are considered largely meaningless, at best a kind of guide to things worth trying. Those who presuppose that culture is within will talk about many cultures; those who believe culture is without will talk of only one objective culture—there can be no such thing as a counter-culture or alternate cultures or multicultures; there is simply culture and varying degrees of ignorance of it or participation in it.

The more radical positions on this continuum may be represented on the right by the person who is led to see culture as residing entirely in a strictly organized hierarchy of objects—so that one could, as it were, acquire culture by buying objects of publicly accepted cultural value and surrounding oneself with them; the higher up the hierarchy, the higher the price. To the left, the radical presupposition leads to believing that what goes on "inside one's head" both is the source and provides the standard of cultural value, regardless of its content—thus drugs or rock-videos can be considered equivalent to Beethoven's quartets if they produce intense feeling.

The central position on this continuum of presuppositions about the "location" of culture leads to the notion perhaps best expressed in Michael Oakeshott's (1962) metaphor of culture as a conversation: "We are the inheritors, neither of a inquiry about ourselves and the world, nor of an accumulating body of information, but of a conversation, began in the primeval forests and extended and made more articulate in the course of centuries. It is a conversation which goes on both in public and within each of ourselves. . . . Education, properly speaking, is an initiation into the skill and partnership of this conversation" (p. 198). Culture, then, is presupposed to be both within and without; cultural objects can provide us with "words" of the conversation, but our individual interpretation and use of them is crucial.

This continuum of presuppositions profoundly determines curriculum issues such as are summed up by the labels "process versus product," or "intrinsic versus instrumental." If one presupposes that culture is within, it is the process one goes through in learning that is important—no future product is more important than present experience because the present experience *is* one's culture. The experience in classrooms must be of intrinsic value in the present. Toward the right of the continuum, because it is the achievement of internalizing the public standards that is important, the process is seen merely as the means to this end, of little importance by itself.

CONSCIOUSNESS: PAST/PRESENT/FUTURE?

Societies and individuals vary in the way they make sense of experience with regard to the flow of time. Three basic positions may be characterized, as indicated by this subheading. Obviously no one locates his or her consciousness exclusively in the past or present or future; we combine them in varying degrees, though we tend to accentuate one or two at the expense of the other(s). I will simply use van Groningen's (1953) characterizations here:

> One person unsuspectingly gives all his attention to the direct present and tries to adapt himself to it with all its delights or sorrows. Another prefers to concentrate on the things which are expected to happen; as a man of the future he is wrapped up in expectations, hope and fear; to him the present, even in its broadest aspect, is above all an approach, a prelude to coming events. There is still a third attitude, the one of the man who is strongly tied down to the past, who finds there the real values of life and who sees the present mainly as a result of that past; recollections and experience are more to him than expectations, he draws his vital energy from the past, borrows his convictions from it, and finds his bearings there. (p. 3)

Clearly this set of presuppositions overlaps, in various ways, with some of those previously discussed, but there is a range of curriculum concerns that is particularly determined by the location of consciousness in time. One way of initially characterizing these is by showing how they influence attitudes toward history in the curriculum.

For the person who is predominantly past-conscious, history is important because knowledge of the past is responsible for securing our very identity; we are what we are and the world is what it is because of what happened in the past. To mix metaphors, it is both the anchor that provides security and the compass that guides us through times of rapid change—the more rapid the change, the more important history is for stability and sound judgment. The past-conscious person will favor a curriculum that not only gives a central place to traditional "academic" history, but also organizes all other subjects on a historical basis; physics, for example, should be taught by introducing the child to Greek ideas of physics, then Alexandrian, medieval, Renaissance, Enlightenment, 19th century, and finally modern. This presupposition tends to lead to acceptance that ontogeny recapitulates phylogeny in the mastery of knowledge and ideas.

To the present-conscious, history is of value in so far as it provides a direct enlightenment of current issues. Thus, most history that cannot be seen to have directly shaped current conditions tends to be considered simply "irrelevant to the needs" of modern children. Our identity is not seen as formed by history, but is seen in terms of current social forms, institutions, ideologies. Teachers who are present-conscious collapse history to social studies, and seek to introduce children directly into the way the world is and works now. Thus, while the past-conscious would prefer to teach children about the Greeks, the present-conscious would prefer to introduce them to the idea of "democracy," and take them out to see a local council working. It is presupposed by the present-conscious person that a better understanding of their world will come from, say, a project that studies the makeup of a local shopping center than a study of Greek or Roman history; urban or environmental studies are preferred to the study of history.

So in Western schools we look a little at early empires, and particularly the Greeks and Romans, then skip to the "birth of the modern world" in the Renaissance and Reformation, pause for the Enlightenment and the 19th century, and finally, as someone put it, come up Main Street foot by foot.

To the future-conscious the study of history is largely irrelevant, except insofar as it can indicate some trend that may be extrapolated into the future. Identity is composed of expectations. Futurology would replace history in a future-conscious curriculum, because it is the future, whose shape can be more or less inferred from present trends, that gives meaning and guidance to the present. The future-conscious teacher is led to prefer a curriculum that will prepare children for what is likely to happen, and so concentrates not on content—who can know what content will be appropriate to the requirements of the future?—but on encouraging critical thinking rather than knowledge acquisition, problem-solving skills rather than familiarity with past problems, openness to change rather than commitment to a set of ideas and institutions.

Most readers are no doubt familiar with the more radical stances with regard to each of the above positions, which I might caricature as the pedant hostile to anything that is not at least a few centuries old, the narrow and ignorant activist, and the mindless "trendy." And the presuppositions that are reflected in these locations of consciousness in time do not only affect history. I use history as an example simply because the effect of these differing presuppositions on its role in the curriculum is quite clear. But all elements of the curriculum are equally affected.

CENTER OF VALUE: BODY/MIND/SOUL?

As with our previous presuppositions, we rarely find a person who exclusively values the body or mind or soul at the absolute expense of the others, but we do find a considerable variation in emphasis. Again, the subheading is very crude and presupposes a Western form of dividing up the self, so I will spend a few lines characterizing people who are imbalanced quite heavily toward each of these centers, and briefly note the curriculum positions influenced by each presupposition.

The person who presupposes that the body is of predominant value sees it as the source of sensation and sees sensation as the predominant form of gratification. The body is not simply an instrument that carries the mind about and needs to be fed, clothed and locomoted; it is rather the source whereby great pleasure may be derived from food, from decorating it, from its ability to move well and powerfully in sports or risky adventures. Ideas are of small importance—it is the sensuousness of music, painting, sculpture that represents their central value. The mind-centered individual, on the other hand, values ideas above all else, and secures greatest gratification from the working of the mind. We are familiar with this attitude in education so need not dwell on it. The soul-centered value the mystical in any of its various forms—that is, that dimension of experience in which we locate our sense of awe, of mystery. For some it comes from contemplating the very fact of existence, for some it is in a set of beliefs about a world other than ours that guides them toward mystical experience, for some it is in the sense of the numinous behind appearances, for some it is in love.

With regard to the curriculum, the body-centered favor activities that lead to sensuous appreciation or physical activity or both; the mind-centered favor a curriculum that engages and leads to the valuing of, and skill in using, ideas; and the soul-centered strive for a curriculum that will constantly lead children beyond the prosaic world of factual knowledge, intellectual skills, and sensuous appreciation to a sense of the mystery and wonder of things. Without going into more detail, it will be evident that people who presuppose one of these centers to be of greater value than the others will conflict with people who hold one of the alternative presuppositions on a range of curriculum issues.

"MAKE PEOPLE LIKE ME!"

Underlying all the above presuppositions, or perhaps constituted by them, is a complex of presuppositions crudely summarized in this subheading. Underlying most curriculum decisions by any person, I am claiming, lies the usually subconscious calculation of what will more likely lead toward children being made like him or her. When this is put in such a crude way, our immediate impulse is to reject such a claim, especially as it refers to ourselves—though it does seem to have some truth when referred to our opponents.

If one examines the stated aims of even the most sophisticated educational thinkers, one will find a curriculum that is clearly designed to produce people like its proposer. Usually this is qualified by our desire to have a curriculum that will produce people like us, but without our "defects"— those, that is, we feel able to acknowledge. It would perhaps be better to say that our decisions about curriculum are largely determined by the desire to produce people like our idealized image of ourselves.

Consider briefly some of the statements of aims or principles for a curriculum expressed by Dewey, Whitehead, Maritain, and Peters in Frankena's *Philosophy of Education* (1965). Dewey wants a product marked by "executive competency . . . by sociability . . . by aesthetic taste . . . trained intellectual method . . . [sensitivity] to the rights of others" (pp. 20–25). Whitehead wants the product of his curriculum "to experience the joy of discovery . . . see that general ideas give an understanding of the stream of events that pour through . . . life," to prove ideas, evoke curiosity, judgment and the "power of mastering a complicated tangle of circumstances, the use of theory in giving foresight in special cases," and to have, above all, "style" (pp. 26–35). Maritain wants "the conquest of internal and spiritual freedom to be achieved by the individual person, or, in other words, his liberation through knowledge and wisdom, good will, and love" (p. 39). He thinks that "no one is freer, or more independent than the one who gives himself for a cause or a real being worthy of the gift" (p. 40). Peters's priorities include "sensitivity, a critical mind, respect for people and facts," and "a rationally held and intelligently applied moral code," so that children will "enter the Palace of Reason through the courtyard of Habit and Tradition" (pp. 44–51).

Our philosophers are writing about themselves—stating aims or principles for curriculum construction that are a kind of covert autobiography, projecting outward into a different form an idealized image of themselves. In a pluralistic society, of course, we acknowledge the desirability of variety, but the amount of variety we are willing to promote is always limited and the basic guide to our curriculum decisions is our calculation of what will most likely make children in our image. And, indeed, why not? What else do we have to go by? It is just important to be clear about it, important for understanding how best to go about dealing with curriculum issues.

CONCLUSION

It would be possible, without much difficulty, to identify a variety of other presuppositions. Indeed, it should be possible to chart a fairly exhaustive set, though the few outlined above suggest that such a set would require organizing in a hierarchy of levels of generalization. No doubt some of those I have dealt with above could be, at least partially, collapsed together, or might be better formulated in different ways. For example, *Center of value: society/individual* might provide a better way of organizing some of the issues touched on above; *Truth: relative/objective* might lead to a more profound way of categorizing some of the content issues. But I will leave this task of elaboration for elsewhere, and go on now to consider the implications of these presuppositions for curriculum arguments and decisions.

If we argue about whether the store on the corner sells paint, and your ground for opposing my claim is your belief that there is no store on the corner, how should we resolve our conflict? It is not an issue that is likely to be resolved by protracted debate, though such a debate might persuade one of the arguers that they had confused corners or something. If I agree that if there is no store on the corner then I will acknowledge my claim is false, then the resolution of this argument is a straightforward empirical matter. We go to the corner and see if there is a store there. If there is not, you win. If there is, we go in and see whether it sells paint.

If I argue on behalf of more child-centeredness, and your basic grounds for opposing my claims, whether you make them explicit or not, are that human nature is generally untrustworthy, that culture is external, and so on, how should we resolve our conflict? It is clearly not a straightforward empirical matter. An attempt at an empirical evaluation of the relative merits of a child-centered school and a "traditional" school might well indicate that on social or "humanistic" measures student freedom, happiness, comfort, feelings about teachers and fellow students, the child-centered school scores higher, and that on academic achievement measures the traditional school scores higher. The obvious problem is that the presuppositions that lead to preferring one kind of school over the other also lead to valuing one kind of measure over the other, so that both sides can claim victory from the comparison. (In such a general comparison the traditional school is more vulnerable; the child-centered school will tend to value its procedures above any product, and thus, as long as it practices child-centeredness in its procedures, there is no way to undermine its confidence; if the child-centered school should show superior academic achievement, the rationale for the traditionalist is entirely undermined.) My point here is the simple one that no general empirical test can resolve our dispute, because our general objectives differ no less than our procedures.

Is the best procedure then to expose our presuppositions to an empirical test? How does one run an experiment to determine whether human nature is generally good or bad? Proponents of the latter position tend to argue that history is the experiment and the results are conclusive—but then the proponents of the "good" human nature position tend to argue that history only proves that institutions dehumanize people and prevent their natural goodness from finding an outlet. To the former, history is a charnel-house of slaughter and cruelty, with moments of relief; to the latter it is the story of the human spirit's increasingly successful struggle for freedom.

But this is not to say that argument about even so general a presupposition must be ineffective. Examples and reasons strongly articulated in debate may occasionally be effective in having someone reassess their position on, say, the likelihood of increased student choice leading to improvements in learning. Also, one could imagine that such debate might lead to agreement on some objective held in common by the proponents of child-centered and traditional education, and that agreement leading to an empirical test of which procedure was better able to bring about the common objective. For example, it might be agreed by both parties that mastery of basic reading and writing skills is a sufficiently important objective that, within limits, each side is willing to sacrifice some degree·of either their rigor or their openness for the better achievement of it. An empirical test could then be conducted to discover which procedure was generally more fruitful in achieving mastery of the specified skills. My point here is simply that it is possible to open up to empirical testing areas of dispute based on differing presuppositions—however restricted the probable result.

It seems to have become generally accepted that curriculum problems are "practical, not theoretical ones" (Walker, 1975, p. 5). An implication of the above argument is that this claim is false. Curriculum problems are theoretical, empirical, and practical. In this they are like the problems of that other common human activity—politics. Underlying political arguments and decisions are presuppositions not unlike some of those I have sketched above. The realm of practical maneuver in politics is perhaps a little greater than in curriculum. Achieving practical results, like winning votes, is sought by various means of persuasion, and exuding of "charisma." Similarly, proponents of a particular curriculum position use various, usually more consciously rational, means of persuasion, and charisma is replaced with a kind of "authority"—the authority and confidence the well-educated person carries in discussion about education. The area for empirical inquiry is somewhat larger in curriculum than in politics. But in both, to differing degrees, the problems have a theoretical dimension that may lead to empirical inquiries that may, in turn, lead to practical decisions or results.

If the basic grounds of disagreements about curriculum issues are differing presuppositions, then are we not reduced to complete relativism? Even though it may be that theoretical discussion and empirical inquiry and practical action may occasionally effect some change in someone's presuppositions, does it not simply boil down to a position where everyone is as right as everyone else—where there are no grounds for saying one area of the continuum of a presupposition is better or worse than any other? No. Only people who require impossible absolutes and certainties will conclude that the impossibility of achieving them leaves us only with the alternative of absolute relativism. The range open to empirical testing and secure theoretical analysis about practical curriculum concerns may be quite small, but that does not mean it does not exist. It does, and it is important to focus a lot of our energy on enlarging it.

This analysis does not lead to relativism for the very good reason that the fact that we cannot show which presupposition about, say, human nature is right or wrong does not at all mean that, therefore, all positions are equally right or wrong. Some presuppositions are right and some are wrong. I have formulated the above set of presuppositions in a way that suggests the middle position is usually right and the further toward an extreme one gets the more wrong one is.

That, ultimately, these presuppositions are like general value positions means that much argument about curriculum problems is likely to be idle, unless the disputes recognize not just the surface content of their argument but also the basic differences in presuppositions from which their disagreement springs. Making these explicit, and trying to isolate components that can be opened to empirical testing or rigorous analysis, will lead to less vacuous idleness in our theoretical discussions, and lead toward greater rationality in both argument and decision making. The fact that our basic values and presuppositions are greatly resistant to change does not mean that they do not change or that they cannot change, or that we cannot change other people's. If curriculum is a kind of political venture whose purpose is to create a system that will tend to produce people like ourselves, let us be as sensible as possible in promoting such a system.

What other implications follow from this brief analysis? One seems to be that when we think about curriculum issues, and imagine that we are dealing with a particular issue on its merits, our view of its merits is determined by the presuppositions with which we approach it. That is, it is an illusion to consider our everyday thinking about curriculum issues to be free. We are not so much thinking as letting our presuppositions think themselves out. We sort the elements of the new problem into the categories prepared by our presuppositions. This metaphor overstates the case, perhaps. It suggests absolute rigidity at the level of presupposition and absolute fluidity at the level of content. In fact, the latter can also, though more rarely and less profoundly, cause changes in the categories created by our presuppositions. We can think about the categories our presuppositions create and we can examine our presuppositions. They are not easy to think about, because they are the things we think with, but there is a sense in which we also think with the phenomena of the world, and it is by being sensitive to the world that we can create some reference system for our presuppositions.

It is dysfunctional, then, to argue about or even think about curriculum problems while failing to recognize the source of our beliefs, arguments, and feelings. Ignorance of our presuppositions, and ignorance that our thinking is largely determined by these presuppositions, blinds us to the real nature of our disagreements about curriculum decisions, and leads us to believe that our opponents are wicked charlatans and idiots because they reach different conclusions based on the same premises. Recognition of our differing presuppositions, however, would show that our premises are in fact different. It would also allow us to focus much more precisely on those areas where we might work toward resolving disagreements, and help us to be more tolerant of persisting disagreements.

CHAPTER 6

The Arts as "the Basics" of Education

This article came to whatever life it has after I had given a talk at the Touchstone Center in New York. In the audience was Monroe Cohen, who was editing a special issue of Childhood Education *on the arts in education. He asked if I could revise some of the material in my talk that seemed to fit that theme. This is the result. It originally appeared in 1997 in* Childhood Education, 73(6), 341–345. *It has benefited from his comments and from the editing of Anne Watson Bauer, who is the editor of the journal and director of publications for the Association for Childhood Education International. I wish to thank her and the association for permission to reprint the article here.*

INTRODUCTION

In its newsletter to parents, a local Canadian school has been boasting that it offers its students "job-ready skills." It has been tailoring its curriculum to "produce" precisely what various local employers seem to want. This responsiveness to the "marketplace," to "the consumers of the schools' products," is considered entirely admirable by many local politicians, who are, after all, the schools' paymasters. This pressure on schools is not only felt at the senior secondary level, but is evident throughout the system. It is also evident in young children. When Cedric Cullingford (1985, 1986) asked a wide sample of primary school children what they were at school for, he was surprised to hear from all the children that they understood the first purpose of school was to prepare them for "jobs."

At present it is easy to justify curriculum time being spent on activities that seem to lead directly to skills that will be of practical use in adulthood. So the "basics" of education are usually thought to be the early development of what will later be skills useful in employment. It is now proving easy for those who promote "computer literacy," for example, to argue for curriculum time on the grounds that computer skills will be of practical value for jobs in the future. It is becoming another basic. How can the arts defend themselves from being increasingly marginalized by the insistence that schools give more and more curriculum time to those basic skills that will be of practical value in future society?

I want to suggest that the problem we find ourselves in—sidelining the arts increasingly even though we recognize their centrality to education—is in part tied up in our having accepted a set of basic educational ideas that are mistaken. That is, I want to make the uncomfortable case that the root of the problem is a set of ideas that most readers of this article probably take for granted.

These ideas have a long history and were put into their modern familiar form by the English philosopher Herbert Spencer (1820–1903). They were then adapted by American psychologists, philosophers, and educators such as William James, John Dewey, G. Stanley Hall, and Edward Thorndike. The ideas also influenced Jean Piaget. These influential thinkers and researchers have reinforced Spencer's ideas and helped to make them taken-for-granted truisms about children's thinking and learning.

These ideas are, in Spencer's (1969) words, that in educating children "we should proceed from the simple to the complex . . . from the indefinite to the definite . . . from the particular to the general . . . from the concrete to the abstract . . . from the empirical to the rational" (p. 75). "Every study, therefore," he argued, "should have a purely empirical introduction . . . children should be led to make their own investigations, and draw their own inferences. They should be *told* as little as possible, and induced to *discover* as much as possible" (p. 75; emphasis original).

The problem with these ideas is that they assume that children's intellectual development follows a path like our biological development. Spencer (1969) adapted these ideas from evolutionary biology (an evolutionary biology since shown to be itself mistaken; see Gould, 1996) and applied them directly to education. Jean Piaget's influential theory is similarly built on a biological conception of development. It is a "hierarchical integrative" theory, in which the child is represented as accumulating skills in stages, each set of which is incorporated and enlarged by the further skills acquired in the subsequent stage. The adult is thus seen as an elaboration of all the capacities that are simply emryonic in childhood.

The result of Spencer's ideas, and the support Piaget has lent to them, is a view of the basics of education as setting in place the skills that gradually grow to maturity and practical use in adult society. What is wrong with this?

WE BEGIN AS POETS

What is wrong is that the human mind does not develop like the rest of the biological world in one educationally very important way. Human children are equipped with some specific intellectual capacities that reach their peak in our early years and remain only in some residual form through the rest of our lives. For example, our ability to recognize and generate appropriate metaphors reaches its peak by age 5, and declines thereafter (Gardner & Winner, 1979; Winner, 1988). Metaphoric fluency is crucial in language development, but also, of course, for a range of other intellectual activities. Those intellectual capacities we rather vaguely refer to as "the imagination" similarly experience energetic deployment early in life and, typically, gradual decline as we grow older. We tend to develop arteriosclerosis of the imagination in adulthood.

Consider for a moment the kind of food you most hated when you were 5 years old, and try to recapture if you can the degree of loathing you felt for it. In my case it was cheese. I couldn't bear to let cheese near my mouth. Now I eat cheese quite appreciatively, and for some time thought this was a triumph of character—when, alas, it's largely the result of a decay of taste buds.

Unfortunately, it isn't only the taste buds that go into decline after about age 5 or 6; a whole range of intellectual capacities that are necessary to quickly orient us to a language, a society, and a cosmos are evolutionarily developed to become less useful after about age 5 and to go into decline. Unfortunately, again, these tools of the imagination are precisely those needed to keep us intellectually flexible, creative, and energetic in modern societies. That is, our evolution is at odds with our educational needs—which helps to explain why the educational job is so hard.

The profile of the development of imagination in our lives seems quite unlike that ever-rising progress from childhood to adulthood that is represented in hierarchical-integrative, biology-derived developmental theories. While we lack any precise image of the development of imagination, even the most casual observation of human beings at various ages suggests that it would be absurd to claim that imagination is only embryonically present in young children and becomes increasingly more evident, elaborate, and rich as we grow older. Give a box to a typical adult and to a typical child and ask them to work out different uses for it; when the adult gives up after a few minutes with 6 uses, the child is into the 50th and just warming up.

If we look at children's imaginative lives, rather than their slowly accumulating logico-mathematical skills, we do not see intellectual activity dominated by the concrete, the simple, the indefinite, the empirical, and so on. We see prodigal metaphoric invention, talking middle-class rabbits, titanic conflicts of good and evil, courage and cowardice, fear and security, and so on.

It seems not unfair to say that current developmental theories that have been influential in education have emphasized what young children do least well—those logico-mathematical capacities that slowly develop through our early lives—and have largely ignored those things that young children do best intellectually, and better typically than adults—those imaginative skills attached to metaphor and image generation, and to narrative and affective understanding.

If we conclude that Spencer's (1969) principles are inadequate in giving us a picture of the child as a learner, and hence are wrongly identifying what are the most secure basics for education, to what alternative can we turn for a more adequate conception of children's development and so the basics of education?

THE ARTS

If language is the crucial fact of early human development—the true basis of all our education—and early childhood is the period during which children are developing oral language at a prodigal rate, let us consider what intellectual capacities—what tools of understanding—are involved in generating and using an oral language. To put it generally, what, intellectually, comes to children along with language?

"Language, in a preliterate society lacking the apparatus of a modern information-state, is basically for telling stories" (Donald, 1991, p. 257). Our inventory of what comes along with language, then, might begin with stories.

What are stories? Stories are unique kinds of narratives in that they have, in their basic forms, ends that satisfy some tension generated by their beginnings. If I tell you that "she was pushed into the water," you will want to know by whom, and why, and, most basically for a story, whether to feel glad or sorry that she was pushed into the water. If I tell you that she was pushed by a big bearded man who snatched her purse and that she hated the water and could hardly swim, you will begin to feel sorry that she was pushed. But if I tell you that someone had planted a bomb in her bag and it was about to go off, and the bearded man was trying to save her life at the risk of his own, you will begin to feel differently about the event "She was pushed into the water." The story is the only form of language that can fix the hearer's affective orientation to the events, characters, ideas, or whatever, that make it up. Stories, basically, are little tools for orienting our emotions.

Language also brings with it a series of techniques to aid the memory to build up a store of knowledge. So rhyme and rhythm can help the process of remembering information in a way that is useful and also enjoyable—"Thirty days hath November." Early language development properly leads to a mind that re-sounds with a store of rhymes and rhythms.

Language can be used to stimulate vivid images in the mind, and knowledge coded into such images is more easily remembered reliably. We remember things best when we can locate them emotionally and associate them with some vivid image. Generating images from words seems invariably to involve some emotional component (Warnock, 1976)—which helps to account for the greater richness we typically experience from generating our own images from text or listening to an oral story than from seeing images presented to us on film or television. Hearing a story is usually an imaginatively active experience, whereas seeing it is usually much less so.

If we consider the kinds of fantasy stories young children are most powerfully engaged by—and it is a rare adult who does not recall in detail, say, Cinderella, while the same adult may remember nothing of the more "relevant," "issues-oriented" stories read to them as children—we may see that their underlying structure is usually a simple binary conflict based on security/fear, courage/cowardice, good/evil, and so on. Three simple observations might be made about these binary structures: First, they are abstract; second, they are affective; and third, they can "expand" understanding to anything in the universe that can be organized in terms of their basic affective concepts.

Their abstractness perhaps merits emphasis in the face of the near-ubiquitous assertion in education that young children are "concrete thinkers." That young children do not commonly use abstract terms explicitly does not mean that they do not constantly use abstractions in their thinking. Indeed, one might reasonably make a case for "the primacy of the abstract" (Hayek, 1970) and for children's ability to make sense of the concrete only to the degree that the concrete elements are tied to some affective abstraction (Egan, 1989). If you tell a young child the story of Robin Hood, you presuppose that the child understands the relationships between oppression, resentment, and revolt. He or she may not know those terms, or be able to define them, but they are meaningful within the story, and, indeed, the story would be largely meaningless to the child without an understanding of those abstract emotional relationships—even though the child may have learned those particular emotions and their relationships within the homes or in play with peers.

The point about the binary oppositions and mediation is that once you grasp from experience such oppositions as solitude/company, for example, you can make sense of a solitary like Obi-Wan Kenobi in *Star Wars*. That is, you don't need to "expand" the child's horizons gradually from something familiar until you can make star warriors, monks, or witches meaningful; they can be grasped directly in terms of such abstract binary terms. So the fundamental principle of much early school curricula, and especially the social studies curriculum, is based on an assumption about children's "expansion" of understanding that is simply inadequate.

These, then, are just a few of the intellectual tools that come to the young child along with language. With metaphor, story, binary opposition and mediation, affective abstraction, image-generation from words, rhyme and rhythm, we are beginning to construct our inventory of "basics" in education. They look very like the basic set of tools we have traditionally associated with the imagination and with the arts in general. They are the tools of the poet within each of us—however energetically, or otherwise, they are used. And we are wise to bear in mind Eisner's (1993) point that "what schools allow children to think about shapes, in ways perhaps more significant than we realize, the kinds of minds they come to own" (p. 5).

By focusing on the intellectual tools that young children use most and best rather than drawing parallels from biological development, the ideas we might form of children's thinking and learning are somewhat different from Spencer's (1969) set. We might state them thus:

1. That children are abstract as well as concrete thinkers.
2. That children's thinking is powerfully *affective*.
3. That children readily understand content organized into story forms.
4. That children are readily engaged by forming images from words.
5. That children are prodigal producers and consumers of metaphors.
6. That children's learning is stimulated by rhyme and rhythm.
7. That children's learning can proceed by forming binary oppositions and mediating them.

There seem to be significant implications for the curriculum and for teaching that follow from these alternative principles (see Egan, 1997). I will here explore just one set of implications for teaching.

IMPLICATIONS FOR TEACHING

The first implication, to quote the title of a book I seem to remember seeing somewhere, is that one might begin to think of "teaching as storytelling" (Egan, 1989). This is not to suggest that we should spend our time telling children lots of fictional stories, though more emphasis on such stories may be one result of this alternative approach, but rather that we think of the content of the curriculum more as great stories to tell than as objectives to attain. We might, then, think of "story" much in the sense a newspaper editor asks a reporter "What's the story on this?" That is, we will not look for a fiction related to the content but rather seek out the affective meaning—the emotional resonance—*within* the content.

For example, instead of using a planning model derived from Ralph Tyler's (1949) useful but industry-influenced (Callahan, 1962) objectives-content-methods-evaluation scheme, we might construct an alternative model derived from some of the principles sketched above. I have called it "mythic" because so many of the poetic features of childrens' thinking on which it is based are shared by the central features of mythic thinking:

Mythic Planning Framework

1. Identifying importance
   What is emotionally important about this topic? What is affectively engaging about it?
2. Finding binary opposites
   What binary concepts best capture the affective importance of the topic?
3. Organizing the content into a story form
   3.1 First teaching event
   What content most dramatically embodies the binary concepts, in order to provide access to the topic? What image best captures that content and its dramatic contrast?
   3.2 Structuring the body of the lesson or unit
   What content best articulates the topic into a clear story form? What vivid metaphors does it suggest?
4. Conclusion
   What is the best way of resolving the conflict inherent in the binary concepts? What degree of mediation is it appropriate to seek? How far is it appropriate to make the binary concepts explicit?
5. Evaluation
   How can one know whether the topic has been understood, its importance grasped, and the content learned?

Let me give a quick example of how this model might be used. I will take the example from a book written by three Australian teachers who have been using the model for a few years (Armstrong, Connolly, & Saville, 1994). Among the units of study they outline in the book is one on the environment.

They identified the importance—the emotional importance to them and to the children—in the sense that what the individual does *can* make a difference to the environment, and that the environment they influence is the one they will grow old in and the one they will pass on to their children.

The binary opposites they identified, based on their exploration of their feelings about the environment, were "despair" and "hope."

They began organizing the content into a story structure by choosing something that provided a dramatic exemplification of those binary opposites. They used the book and video *The Man Who Planted Trees* by Jean Giono. It tells the story of Elzéar Bouffier, who, over a lifetime, filled a whole region with hope by his solitary efforts to reafforest a desolate area of the French Alps. From this beginning they built activities and knowledge that conveyed an understanding of the environment by constantly contrasting hope with despair.

These activities involved the students in regenerating some wasteland, and the conclusion was in seeing the positive results of their work, feeling the hope that working along with nature gave them, and recognizing that over the years what they had done would have significant beneficial consequences. Their purpose was less mediation than the confirming of hope. The unit of study also involved personal-development activities, religious study, science and mathematics, language arts, and so forth, all integrated into the single extended story about human hopes and despairs concerning the environment.

Evaluation was based on the students' sense of the story of regeneration they played a part in; the clarity and accuracy of their predictions for the results of their work; discussion of their emotions and thoughts about their work; their enthusiasm, commitment, and involvement; their ability to extract relevant information that would have practical beneficial effects and to be able to present this in confident and competent oral and written forms; and an ability to cooperate in a group to achieve agreed-on goals.

CONCLUSION

Spencer's (1969) principles derive from thinking of children's minds largely in terms of logico-mathematical capacities, and forgetting that before they develop these to any significant degree, and also after they have done so, children also have more richly the capacities of poetic thinking. The central fact of our minds from an educational point of view is not their biological nature, and all that has been assumed to follow for our slow development of logical skills, but their poetic nature. We begin as poets, using the techniques that language allows us to make sense of our world. The basics of our educational development, then, are the arts. It is through deployment of those tools and skills that are central to early language development—story, metaphor, rhyme and rhythm, binary structuring and mediation, image formation from words, affective abstraction, and so on—that we lay down the true basics of education.

CHAPTER 7

Clashing Armies in the Curriculum Wars

This chapter, like Chapter 5, began life as an introductory talk to my curriculum course. It was then elaborated into a talk I gave to the Seven Oaks School District in Winnipeg—which accounts for the mention of that city in the text. From there it was elaborated further as my contribution to a set of papers delivered as a part of a panel made up from the Canadian Society for the Study of Education and presented at the American Educational Research Association in 1995. Those papers and some others were then gathered into a book co-edited by Marvin Wideen and Mary Claire Courtland and published in Canada. Then, altered again, it appeared early in The Educated Mind *(Egan, 1997). I do like to get a bit of mileage from ideas. Like Chapter 5, it explores presuppositions. In this case, I try to expose the most general set of presuppositions or ideas that constitute our very conception of education today. My aim was to show, in a somewhat unfamiliar way, what is really at the root of the arguments, frustrations, and practical difficulties in education today. I've been surprised at the number of people who have responded positively to what is, basically, a grim picture of incompatible ideas ineffectually battling each other. I am grateful to Dr. Marvin Wideen and the Canadian Association for the Study of Education for permission to reprint the essay here. It first appeared as "Competing Voices for the Curriculum" in* The Struggle for the Curriculum: Education, the State, and the Corporate Sector *(Burnaby, B.C.: Canadian Association for Curriculum Studies and the Institute for Studies in Teacher Education, Simon Fraser University, 1996). The revised title here suggests echoes with Matthew Arnold's "Dover Beach" and beyond to Thucydides' account of ignorant armies clashing by night.*

INTRODUCTION

The competing voices the title refers to are those of parents, governments, press, professional educators, the corporate world, "the public" as an entity somehow supposed to be distinct from each of the above, and others that emerge from time to time making claims on the school curriculum. These are often referred to as the "stakeholders," who, as stakeholders, are assumed to have a right of influence on the school curriculum. The state, the corporate sector, and the educational community are supposed to have interests in common but also somewhat different, such that the ideal curriculum of each group would vary somewhat, though perhaps with a more or less common core. Analyses of the "rights," the claims, and the influences of the different stakeholders tend to focus on their political clout, the means they have of influencing the curriculum, their demographic makeup, the particular curriculum revisions their interests dictate, and so on.

I want to suggest that a lot of this focus is misplaced, and that it is probably not very useful if considered without analysis of the ideas that these stakeholders have available to think with. If we know about the ideas they have to think with, we can make a much more economical and effective analysis of their influence on the curriculum. Dealing with general theoretical issues may seem remote from the activities in that school down the road to practical people, and may seem remote from the pragmatic issues of power over the curriculum. I will try to show that unless we get these theoretical issues front and center, much of our commonsense, pragmatic discussion of the struggles for the curriculum will be so much waste of time. In this I am following in the wake of Elliot Eisner's discussion of "Five Basic Orientations to the Curriculum" (which appeared first in the 1979 edition of *The Educational Imagination*). He points out that the issues the stakeholders discuss "seldom broaden into an examination of principles" (p. 50) and that it is by trying to make explicit the values, premises, and ideas that underly them that we can develop a more adequate basis for dealing with them.

I will take as my starting point J. M. Keynes's (1936) famous, or infamous, conclusion to his *General Theory of Employment, Interest and Money*— (I will change the words slightly to fit an educational rather than an economic context):

> The ideas of educational theorists, both when they are right and when they are wrong, are more powerful than is commonly understood. Indeed education is ruled by little else. Practical people, who believe themselves to be quite exempt from any intellectual influences, are usually the slaves of some defunct educational theorist. Mad people in authority, who hear voices in the air, are distilling their frenzy from some academic scribbler of a few years back. I am sure that the power of educational stakeholders is vastly exaggerated compared with the gradual encroachment of ideas. Not, indeed, immediately, but after a certain interval; for in the field of education there are not many who are influenced by new theories after they are twenty-five or thirty years of age, so the ideas which administrators and politicians and even teachers apply to current schooling are not likely to be the newest. But, soon or late, it is ideas, not "stakeholders," which are dangerous for good or ill.

To understand the struggle for the curriculum, then, one needs to have a clear idea of what ideas govern the actions of those engaged in the struggle, what the stakeholders think they are doing. And so one needs to be clear about what they have to think with about issues of the curriculum, what ideas detemine their actions. What follows, then, is a brief and very general attempt to get some handle on the prime determiner of the behavior of the various educational stakeholders, the dominant ideas of education that they use. I will argue that there are only three significant educational ideas, and that we can better understand the moves of the various stakeholders by seeing that they tend to hold these three different ideas in different proportions. I will discuss these ideas briefly, putting them in the context of their initial appearances, so that we might also have some sense of whose ideas shape current struggles, of which academic scribblers are the real combatants, the real proponents in the stakeholders' mimic battles.

The three ideas are that we must shape the young to the current norms and conventions of adult society, that we must teach them the knowledge that will ensure their thinking conforms with what is real and true about the world, and that we must encourage the development of each student's individual potential. These three ideas have rolled together over the centuries into what is our currently dominant conception of education.

I will try to show, furthermore, that not only does this analysis of ideas give us a better grasp on what is at stake in battles for the curriculum, but it also can give us a better understanding of why we have such practical problems in making schools more educationally effective institutions. Commonly each group of stakeholders tends not only to have a particular interest in the curriculum, but also tends to blame some other stakeholder or stakeholders for the ineffectiveness of schools. (Among the various stakeholders, only professional educators will sometimes claim that schools are doing a good educational job. The various reports, task forces, and commissions that have pronounced on public education in the Western world for the last half century have been almost unanimous in their condemnations of schools.) There is certainly no shortage of candidates recommended to our blaming attention. We are told that inadequately educated teachers are to blame, or the absence of market incentives, or the inequities of capitalist societies, or the lack of local control over schools, or the genetic intellectual incapacity of 85% of the population to benefit from instruction in more than basic literacy and skills, or drugs, or the breakdown of the nuclear family and family values, or an irrelevant academic curriculum, or a trivial curriculum filled only with the immediately relevant, or short-sighted politicians demanding hopelessly crude achievement tests while grossly underfunding the education system, or a lack of commitment to excellence, or

vacuous schools of education, or mindless TV and other mass media, or failure to attend to some specific research results, and so on.

Along with the cacophony of blame comes a panoply of prescriptions:
introduce market incentives, make the curriculum more "relevant"/aca-
demic, reform teacher training, ensure students' active involvement in
their learning, and so on. I will try to show that none of the above, nor
any of the other suspects that are usually rounded up, is the cause of
schools' ineffectiveness, and consequently, that none of the related prescriptions is likely to make things better. Rather, our problem can be better identified by focusing on the ideas that are in conflict, and, in our current case, we may see that our problem derives from schools' trying to
implement a fundamentally incoherent conception of education. I will try
to indicate the incoherence of the general conception of education that
governs most people's ideas of what schools ought to be doing. So, I will
outline the three general ideas that determine people's thinking about
education today, and I will then try to show in what ways these three great
ideas are mutually incompatible, and I will conclude by trying to show
how this abstract theoretical discussion can help us better understand our
current educational disputes and our practical educational problems.

EDUCATION'S THREE IDEAS

The First Idea: Socialization

Central to any educational scheme is initiation of the young into the
knowledge, skills, values, and commitments common to the adult members of the society. Oral cultures long ago invented techniques to ensure
that the young would efficiently learn and remember the social group's
store of knowledge and skills and would also take on the values and emotional commitments that sustain the structure of each particular society
and establish the sense of identity of its individual members.

Prominent among the techniques developed in oral cultures for socializing the young were the use of rhyme, rhythm, meter, and vivid images, to help fix important lore in the minds of the young. Perhaps the
most powerful technique invented, and perhaps the greatest of all social
inventions, was the coding of lore into stories. This had the dual effect of
making the contents more easily remembered—crucial in cultures where
all knowledge had to be preserved in living memories—and also of shaping the hearers' emotional commitment to those contents at the same time.
So once one could code the lore that was vital to one's society into stories—lore concerned with such things as proper kinship relations and

appropriate behavior, economic activities, property rights, class status, medical knowledge and its application, and so on—one could ensure greater cohesiveness within the social group.

Human beings have an enormous plasticity early in life to adapt to a kaleidescopically indeterminate range of cultural forms, beliefs, and patterns of behavior. The central task of socialization is to inculcate a restricted set of norms and beliefs—that set which constitutes the adult society the child will grow into. Societies can survive and maintain their sense of identity only if a certain degree of homogeneity is achieved in shaping its new members, and "education perpetuates and reinforces this homogeneity by fixing in the child, from the beginning, the essential similarities that collective life demands" (Durkheim, 1956, p. 70).

Whoever governs the initiation process—the storytellers or the ministry of education and the school board—acts on behalf of the norms and values that are dominant in the society at large. Their job is to perform the homogenizing task Durkheim (1956) refers to; it is a process of convergence toward particular norms and values. To put it at its simplest, socializing aims to make people more alike. If a school today in Cuba or Iran routinely graduated liberal, capitalist entrepreneurs, it would be considered a disaster. In Winnipeg, Wigan, Wabash, or Wollongong, this would not be considered so bad. Indeed, what would be considered outrageous in Iran is a deliberate aim of Wollongong schools.

The process of socialization is central to the mandate of schools today. Our schools have the duty to ensure that students graduate with an understanding of their society and of their place and possibilities within it, that they have the skills required for its perpetuation, and that they hold the values and commitments that are common to the society at large. While we might not feel comfortable with the term, we accept that a prominent aim of schools is this homogenization of children.

The spokespersons of governments, taxpayers, and businesses that require the schools to produce a skilled workforce of good citizens echo those who learned long ago the techniques for reproducing in the young the values and beliefs, the skills and lore, that best contribute to the untroubled perpetuation of the tribe. The public voices that primarily associate education with jobs, the economy, and the production of good citizens reflect a predominantly socializing emphasis.

The very structure of modern schools in the West, with their age cohorts, class groupings, team sports, and so on, encourages conformity to modern Western social norms. Such structures can accommodate only a limited range of nonconformity. Students learn, more or less, to fit in for their own good. We need not see this process of socialization and homogenization as the dehumanizing, right-wing conspiracy it was "exposed" to be by 1960s romantic radical writers on education (e.g., Goodman, 1962; Kozol, 1967; Roszak, 1969; Young, 1971). Of course, pushed to extremes— which is where the sixties and modern radicals consider the regular public school to be—the socially necessary homogenizing process can become totalitarian in its demands for conformity. But most pluralistic Western societies build defenses against those who are most eager to censor children's reading or restrict their behavior and shape their beliefs excessively.

So, the currently dominant conception of education includes as one of its main constituent ideas the socialization of the young. This constituent is evident in those voices that support curriculum time being given over to such subjects as consumer education, programs combating drug use, programs in auto maintenance and computer use, and other areas that promote useful knowledge and skills. Sometimes they may argue that schools should graduate students only when they are equipped to do a job. I have kept an old letter from an Ann Landers column from someone who signed, sadly, as "Too soon old—too late smart." The letter expresses frustration with schools in which "our children are subjected to 12 years of 'education' without learning how to conduct themselves in real-life situations" and suggests as a remedy that schools introduce a course on the hazards and consequences of shoplifting in the fifth or sixth grade, that several days a week be devoted to the subject of cigarette smoke, that there be instruction in the dangers of alcoholism, that sex education be a "must" in every school not later than the seventh grade, that there be courses on "life"—how to settle arguments, how to express anger and hostility, how to deal with competitive feelings involving brothers and sisters, how to live with alcoholic parents, what to do about "funny uncles" and passes made by homosexual peers. The writer concludes that of course algebra and geometry are important, but that information on how to handle one's life should take precedence.

Too soon old—too late smart expresses very clearly how the curriculum would be changed if socializing were made more prominent in the schools' mandate. Those who share this view see the school as primarily a social agency that should be ever sensitive to society's changing needs, and flexible in changing its programs to respond to those needs. Recently their voices have been prominent in demands that schools ensure that students become familiar with computers and their range of applications. They support counseling programs and like to see school counselors, working with parents, helping students adjust to the strains and challenges of modern society. Sports, travel, exchanges, visits to monuments and courts and government buildings, social studies activities that help students understand their local environment, tend all to be supported as helping to socialize the young. The teacher, from the perspective of this idea, is an important social worker, primarily valuable as a role model who exemplifies the values, beliefs, and norms of the dominant society; knowledge of subject matter cannot substitute for "character," wholesomeness, and easy and open communication with students.

The Second Idea: Plato and the Truth About Reality

Plato (c. 428–347 b.c.e.) had a new idea about how people should be educated. He wrote *The Republic* (trans. 1941) as a kind of elaborate prospectus for his Academy. Not conforming with the best modern advertising practice, he laid out his ideas in a manner that involved constantly arguing the inadequacy of the forms of education offered by his competitors. Plato wanted to show that the worldly-wise, the well-socialized, practical person equipped with all the skills of a good and effective citizen was not just educationally inadequate, but actually contemptible. The assertive and confident Thrasymachus of *The Republic* and the worldly-wise Callicles of the *Gorgias* are shown to be other than the masters of affairs they seem; they are shown to be slaves of conventional ideas because they cannot reflect self-critically on those ideas. That ability to reflect on ideas, to pull them this way and that until some bedrock of truth and certainty is established, was the promised result of the curriculum described in *The Republic* and offered in Plato's Academy. Plato certainly wanted the graduates of his school to be politically active and to change the world, but first they had to be philosophers and understand it.

Plato's revolutionary idea was that education should not be primarily concerned with equipping students to develop the knowledge and skills best suited to ensuring their success as citizens, sharing the norms and values of their peers. Rather, education was to be a process of learning those forms of knowledge that would give students a privileged, rational view of reality. Only by disciplined study of increasingly abstract forms of knowledge could the mind transcend the conventional beliefs, prejudices and stereotypes of the time, and finally see reality clearly. He proposes that the everyday world disclosed by our perceptions and conventional beliefs can somehow be better understood by a rational grasp of some transcendent world of abstract theoretic ideas, which are accessible only after decades of refined scholarly activity guided by a kind of spiritual commitment. Now this hasn't been everyone's cup of tea by any means. And it wasn't the whole of Plato's idea of education, but it is the part that has become institutionalized within what is commonly called the "traditional" or "liberal" conception of education.

Plato succeeded in expressing this central idea with such clarity, force, vividness, and imaginative wit that everyone who has written about education in the West since has been profoundly influenced by it. He bequeathed to us, however it has been interpreted, a disturbing idea. Who, after all, wants to live and die a prisoner to conventional prejudices and stereotypes, frightened of reality, never seeing the world as it really is? And how can one know that one is dealing with reality rather than with illusions and stereotypes? Plato's claim that his "academic" curriculum alone can carry the mind to rationality and a secure access to reality has been so influential that we can hardly imagine a conception of education without it.

And, indeed, nearly everyone today takes it for granted that schools should attend to the intellectual cultivation of the young in ways that are not justified simply in terms of social utility. We include in the curriculum a range of subject matter that we assume will do something valuable for students' minds and give them a more realistic grasp of the world. So, we consider it important to teach them that Saturn is a planet that orbits the sun, rather than have them believe that it is a wandering star erratically orbiting the earth and influencing their daily fortune by its association with other stars. We teach division of fractions, algebra, drama, ancient history, and much else for which most students will never have a practical need. The place of such topics in the curriculum is usually justified in rather vague terms, variously argued by those who claim that they are of "educational value" and benefit the minds of students. In Plato's idea, the mind *is* what it learns, and so selecting the content of the curriculum is vital. Consequently, too, he seems reluctantly to have concluded that women should be educated equally with men.

So, how is the Platonic idea of education represented today? One prominent conception can be introduced via an image suggested by the work of the astronomer Carl Sagan. Sagan has been energetic in organizing a search for signs of extraterrestrial intelligence by means of radio telescopes. He presents a vividly romantic picture of a conversation among intelligent beings in our galaxy, which we are just now developing the technology to enter. By plugging in, we might suddenly have access to a conversation of unimaginable richness and wonder. In a more immediately possible sense, modern proponents of the Platonic idea of education suggest that accessing a transcendent conversation is precisely what education does for the individual. Michael Oakeshott (1991), for example, represents education as entry into a conversation that began long ago in the jungles and plains of Africa; gathered further voices, perspectives, and varied experience in the ancient kingdoms of the east, then additional distinctive voices and experience in ancient Greece and Rome, and so on and on. The conversation is now one of immense richness, wonder, and diversity. An individual can live and die happily, be socialized harmoniously in her or his special milieu, but remain almost entirely ignorant of this great cultural conversation—as we will probably do with regard to Sagan's imagined galactic interchange. But if it were really there in radio waves across the galaxy and we had the means to join it, would we not be foolish to ignore it? Would we not be culpably impoverishing our experience? The task of education, in this view, is to connect children with the great cultural conversation that very definitely is there, and that transcends any particular political society or special milieu or any particular form of local experience or conventional sets of norms and values. To pass up the chance to engage in this conversation is culpably to impoverish our experience; it is to live like Proust's dog in the library—possibly content, but ignorant of the potential riches around one.

Those who want the schools to connect children to this great cultural conversation, and to serve as bastions of civilization against the cretinizing mindlessness of pop culture (these are the kind of terms they like), who want students to be engaged by the disinterested pursuit of truth through the hard academic disciplines that will make them knowledgeable, discriminating, and skeptical, give new voice to the idea Plato bequeathed to us. These are people who value Plato's idea higher than the other two. For them, school is properly a place apart from society: a place dedicated to knowledge, skills, and activities that are of "persisting value," transcending the requirements of current social life. Indeed, what students learn is to establish the grounds from which they can judge the appropriateness of the values, norms, beliefs, and practices of society. Schools dominated by this idea consequently tend to be called elitist.

This idea leads its proponents to infer that the institutions that should give direction to the school curriculum are not those of society at large but those of higher education, particularly the university. Knowledge is valued less for its social utility and more for its presumed benefit to the mind of the student—so Latin will have a higher status than auto maintenance in such a view. "Excellence" has recently been a prominent slogan for modern neoconservative promoters of this Platonic idea. Their outrage is directed particularly at students' ignorance of their cultural heritage (e.g., Hirsch, 1987; Ravitch & Finn, 1987). They would like to refocus schooling on teaching an academic program and remove or downplay programs that do not serve that central purpose of the school. The curriculum would be constructed primarily on grounds of intellectual and cultural, rather than more generally social, value, and so literature and history, the sciences and mathematics, will receive most curriculum time, and subjects like Latin, Greek, and art history will stake a claim to a presence in the curriculum denied them when the other ideas have been predominant. In schools dominated by this idea, the teacher will tend to occupy a more distant, authoritative (and even authoritarian) role because teachers properly embody the authority that comes from being an expert in the relevant subject-matter.

The Third Idea: Rousseau and Nature's Guidance

Jean-Jacques Rousseau (1712–1778) thought that most of the educational practice he saw around him was disastrous. He was happy to acknowledge that Plato's *Republic* "is the finest treatise on education ever written," but he concluded that it lacked something, and that lack was undermining its implementation. What happened when dull pedagogues took hold of Plato's idea at sixth or seventh hand was that they focused on the forms of knowledge that made up the curriculum, organized those into what seemed the best logical order, then beat them into the students. The typical result was misery, violence, and frustration—a syndrome not unknown today, though we may mark some success, influenced by Rousseau, at reducing the physical violence inflicted on children in the name of education.

Pedagogues, Rousseau (1911) observed, "are always looking for the man in the child, without considering what he is before he becomes a man" (p. 1). In *Emile*, he focused attention instead on the nature of the developing child, concentrating less on what ought to be learned and more on what children at different ages are capable of learning and on how learning might proceed most effectively. He saw his book, *Emile*, as a kind of supplement to the *Republic*, rectifying its major omission and updating the master's work. But, as we'll see, *Emile* was built on assumptions profoundly at odds with Plato's.

Rousseau's (1911) central and continuous theme was that if you want students to understand what you teach, then you must make your methods of teaching conform with the nature of students' learning: "The internal development of our faculties and organs is the education of nature. The use we learn to make of this development is the education of men" (p. 11). So, to be able to educate, we must first understand that internal development process. The most important area of educational study, then, is the nature of students' development, learning, motivation, and so on. The more we know about these, the more efficient and humane we can make the educational process. The key is that underlying natural development: "Fix your eye on nature, follow the path traced by her" (p. 14).

As nature was to be our guide, and Rousseau clearly believed the nature of males and females to be significantly different, "nature" thus dictated a quite different education for Sophie from that of Emile—an education that encouraged the "domination and violation of women" (Darling & Van de Pijpekamp, 1994).

Emile was published in 1762, and promptly ordered to be burned in Paris and Geneva. This no doubt helped sales considerably, as it went from printing to printing. The sentimental image of the child clearly helped the book's popularity too (Warner, 1940), even while Rousseau himself was dispatching his own unwanted children to foundling hospitals. But the rhetorical force with which *Emile* conveys its conception of the benefits that follow from attending to the nature of the student carried his ideas across Europe. In more recent times, John Dewey and Jean Piaget have been profoundly influenced by Rousseau, and the degree to which their ideas have affected practice is one index of his continuing influence.

Careful observation and study of students, recognition of the distinctive forms of learning and sense-making that characterize different ages, construction of methods of teaching that engage students' distinctive forms of learning, emphasis on individual differences among learners, observation that students learn much better when they are themselves active, and insistence that the student's own discovery is vastly more effective than the tutor's "words, words, words" are all features of Rousseau's educational scheme. While it would be false to claim him as the originator of all these ideas, he did bring them together into a powerful and coherent conception of education. These are ideas that have become a part of the "common sense" or the taken-for-granted folklore of so many educationalists today. It would now be considered strange not to recognize the importance of students' varying learning styles, or not to recognize the value of methods of teaching that encourage students' active inquiry, or not to accommodate to the significant differences among students at different ages. Rousseau's central idea, that is to say, provides another of the main constituents of the dominant conception of education that schools today try to implement.

The modern voices that encourage schools to focus on fulfilling the individual potential of each student, that emphasize that students should "learn how to learn" as a higher priority than amassing academic knowledge, that support programs in "critical thinking," that evaluate educational success not in terms of what knowledge students have acquired so much as in terms of what they can do with what they know, reflect this third educational idea. Active, inquiring students who are enjoying learning are the ideal of schools dominated by this idea. The focus of education, in this view, is the experience of the child. The construction of a common core curriculum for all children is not simply undesirable to promoters of this idea, but impossible. Each child's experience, even of the same curriculum content, is necessarily different. We should recognize this, and let the unique experience and needs of each child be the determiner of the curriculum, even to the radical point of making the curriculum a response to the questions students raise (Postman & Weingartner, 1969). The educator's attention should be focused on the individual development of each child and on the provision of the experiences that can optimally further this development. The commonest expression of this idea today combines the variously interpreted progressivism of John Dewey (Kleibard, 1986) with Piaget's developmentalism and the psychologizing of the study of children—the modern form of discovering their "nature" that Rousseau recommended. In the classroom, and outside it, "discovery learning" is valued, manipulables and museums are recommended for students' exploration, discussion is encouraged, project work by individuals or groups is provided for. Careful attention is given to the results of empirical studies of children's learning, development, motivation, and so on, and teaching and curricula are adjusted to conform with such "research findings." The teacher, in such a school, is not an authority so much as a facilitator, a provider of the best resources, a shaper of the environment from the responses of their actions on which the students will learn.

INCOMPATIBILITIES

Are these three ideas really incompatible? Surely we can find a way of addressing these somewhat distinct aims for education without having them undermine each other. Why can we not socialize students to prevailing norms and values, while also ensuring that they accumulate the kind of knowledge that will give a truer view of the world, and also help them to fulfill the potential of each stage of development? A rigorous academic program surely does not conflict with society's needs, and facts about learning, development, and motivation surely can only help us better implement both the academic program and socialization. At least, Plato's concern with the *what* of education is surely not at war with Rousseau's concern with the *how*. Don't they properly complement each other? Looked at in sufficiently general and vague a manner, it may indeed seem that the distinctive ideas that constitute our conception of education are not as incompatible as I have been suggesting. Certainly the everyday business of schooling in Western societies has been going ahead on the assumption that evident problems are due to improper management, or poor teaching, or genetic constraints on students' abilities to learn, or flawed curriculum organization, and not to some profound theoretical incompatibility among constituents of our concept of education. But I think the incompatibility is there, and it is at the root of our practical problems. Let us consider the incompatibilities of each constituent idea with the others.

Plato and Socializing

The homogenizing aim of socialization, which is to reproduce in each student a particular set of beliefs, conventions, commitments, norms of behavior, and values, is necessarily at odds with a process that aims to show the hollowness and inadequacy of those beliefs, conventions, commitments, and so on. They are, after all, the glue that holds society's foundations in place. If Socrates was Plato's ideal example of the educated person, it is evident why the democratic citizens of Athens condemned him to death. The radical skepticism that his kind of education engendered threatened the foundations of society. He was condemned for corrupting the youth. What he was corrupting, or corroding, was their acceptance of the conventions, beliefs, values, that were fundamental to the life of their society. His fellow citizens saw his behavior as a kind of treason.

Few now believe that Plato's ideal aim of direct knowledge of the real, the true, the good, and the beautiful is attainable. What is attainable, though, is the skeptical, philosophical, informed mind that energetically inquires into the nature and meaning of things, that is unsatisfied by conventional answers, that repudiates belief in whatever cannot be adequately supported by good arguments or evidence, and that embodies the good-humored corrosive of Socratic irony. This kind of consciousness has not often been greatly valued by those who govern societies; it is a disruptive force. Everyday social life, particularly in complex modern economic systems, proceeds more smoothly and blandly without the irritant created by following Plato's educational prescription too closely. If people are busy asking "but is this really the best way to live?" all the time, they simply can't get on with everyday business with single-minded efficiency.

Of course we want the promised benefits of both educational ideas. We want the social harmony and the psychological stability that successful socialization encourages, but we also want the cultivation of the mind, the skepticism and dedication to rationality that Plato's program encourages. Designing schools to achieve either one is difficult. Our schools today are supposed to encourage conformity to specific norms and values while encouraging skepticism of them at the same time.

Rousseau and Plato

But if we see Plato as dealing with the *what* of education and Rousseau with the *how*, then need we consider them incompatible? This common resolution of apparent conflicts would be fine were it not the case that it falsely represents both ideas. The above compromise, leaving Plato's descendants with the content and aims of education and Rousseau's with the methods, appeals to many as a neat division of labor. So the educational philosophers can deal with content and aims, drawing on the knowledge generated by the educational psychologists about learning and development. It seems so obvious that facts about students' development can blend with philosophers' research into the nature and structure of knowledge to yield a more easily understood math or history curriculum. It seems so obvious that such collaboration should be common that one would expect the absence of it to compel reassessment of what looks, but clearly isn't, obvious.

One problem for the neat compromise is that, in the Rousseauian and Deweyan view, the means and ends of education are tied together. They argue that distinct means cannot be employed in education to achieve distinct ends. The means used in Rousseauian and Deweyan instruction are *parts* of their educational ends. They favor discovery procedures, for example, not because they are more efficient means to some distinct educational ends, but because they are a component of their educational ends. Discovery procedures, in Rousseau's terms, disclose nature and in so doing stimulate the development of a pure, uninfected reason. In Dewey's terms, discovery procedures mirror the scientific method whose acquisition by students is a crucial component of their education. We have incorporated this idea into our currently dominant conception of education. Put crudely, we recognize the inappropriateness of beating children who have failed to memorize the text on compassion; we feel a bit uncomfortable about compelling attendance at institutions that try to teach the values of liberty and democracy; and it is increasingly clear that choice of method of teaching is not a simple strategic matter disconnected from our educational ends. In our educational means are our ends; in our educational ends are our means.

A further problem may be seen by observing that Plato and his descendants have their own conception of educational development. Students progress, in Plato's scheme, from *eikasia*, to *pistis*, to *dianoia*, to *noesis*. But these stages are interestingly different from Rousseau's and from Piaget's. Plato's stages represent greater clarity in understanding. Education, in Plato's view and in that of modern proponents of the academic idea, is marked by students' progress through stages of mastery of increasingly sophisticated knowledge—regardless of how they may be progressing through some putative psychological developmental stages. For Rousseau, and Piaget, it is precisely the psychological developmental stages that mark education, and that must determine what kind of knowledge the student needs; as the development of the body proceeds almost regardless of the particular food it eats, so the mind will develop almost regardless of the particular knowledge it learns. For the Platonists, the only development of educational interest is the accumulation of the particular knowledge learned; the mind is nothing much else.

So Rousseau and his modern followers are not simply making methodological or procedural recommendations, which might allow us to do the Platonic academic job more efficiently. They are actually recommending a different job. Rousseau's idea is not one that yields us an easy accommodation with Plato's. These ideas conflict—most profoundly in identifying the cause and dynamic of the educational process. In the Platonic idea, learning particular forms of knowledge carries the educational process forward; in the Rousseauian idea, education results from an internal developmental process unfolding within a supportive environment. In the Platonic view, knowledge drives development; in the Rousseauian view, development drives knowledge; it determines what knowledge is learnable, meaningful, and relevant. In the Platonic view, education is a time-related, epistemological process; in the Rousseauian view, it is an age-related, psychological process.

We could design schools to implement either of these conceptions of education, but we require our schools to implement both together. Our practical difficulties arise from our acceptance that both the Platonic and the Rousseauian ideas are *necessary* for education, but the more we try to implement one, the more we undermine the other.

The conflict between these two ideas has been the basis of the continuing struggles between "traditionalists" and "progressivists" during this century. One sees them at odds in almost every media account of educational issues, where the Platonic forces argue for "basics" and a solid academic curriculum, and the Rousseauians argue for "relevance" and space for students' exploration and discovery. A key battleground as I write this is the elementary social studies curriculum in North America; the traditionalist forces are pressuring for a revision that will reintroduce history and geography in place of the progressivists' preferred relevant focus on families, neighborhoods, communities, interactions among communities, and so on; the progressivist forces argue that history and geography require abstract concepts and are not "developmentally appropriate" for young children and the traditionalists argue that any content can be made comprehensible if presented sensibly.

Socializing and Rousseau

When socializing, we derive our educational aim from society's norms and values; in the Rousseauian view, we should keep the child from contact with society's norms and values as long as possible, because they are "one mass of folly and contradiction" (Rousseau, 1911, p. 46). If we want to let the nature of the child develop and flower as fully as possible, we will constantly defend him or her against the shaping pressures of society. An aspect of this conflict is apparent today in many educators' attitudes to the general influence of TV on children. TV provides a powerful shaping to a set of prominent social norms and values, but educators resist much of this shaping in favor of activities that seem to them less likely to distort proper or "natural" development. Natural is not, of course, the term much used today, but it lurks around the various ways the Rousseauian position is restated, as in a number of books that appeal to a conception of a more natural kind of childhood that is being distorted or suppressed by current forms of socialization (e.g., Elkind, 1981; Postman, 1982). Some of the 1960s radicals were even plainer—Paul Goodman (1970) put it this way: "The purpose of elementary pedagogy, through age twelve, should be to delay socialization, to protect children's free growth. We must drastically cut back formal schooling because the present extended tutelage is against nature and arrests growth" (p. 86).

No one, of course, is simply on the side of Rousseau against socialization, or vice versa. We all recognize that any developmental process has to take place within, and be influenced by, a particular society. Our problem comes about because of the attraction of Rousseau's ideas about a kind of development that honors something within, something uninfected by the compromises, by the corruptions and constrictions, that social life so commonly brings with it. We do not have to share Rousseau's own disgust with society (which returned him high regard and money) to recognize the attraction of his ideas. This Rousseauian idea of development entails the belief that the most important shaping of the individual must come from a natural, spontaneous, internal process, and proper education requires that all influences from society either conform with that process or be held at bay.

There doesn't seem room for much compromise here. We can't sensibly aim to shape a child's development half from nature and half from society. That creates the same problems as half punishing and half rehabilitating a prisoner. Such treatments interfere with one another. The more we do one, the more we undermine the other. By trying to compromise, we ensure only that neither is effective.

There are, of course, a number of ways of seeing this conflict that do not lead to the conclusion of incompatibility I am urging. We can "solve" the problem by observing that our nature is indeterminately plastic in our early years and socialization is a condition of our nature being realized. We are, after all, social animals; there is no natural form that we will develop toward if we are kept apart from society. We can solve this conflict also by seeing it not as one between nature and society but much more simply as the kinds of disagreements one must expect in a pluralistic society about the preferred norms and values into which children should be socialized. But the incompatibility I am concerned with is only within the conception of education, and it seems to me inevitable so long as people conceive of children as going through some regular, spontaneous, process of intellectual development that can be optimized by shaping their learning environment to suit it. One cannot derive one's educational principles both from some conception of an ideal developmental process and from some current norms and values of adult society; they are bound to be incompatible unless one lives in a perfect society. They are incompatible because socializing has a distinct end in view and is a shaping, homogenizing, narrowing process toward that end, whereas supporting the fullest development of students' potentials involves releasing them to explore and discover their uniqueness; it is an individualizing process that encourages distinctiveness even to the point of eccentricity if necessary, and is expansive without predetermined ends.

CONCLUSION

As I noted above, nobody holds to one of these ideas exclusively. The different positions of education's stakeholders can be seen in the different degrees to which they hold the three ideas. Also, the fact that they all hold the three mutually incompatible ideas in whatever degrees ensures that their related prescriptions for improving education are likely to be unsuccessful.

We could characterize the positions of the various stakeholders in terms of the three ideas. So, in general, corporate stakeholders want lots of socialization, basic Plato (but not enough for systematic skepticism), and cautious dribbles of Rousseau. Professional educators today tend to want lots of Rousseau and a fair bit of Plato with judicious amounts of socialization. Parents want lots of everything. Upper-class conservatives tend to support lots of Plato, lots of socialization, with small amounts of Rousseau, whereas radicals want lots of Rousseau, a fair amount of socialization, with a little Plato. Well, this is at one level silly, but it could be elaborated in ways that would more clearly establish the ways in which the major positions we see in the press or in policy documents simply reflect different amounts of these three ideas. Most familiar is the Plato/Rousseau battle, which has been prominent during this century in terms of traditional versus progressive stances. These positions, when held unconsciously (as is usually the case), function like the presuppositions discussed in the Chapter 5.

So what is the point of this kind of exercise? We are left with the problems we started with, only seeing in them more abstract, theoretical terms. Well, this is the point of ivory towers, in which one can abstract oneself from the details of the particular battles that are going on among, in this case, education's stakeholders and try to see in a more fundamental sense what they are about. If we leave it like this, of course, the exercise is futile. The point about understanding the world is that it better enables us to change it. The problem with not understanding it adequately is that one's suggested solutions to problems will themselves be inadequate, and often cause even worse problems. This seems to me the case for the panoply of recommendations for educational change that are touched on in the introduction to this chapter. Our problem is that we have three profound and important ideas, which are all indispensable, but which are also in significant ways incompatible. The solution will have to start from resolving this theoretical incompatibility. Proposals that fail to do this will be futile.

CHAPTER 8

Educating and Socializing:
The Curriculum Wars Continued

This is rather an odd essay. I can't now remember why I wrote it, except that I was thinking about these issues after co-authoring with David Nyberg The Erosion of Education *(New York: Teachers College Press, 1981). I commonly find that it is only after finishing a book that I try to sort out what I was writing about. Not a very useful way of proceeding, I acknowledge, but as I only seem to think when writing. . . . Well, I wouldn't today focus on the distinction between educating and socializing like this, but—following other essays in this section—it is another example of trying to excavate the ground on which people argue in education. As is clear from the previous chapter, I think it more fruitful to see socializing as one of the three great ideas that constitute the currently dominant concept of education. The essay first appeared as "Educating and Socializing: A Proper Distinction?" in* Teachers College Record *(Vol. 85, No. 1, 1983, pp. 27–42), and I am grateful to the editor and publishers for permission to reprint it here.*

INTRODUCTION

Distinctions between educating and socializing have been made a number of ways, and the two have also been treated by some people more or less as synonyms. Usually the distinctions hold socialization to be the process of preparing someone to be a competent social agent within a particular society, and education to be something in addition to this, which might include being able to reflect critically on one's particular society or might include a range of more or less refined cultural attainments whose value to the individual might seem clear but whose value to society at large is less clear. Underlying most of the distinctions is an implication—though it has not perhaps been put so starkly—that anything that may reasonably be called socializing has implicit in it the impulse and tendency to make people more alike, and the contrasting impulse and tendency in education is to make people more distinct. (So we say of those we recognize as most highly educated that they are "distinguished.")

111

Whether one considers the distinction important to make seems connected to what one encompasses within one's idea of society. If one's idea
of society is so encompassing that all aspects of all members of society's
lives and their meanings are included within it, then education will undoubtedly be seen as only a part of a more general socializing process or
as a synonym for socialization. If one's idea of society includes mainly a
set of economic, industrial, legal, political, and commercial transactions
and a set of relationships determined by them, yet holds distinct a cultural
world of knowledge, understanding, and appreciation that provides particular pleasures that transcend the relationships and transactions of particular societies at particular times, then one will undoubtedly want to
distinguish initiation into "society" by "socialization" and initiation into
the cultural realm by "education." One may say perhaps that the importance or otherwise of the distinction turns on one's response to what has
been called the "problem of the culture-boundedness of meaning" (Wilson,
1970, pp. viii–ix).

This chapter explores why some people consider it important to make
the distinction and why others think it unimportant, and why others again
think it important not to make it. It also considers whether it is proper to
make such a distinction and, if so, the proper way to make it.

DURKHEIM, DEWEY, AND SOCIALIZATION

One of the contributions of sociology has been to show the extent to
which we become recognizably human by being initiated into a society.
As Durkheim (1965) puts it, "Man is man, in fact, only because he lives in
a society" (p. 76). Becoming socialized is the process of being fitted into a
complex social environment and in this process a certain limited set from
the indeterminately large range of human potentialities is evoked and
actualized. The limited set comprises those potentialities that are shared
by other members of the society into which the child is being initiated:
"Society can survive only if there exists among its members a sufficient
degree of homogeneity; education perpetuates and reinforces this homogeneity by fixing in the child, from the beginning, the essential similarities that collective life demands" (p. 70).

Social life is concerned not merely with the basic necessities of physical existence and the regulating mores of the group, but also with what
we call our culture. "Of what an animal has been able to learn in the course
of his individual existence, almost nothing can survive him," but human
beings accumulate knowledge, skills, records of many kinds, and "this
accumulation is possible only in and through society" (Durkheim, 1965,

pp. 77, 78). Nor is it merely crude information that is passed on in socializing, but also how that knowledge and those skills and understandings are to be interpreted: "Society frequently finds it necessary that we should see things from a certain angle and feel them in a certain way" (p. 83). The initiation of children by adults into society, in this general sense, is what Durkheim calls education: "Education consists of a methodical socialization of the young generation" (p. 71).

Durkheim (1965) appears, then, not to make any distinction between socializing and educating: They serve as synonyms for him. He seems not to admit of anything that is of human value that is outside of society, and so any initiation into any aspect of human life must be socialization. In stressing the absolute importance of a society to human beings and the role of education in initiating the young into particular societies, he is, incidentally, trying to expose the shallowness of notions of education—such as James Mill's—that focus on the cultivation of the individual as though people had free choices about what characteristics they would encourage in the young: "Even the qualities which appear at first glance so spontaneously desirable, the individual seeks only when society invites him to, and he seeks them in the fashion that it prescribes for him" (Durkheim, 1965, p. 75).

But this is not to say that society inhibits the development of the individual; society makes development possible and, given our social nature, it is only within the collectivity that the individual can develop properly:

> Whereas we showed society fashioning individuals according to its needs, it could seem, from this fact, that the individuals were submitting to an insupportable tyranny. But in reality they are themselves interested in this submission; for the new being that collective influence, through education, thus builds up in each of us, represents what is best in us. (Durkheim, 1965, pp. 75–76)

Sometimes those who see education as entirely an instrument of social initiation and who thus categorize individual cultivation entirely within a social context tend toward conclusions about "society's" rights and duties in governing individuals' education that can make others distinctly uncomfortable. Thus "since education is an essentially social function, the state cannot be indifferent to it. On the contrary, everything that pertains to education must in some degree be submitted to its influence" (Durkheim, 1965, p. 80). Even in private schools, "the education given in them must remain under [the State's] control" (p. 80). The alternative to this all-pervasive state control of education, according to Durkheim, is disaster:

If [the State] were not always there to guarantee that pedagogical influence be exercised in a social way, the latter would necessarily be put to the service of private beliefs, and the whole nation would be divided and would break down into an incoherent multitude of little fragments in conflict with one another. (Durkheim, 1965, p. 79)

One way of viewing the history of schooling over the past century and a half in the West is as a generally successful struggle waged by the centralized states against church, family, locality, and class interests for control of the schools. Prominent among the weapons of the state have been the slogan "equality of opportunity" and arguments such as Durkheim's. We might be wary, however, of Durkheim's easy move from his general, normative concept of society to seeing particular centralized nation-states as instantiations of that normative concept. The problem with that move is summed up by Dewey (1916/1966) (though not referring especially to Durkheim): "The social aim of education and its national aim were identified, and the result was a marked obscuring of the meaning of a social aim" (p. 97).

Some might think that a lot of confusion could be avoided if Durkheim and Dewey made a distinction between education and socialization. The previous quotation might then be written something like this: "Education was confused with socialization and the result was a marked obscuring of the meaning of education." But Dewey no less than Durkheim uses *education* for the process of growth into social life. Those who want to distinguish education from socialization need to define the two terms. But for Dewey the "conception of education as a social process and function has no definite meaning until we define the kind of society we have in mind" (Dewey, 1916/1966, p. 97). For the person who wishes to distinguish between education and socialization, Dewey's claim might well be true for socialization, but not for education. Those philosophers of education who labor to clarify their "concept of education" without constant reference to the particular social context in which it is to be embedded are, in Dewey's view, engaged in a futile scholastic exercise. His aim in *Democracy and Education* was to show that education was not the kind of process that could be defined apart from social experience and to show that if it was allowed to become untied from that experience one was left with "an unduly scholastic and formal notion of education" (p. 4).

In this view, then, a society in which a distinction could readily be drawn between educating and socializing is a society in which an elite will be educated and the rest will be socialized: "The result is that which we see about us everywhere—the division into 'cultured' people and 'workers'" (Dewey, 1956, p. 27). Rather, what we have to do is to so describe the qualities of a truly democratic society that socialization to such a society would encompass all that anyone might wish to include in a proper concept of education.

"Not only is social life identical with communication, but all communication (and hence all genuine social life) is educative" (Dewey, 1916/1966, p. 5). Given such a vision of a constantly educating social experience, the desire to distinguish socializing from educating threatens to drive apart aspects of social initiation that Dewey was most concerned to hold together. The idea of a *distinct* process of education involves "the standing danger that the material of formal instruction will be merely the subject matter of the schools, isolated from the subject-matter of life-experience" (p. 8). The idea of a distinct process of socialization leads to the danger of "a narrowly conceived scheme of vocational education to perpetuate the division between rich and poor" (p. 317). The means of overcoming these dangers was to tie both formal instruction and vocational education to the living reality of present social experience. Thus there follow those pedagogical recommendations for preserving the social character of all learning that became, or were perverted in, the program of progressivism.

In the literature of progressivism, then, we find no form of the traditional distinction between education and socialization because education is seen as having a fundamentally social character. Its role is seen as preparing people to be at home in the social world that is constantly coming into being, in order "to naturalize, to humanize, each new social and technical development" (Goodman, 1962, p. 40). To ignore that social reality and to try to "educate" children into a distinct dead or dying culture—which is what the traditional "liberal" or "classical" education was conceived as doing—is to guarantee the preservation of ignorance and helplessness for the many and a dehumanized exploitativeness for the few. Similarly, the institution that is primarily charged with the more or less formal part of this initiation needs to be closely integrated with society's experience; it is not to be a place apart where students undergo an artificial and difficult initiation to a culture not alive in the society at large. The society must constantly invade the school so that children may grow easily into that social experience by directly doing things that are a part of its reality.

EDUCATION AS DISTINCT FROM SOCIALIZATION

Above, then, is an attempt to sketch in general terms why some people do not distinguish between educating and socializing. It may be useful here to try to sketch in a similarly general way how and why others do make the distinction.

   Socializing and educating have been distinguished in a variety of ways, sometimes quite casually and vaguely. To try to uncover the main grounds for the distinction it may be useful to begin with the strong distinction suggested in the introduction to this chapter: Socializing activities are those whose aim is to make people more alike; educating aims to make people more distinct. The first great socializer, then, is learning a language. Those who share a language share a considerable part of their view of the world, which is encoded at a level of presupposition in the terms, distinctions, and grammatical structure given in that language. Teaching people to be functionally literate is, in this form of the distinction, to socialize, in that it teaches conventions that are shared by everyone who aims to communicate by writing. Teaching to write with style, talk with eloquence, and read with critical awareness is, then, to educate. Such things stress individual distinctness from the basic conformities that make communication possible; they stress distinctness from the current clichés and conventional forms. A homogeneity in conventional forms of expression serves social utility; there is less complexity, less ambiguity, less likelihood of misunderstandings, and also less richness and diversity. Writing with elegance and reading with discrimination are not matters of social utility. They are, however, matters of educational importance. (Eccentricity is a kind of disease of education; it focuses on the formal characteristics of distinctness at the expense of the content that might make one "distinguished.")

   In schools, then, we might expect all activities to have both socializing and educating aspects—the degree of which will vary from activity to activity. In woodwork or metalwork, for example, learning to use tools is a matter of socializing. Learning to use them with elegance, with individual style, and seeking therethrough an aesthetic quality in one's work above and beyond what utility requires is an educational matter. In learning, say, Greek there is a level of learning conventions of letters and basic expression that involve a socialization to that language, but the aim of fluency and subtlety in understanding a different view of life and the world is an educational matter. Usually in schools the distinction can be made more easily and clearly. Those activities that are engaged in so that people can get on more easily in society at large—can get jobs, can fulfill the basic responsibilities of citizenship, parenthood, and so on—will tend to be mainly a matter of socialization. Those activities that lead to personal cultivation will tend to be mainly educational.

   We may also distinguish between educating and socializing activities by the grounds on which we justify their place in the curriculum. Socializing activities are justified on grounds of social utility, educational activities on the grounds of cultivation of individuals. Both are worthwhile. The former are worthwhile because they are the homogenizing activities that Durkheim (1965) pointed out were necessary to keep a society working; the latter are worthwhile for the refined pleasures they provide us individually.

The distinction is important to hold, in the view of those who hold it, because we need to be able to refer to separate criteria in judging whether curriculum time should be allowed for any particular socializing or educating activity. Thus, if we face a conflict between some who want to add a course in, say, Consumerism or Driver Training and some who want to add a course in, say, Greek or music appreciation, we need to be clear that we do not decide which to include and which to exclude by reference solely to a socializing criterion. We do not ask which is more relevant to students' ability to get by in the daily adult world. Rather we need to recognize that schools both socialize and educate, and a conflict between Consumerism and Greek cannot sensibly be settled by applying a criterion appropriate to deciding which among various socializing activities should be included. This sharp distinction, then, is seen as a defense of education in schools, a defense sorely needed in light of the erosion of educational activities in schools in favor of increasing socialization.

This erosion has been especially severe, in this view, in North America, where the schools were willing instruments in the homogenizing of diverse immigrant populations—*e pluribus unum*—and where the society at large is seen as appropriately demanding that the schools pay increasing attention to socializing concerns. This perspective is expressed most boldly by Michael Oakeshott (1971):

The design to substitute "socialization" for education has gone far enough to be recognized as the most momentous occurrence of this century, the greatest of the adversities to have overtaken our culture, the beginning of a dark age devoted to barbaric affluence. It emerged from a project, embarked upon about three centuries ago (which was neither stupid nor itself menacing to the educational engagement) to provide an alternative to education for those who, for whatever reason, fell outside the educational engagement. Since those times this alternative has been adjusted to respond to changing circumstance, it has been improved and extended to compose an apprenticeship to adult domestic, industrial and commercial life, it has generated a variety of versions of itself, and for the most part it has submitted to the direction of governments. Indeed, it has become what the world it has helped to create can recognize as a "service industry". It was designed as a contribution to the well-being of "the nation"; it has been welcomed or endured on account of the affluence it is alleged to be about to procure, and attempts have been made to calculate its product in terms of costs and benefits; and it has been defended on the ground of what it is designed to produce and upon the more questionable plea that it is the most appropriate apprenticeship for certain sorts of children. This makeshift for education, however, was permitted to corrupt the educational engagement of European peoples; and it is now proclaimed as its desirable successor. The usurpation has everywhere been set on foot.

But the victim of this enterprise is not merely an historic educational engagement (with all its faults and shortcomings); it is also the idea of education as an initiation into the inheritance of human understandings in virtue of which a man might be released from the "fact of life" and recognize himself in terms of a "quality of life". The calamity of the enterprise is matched by the intellectual corruption of the enterprisers. (p. 71)

The reason for holding fast to a clear distinction between socializing and educating, as may be seen from Oakeshott's (1971) words, is that it is the only way of making clear that human beings may engage a refined culture that transcends the relationships and transactions of any particular society. To use another of Oakeshott's images, this culture that transcends particular societies is like a conversation: It began long ago in the primeval forests and was elaborated in the earliest towns and in the city-states and empires around the Mediterranean; it has continued to grow and be enriched through the centuries. Some parts of it are in poems, plays, music, painting, sculpture, until in the present we have around us this enormously rich cultural conversation continuing, in which we can engage. Education is learning the language of this great civilized and civilizing conversation. We can of course live and die without engaging it, as our cats and dogs do. For a human being to live and die without engaging in this conversation, however, is to miss the best that life has to offer.

In North America there has prevailed a powerful resistance to seeing the schools merely as socializing institutions. A strong statement of this view from the earlier part of this century runs:

> The fundamental theory of liberty upon which all governments in this Union repose excludes any general power of the state to standardize its children by forcing them to accept instruction from public teachers only. The child is not the mere creature of the state; those who nurture him and direct his destiny have the right, coupled with the high duty, to recognize and prepare him for additional obligations. (Pierce v. Society of Sisters 268 U.S. 535, 1925)

PROGESSIVE RESPONSES

Everyone recognizes a distinction between learning to use a tool in a utilitarian fashion and learning to use the tool to produce an aesthetically satisfying product. What has been wrong with some parts of the traditional form of education is that this distinction has been complacently accepted and built into practice, such that it is seen as perfectly proper for the masses to be taught in a utilitarian fashion—if indeed an acceptable proportion can be taught to use tools, read, compute, and so on, adequately for the demands of their jobs and social roles—and proper for a much smaller number of others to receive instruction beyond, or different from, utility's requirements. The traditionalist might well say that it would of course be desirable if everybody could learn the more refined uses of tools, more sophisticated literacy, and so on, but, unfortunately, these higher abilities are accessible only to a small proportion of citizens, a proportion often calculated at about 15%. What is wrong with this from the progressive point of view is the acceptance of the division between utilitarian skill and cultural achievement. The progressive program is designed to prevent precisely that traditional theoretical distinction's becoming realized in social life. No one is to be trained simply to utilitarian skills with no sense of the intrinsic value of their functions; no one is to be allowed to develop a frivolous, effete aesthetic sensitivity with no sense of social functions and utility. The educational vision of Dewey is seen reflected in architecture by "the functionalism of Louis Sullivan and Frank Lloyd Wright, that was trying to invent an urbanism and an aesthetic suited to machine-production and yet human" (Goodman, 1962, pp. 41–42).

There is an apparent ambivalence in progressivist thinking, which will be explored later, about traditional high culture. There is a strain of progressivism that sees this elite pleasure as properly the inheritance of everyone, and among the complex mix of programs that are identified as progressivism is a set of methodological reforms that will make high culture accessible to everyone. Another strain of progressivism is hostile to high culture, seeing it as miseducation and a sham. Both recognize that a product of high culture is social division; the former consider this a contingent matter, a historical coincidence that can be rectified by proper democratic procedures. In the process, the artificial aesthetic that creates for traditionalists a hierarchy of cultural objects "out there," which have to be internalized in appropriate hierarchies inside, will become purified; the artificial crud, associated with unreflective snobbery, will be wiped away, and the new democratically educated person will be able to see the contents of this high culture afresh and with a purer aesthetic make appropriate, authentic responses. So the baroque extravagance and oversophistication, the diseased aesthetic and its associated rottenness, may be overthrown and the inheritance of high culture may be brought fresh and clean into the American democratic experience. Frank Lloyd Wright did not ignore the traditions of architecture; what he did was see them with a clear eye, one that was alive to the present reality of social experience, and so he could fashion buildings that preserved elegance but forged that elegance in alliance with their new function, sweeping neo-Gothic absurdities away.

The other strain of progressivism saw high culture and class-based divisions as necessarily connected. The stress on personal cultivation was possible only to a class that had leisure, and the money to support it, and so personal cultivation was simply a means of distinguishing, distancing, oneself from the masses and the society around one. The distance, and the preservation thereby of a sense of *real* difference, was achieved by the use of leisure and education for initiating one's children into an arbitrarily chosen dead culture. It has been purely a matter of fashion which dead culture is chosen. In the 18th century the social division was marked and preserved by artificially resurrecting Roman culture as the *differentium*; in the 19th century the fashion shifted to Greek culture as the distinguishing criterion; in the 20th century, ironically, it is 18th- and 19th-century cultures that are resurrected—cultures that, when living cultures, were derided by the predecessors of those who now use them to mark themselves off from the living culture of today. The central characteristic of this culture—what Oakeshott (1971) so inappropriately likens to a conversation—is that it is mainly passive; its appropriate response is "appreciation." It is dead and gone so one cannot do anything to it, with it, or about it, except "appreciate" it. The "personal cultivation" that results from initiation into this high culture is likened to 18th-century upper-class clothing: vastly ornate and impracticable for any activity except being looked at or standing and looking at others.

What Oakeshott (1971) presents as an ideal of education, the progressives see as precisely the social problem. Oakeshott approvingly quotes Ortega y Gasset's tag: Man does not have a nature, what he has is history. The progressives would rather say: Man does not have a nature, what he has is society (and thereby a future). It is only the upper and middle classes, and the male parts of these, that have a history. The working classes, peasantry, and women are relatively history-less and, in the progressives' view of the traditionalist position on education, they are thus treated as less human. Given Oakeshott's claim that we become human as we are initiated into the fullness of human culture, it is clear that some are much more human than others. The working classes and peasantries, however, have had and have a society no less than the upper classes, and on this criterion are no less human and have no less claim on the future.

The traditionalist acceptance that only 15% of the population can hope to be properly initiated into high culture leaves the rest to Oakeshott's (1971) "alternatives to education," and so they should be carefully socialized in a way that makes them useful to themselves and their fellows and preserves the social and economic conditions that support the leisured class and their personal cultivation. These are among the conditions "which split society into classes, some of which are merely tools for the higher culture of others" (Dewey, 1916/1966, p. 98). So the taxes levied on the working and lower middle classes may go to state support of opera, ballet, orchestras, poets (sometimes through universities—which are themselves instruments of the divisive process), while should hockey or football or boxing get into financial difficulties there will be no state subsidy for them. So the artificial entertainments of those educated into dead cultural forms are preserved. Those with a Marxist/Freudian bent see this form of culture in terms of a rather nasty psychosis compounded of narcissism and necrophilia.

CONDITIONING AND DETERMINING

It would be possible to give an account of the conflicting positions about the appropriateness or otherwise of a distinction between socializing and educating in historical terms. In such an account the distinction between those who see knowledge, culture, and aesthetic responses as being socially conditioned and those who see them as being socially determined would come only recently into the story with any sharpness. The conflict is prefigured in Dewey, of course, in that he seems to hold both positions, each at different points. But the arguments are all contemporary; the traditionalists have not gone away nor have the progressives conceded defeat with "back to basics." What is more significant of late is the harder progressive position sketched above—the position that, to put it starkly, holds that high culture is a political commitment, and that any institution that seeks to preserve it is necessarily reactionary and hostile to the interests and proper education of the working class. It is a necessary connection because knowledge, culture, and aesthetic responses are socially *determined*.

Pursuing what in other, connected, arguments is called a synchronic rather than a diachronic approach, we may lay out a continuum with two apparent discontinuities along its length. On the right is the desire to distinguish sharply between educating and socializing, because in the distinction lies a defence of high culture, civilization, and what makes life most worth living. In the middle is a weak form of progressivism that tends to recognize some kind of distinction between cultural initiation and utilitarian training in job skills, and whose adherents believe that high culture can be incorporated into present social life and provide its pleasures to the working classes, as long as schools are careful in tying it always to present experience. There is some discomfort about all this, however, and there is no commitment to initiate children into high culture, only the vague sense that working-class (and other), children should be "exposed" to it, and if it "takes" so much the better, and if not, it doesn't much matter. On the left, there is the belief that the distinction between socializing and educating is a political tool to preserve an unequal, divisive, and exploitative social system. It would be useful to consider this left position in more detail. Perhaps we might usefully call this group radical as distinct from progressive—though their position has been now and then articulated within what has traditionally been called progressivism.

The radicals believe, most radically, that "every society has its specific way of defining and perceiving reality" (Berger & Kellner, 1979, p. 51). There is no such thing as an objective reality; objectivity and reality are created by each society and they are what they are believed to be by each social group. This perspective allows its user to see why the progressives were ineffectual in changing in any serious way the traditional educational system and the class-based social system it supported: The progressives failed to see that knowledge and objectivity and reality were not simply *conditioned* by social experience but were indeed created in it and *determined* by it. In accepting the traditional epistemology with its assumptions about scientific method's establishing an objective view of the world, about how one can secure certain "facts," about the very tenets of rationality, the progressives lost the ability to do anything but reform and so strengthen the social system they worked to reconstruct. The more radical perception that social life *determines* what counts as a fact, as objectivity, as rationality, leaves the way open for rejecting the grounds on which the traditionalists have so far preserved the dominance of their social view. So: "It is necessary that . . . criticism should be extended even to such apparently neutral, common ground as the concepts of science, fact, objectivity and rationality" (Arblaster, 1975, p. 6). By accepting the "bourgeois forms of these concepts," the socialist position is undermined.

Thus one may also see, from this position, why the traditionalists were able to continue their control of education and extend their view of reality under the slogan "equality of opportunity." This did nothing to break down class-based society, but became simply an instrument for co-opting cleverer children from the working class into the traditional view of reality through initiation into its culture. Equality of educational opportunity, while seen by many socialists as a tool in their kit, became a more effective way of preserving the social status quo.

The radical challenge is to deny all the grounds that have been accepted as common by traditionalists and progressives: the belief in the "accepted" (by whom and for what purpose?) canons of rationality, what counts as a fact and how is it established, the ideal of objectivity, and so on. Similarly, the radicals have serious doubts about whether one can hope to use the schools to transform our sense of social reality, because the public schools are at heart middle-class institutions. They have only been good for the middle-classes and their interests; they have always been hopeless institutions for the working classes. Thus the radicals are driven toward a program of deschooling and finding new ways of bringing children to be at home in a better social reality.

In debate with traditionalists the radical responds: "While agreeing that our educational dilemmas are about culture and meanings, these are not separable from the political and economic struggles of which such meanings are an expression" (Young, 1977, p. 8). So for the radical "the curriculum is a social construction" (p. 9), with all that "social" implies in the radical lexicon. Thus traditional educationalists who have uncomplicatedly pursued the task of clarifying and elaborating their conceptions of education find themselves engaged by what seem irrelevant questions about their political motives, their ideological commitments, their very way of life, in which their relationships with wife and children, the kind of car they like to drive, and so on and voraciously on, are inserted into what they thought was to be a traditional academic debate conducted by the old ground rules that the progressives, to their cost, accepted. A typical response of traditionalists at this point is to throw up the hands. This is fine by most radicals, as they see their job not to argue with traditionalists—they know all those arguments—but to elaborate their newly perceived social reality and destroy the institutions that preserve the unjust and inhumane traditional social reality.

A TRADITIONALIST RESPONSE

There are two main connected lines of traditionalist response. One may start with an appropriately Latin slogan, from Terence: *Nihil humanum alienum mihi puto* (I consider nothing human to be alien to me). If human nature is plastic and shaped so greatly by experience, goes the argument, meanings can be shared, and translated and interpreted, only if there is an objective world out there that is unaffected by our culture and social experience. Also, we must have a common set of human characteristics that at some level are unaffected by cultural conditioning. Of course we cannot translate the meanings of one society with absolute precision and clarity into those of another, but that does not mean that we absolutely cannot do it. We can recognize greater and lesser degrees of "ethnocentrism."

The lesser degrees are due to our more truly translating the meanings of one culture into those of another than those who absolutely reduce the meanings of one to another. If all meanings were socially *determined*, we would only be able to absolutely reduce the meanings of one culture into another, and we would not be able to distinguish degrees of ethnocentrism. So the scholarly tradition that increasingly uncovers for us the meanings of, say, Homer, is not merely an illusion. Of course we cannot absolutely recover Homer's meanings, and we can see how in previous generations there was a very large reduction of his meanings to those of the society at the time. Success at reducing the reduction is a success at expanding the meanings of our culture. The argument for high culture in the Western tradition is that it is the greatest expansion of meanings. One of its latter-day tools is scientific method, which may fail in absolute objectivity but is not thereby absolutely relative. The use of scientific methods in exploring other cultures has been a proof that there are degrees of reductionism and objectivity, and this fact of clearly perceptible degrees is evidence that societies certainly condition but do not determine what can count as knowledge. That *nihil humanum* is alien means that at some level we may find psychological analogues to the behaviors, the myths, the literatures, the conversations of others and so find something of their meaning and bring that meaning into our culture. The absolute separation of cultures suggested by the image of each society creating its own reality is contradicted by these observations.

The connected attack concerns the status of the radical's own arguments. It is the old "and relativity to you!" response. If knowledge is socially determined, then the radicals' claim that knowledge is socially determined becomes undermined by itself. What kind of claim on truth can this claim that knowledge is socially determined make if its purpose is to undermine the notion that such knowledge can be true? The excellent line of attack represented by the relativist position is disastrous to any attempt to construct something in the place of what has been attacked, and it serves to undermine the attack as well.

A further part of the traditionalist response is that the radicals systematically confuse contingent associations with necessary connections. Thus the traditionalist would accept as fairly obvious that the contents of high culture, let us say Schubert's piano trios, were produced at certain times in a certain kind of society and tend to be enjoyed now by people who have had a certain kind of education that is associated with a certain social class. To the traditionalist, the connections among the social, economic, and political conditions of Schubert's time and between the social class and forms of education that make Schubert's trios accessible to people today are all contingent relationships. Yes, of course, a certain economic system was necessary to create the leisure that shaped the developing forms of the musical tradition in which Schubert's trios figure, and, of course, certain social forms conditioned the conventions of this tradition, and, of course, a certain kind of education seems necessary today in order to make this music accessible. The form and content of Schubert's trios are clearly causally connected to particular economic, social, and educational systems. All these systems, however, do not *explain* Schubert's trios; nor do they affect what is most culturally significant about them. Explanations derived from such sources can only explain equally all the trios produced at that time in that tradition. We do not, however, prize "piano trios": The category, which *is* subject to explanation, is not what provides the content of high culture. It is particular trios that are prized—and the variability of taste over time and among any social group does not demonstrate some absolute relativity of taste. That there is not absolute agreement in matters of taste does not mean that there is absolutely no agreement. This indicates the logical flaw with the radical position in general: They assume "if not absolutely x, then absolutely not x."

We may note that during the 18th and 19th centuries people walked on two legs. It is clear that this bipedalism was a necessary condition of the development of advanced capitalism and its high culture. It would obviously be absurd to suggest that the best route to destroying capitalism would be to prevent bipedalism. Certainly, if it were possible, it would have the desired effect. But while bipedalism is indeed causally related to capitalism, the fact that person X walks with a slow shuffle and person Y walks with a rolling gait cannot be seen as causes of capitalism.

The traditionalist would defend this case as analogous with that of high culture's relationship to capitalism. High culture is, by analogy, the residue of styles of walking, not walking as a generic condition. Particular styles are only contingently associated with economic and social conditions. (The Monty Python Ministry of Funny Walks would appear to cater largely to middle-class clients.)

Goering, Goebbels, and sometimes Bismark are claimed to have observed: "When I hear the word culture, I reach for my gun." The former two probably did say it, quoting apparently Hanns Hohst's *Schlageter*, but it was not so much the particular cultural forms (or "Jewish physics") that concerned them but the social, political, ideological, and racial ideas *associated* with them that they disliked. The radical makes a doctrine of not recognizing a distinction between cultural forms and associated political and ideological claims and conditions. The traditionalist position, however, is to reassert the principle that where we can make distinctions we should. The traditionalist thus favors Yeats's response to the radical claim that in the future social reality will have to be viewed in political terms. He found that this perspective was inadequate as a means of making sense of much of his social reality. However he might consider the political perspective on things, he would sometimes see a girl standing there and his nonpolitical response was simply "Oh that I was young again and held her in my arms."

But, for the radical, such a response is not nonpolitical. At its simplest, the aesthetic response to particular forms of beauty is socially learned—whether determined or conditioned is at the crux of the dispute. Had Yeats been an old Greek in an earlier time, the response would probably have been to a young man, not a young woman. So there is not even here an escape from the more evident socially determined thinking seen in his overt political statements.

The traditionalist, acknowledging the obvious conditioning influence of social experience, will want to argue that there is below this social conditioning a level of basic human realities not open to determining. The passionate response Yeats makes to that girl standing there could not *equally* well have been evoked by a wrinkled old man. Indeed, the traditionalist concedes, our notions of beauty and appropriate objects of sexual desire are socially conditioned; we can, however, only claim that they are socially determined if we can show that the conditions affecting what objects are found desirable are relative only to existing social forms. If we can show that there are aspects of human thinking and feeling that are *more resistant* to finding some objects rather than others desirable, then we must acknowledge that such things are socially *conditioned*, not socially determined. We may disagree about the extent to which they may be conditioned, but that returns us to the argument between traditionalists and progressives, and undermines the ground on which the radicals stand.

CONCLUSION

In general, the traditionalists' response to the radicals is not altogether satisfactory. It is not enough to show the radicals hoist by their own relativist petard; the traditionalists must show that they are not also hoist by it. The challenge of relativism, and the degree to which social conditioning affects what counts as knowledge, seems to me underestimated by traditionalists, who too complacently seem to adopt remnants of 19th-century positivist epistemology.

The next moves for this line of thinking would be to outline the traditionalist response to the progressivists and then the radical response to the above traditional's arguments. The former argument is ongoing and its constraints are spelled out above; the radicals' responses to the above points are not spelled out here, however sketchily, because I don't know what they are. One does not find responses to such arguments in the radical literature, merely repetitions of the basic set of assertions and a refusal to accept the terms in which the arguments have traditionally been conducted.

Should we distinguish between educating and socializing, and, if so, how? Yes; carefully. Yes, because no one will gain if we sacrifice civilization to justice; and carefully, because civilization will be rotten if we sacrifice justice to culture.

Clockwork Oranges

CHAPTER 9

Social Studies and the Erosion of Education

You might want to turn the volume down for this essay. I must have been feeling a bit dyspeptic when I wrote it. The theme is a sustained attack on social studies as a generally antieducational curriculum subject, which we would be better off without. When it first appeared, in Curriculum Inquiry, *Vol. 13, No. 2, 1983, pp. 195–214, it stimulated some discussion, and a lot of hostility from social studies professors. I suppose I should not have been surprised that an argument for removing the source of their livelihood would elicit hostility. Perhaps some of the purple passages stimulated much of the irritation: "The social studies curriculum . . . has not worked, does not work and cannot work"; social studies did "for the cultures of immigrant peasantries of Europe what the U.S. cavalry was busy doing for the native cultures of this continent"; perhaps what irritated them even more was the attack on John Dewey's "flabby generalities."*

I use Dewey as a stalking horse in much of what follows. To someone not brought up in America, the place of Dewey in American educational thinking is a cause of some bemusement. He is held in the highest regard by people who take opposing positions on education and both sides claim Dewey as foundational to their position. Any criticism is met with the claim that Dewey did not mean what the critic has inferred, or that one has failed to understand him. When one searches for what he did mean, or why he did not mean some of the things he seems to have plainly written, it is impossible to find any agreement among his interpreters, or indeed much coherence. I concluded that Dewey's writings served American professors of education as a Rorschach test—in which they read their own vision of education. (This is section 42 of my "How to make friends and influence people.") Mind you, I should add that I am no less immune to Dewey's enchantment than anyone else. His is clearly the richest body of educational writing that has been produced on this continent, full of particular insights along with an unequalled synoptic vision of education's role in a democratic society.

I am grateful to the editor and publisher of Curriculum Inquiry *for permission to reprint this essay here.*

INTRODUCTION

Even the more modest statements of aims for the social studies curriculum promise the world, or worlds. The 1984 (U.S.) National Council
for the Social Studies' statement of the "essentials of the social studies"
lists "knowledge of the world at large and the world at hand, the world of
individuals and the world of institutions, the world past, the world present
and future" (p. 11). In addition, the social studies curriculum is to equip
students with the appropriate attitudes and skills to partake in and further the values of their democratic form of life, while also inculcating the
ability to think critically and effectively about the major problems of the
past, present, and future.

Criticizing statements of aims for the social studies curriculum might
easily qualify as a blood sport or seem like shooting fish in a barrel. Yet
the vacuous generalities, their mind-numbing vagueness, and their ideological innocence persist despite the criticisms. Clearly the extraordinary
vagueness of typical statements of aims for the social studies curriculum
serves some purpose for its defenders and promotors. That purpose, I will
argue, is to hide a fundamental conceptual confusion inherent in social
studies. What may seem merely a conceptual confusion, however, exacts
a brutal practical price. The price is that the social studies curriculum, which
is designed to achieve aims such as those listed above, has not worked,
does not work, and cannot work.

In this chapter I will try to support these claims in a three-part argument. First, I will argue that the basis for the general form of the typical
social studies curriculum is psychologically flawed—that it embodies assumptions about what children can learn and how best they learn that
might have seemed plausible at the beginning of this century but that
cannot bear much scrutiny today. Second, I will argue that the social studies
is designed primarily to socialize students, but it seeks to do so in a way
that both erodes education and, connectedly, undercuts its own stated aims.
Third, I will argue that we would be educationally better off letting the
early 20th-century curriculum experiment called social studies quietly die.

In what follows I will focus mainly on history, because I consider history to be the main victim of the rise of social studies—or rather students'
historical understanding is the victim: We can't do anything to history, except
not use it. I realize of course that in some parts of North America, history
appears on the curriculum as a separate entry from social studies. It will
become clear as the argument moves forward that, while I support this separation, what typically happens in such history curricula at present is much
the same as what happens to history within social studies, and so my argument is equally against such history curricula. (Mind you, I am not at all

arguing for a return to traditional history curricula. For my sense of what a history curriculum that avoids both the traditional "content accumulation" and the progressivist reduction to social studies, see Egan 1997.)

THE PSYCHOLOGICAL BASIS
OF THE SOCIAL STUDIES CURRICULUM

There is one major idea evident in the typical structure of the social studies curriculum. That idea is summed up in the term "expanding horizons." The source of this idea in curriculum thinking seems to lie in a mixture of child-centered, late 19th- and 20th-century early developmental psychology and some confusion about Herbert Spencer's (1861) principle that one must work from the known to the unknown. Dewey (1963) gave these ideas their definitive American form, observing, for example, that

it is a cardinal precept of the newer school of education that the beginning of instruction shall be made with the experience learners already have; that this experience and the capacities that have been developed during its course provide the starting point for all further learning. (p. 74)

He adds that there should be "orderly development towards expansion and organization of subject matter through growth of experience" and that it is "essential that the new objects and events be related intellectually to those of earlier experiences, and this means that there be some advance made in conscious articulation of facts and ideas" (pp. 74, 75).

When this is translated into content for the social studies curriculum, we get that familiar focus on the local experience and knowledge that children are assumed to bring with them to schools. They begin from this. So we study families, neighborhoods, then larger communities, then interactions among communities, and so on "outward," expanding children's knowledge along lines of content associations from what they know and experience in their daily lives. One problem with this lone organizing principle is that it begins to lose its determining force by about grade six, once children have made contact with other "culture realms" of the world. By then, however—I will argue—quite enough erosion of education has already taken place.

Throughout this section I will quote John Dewey as the source of ideas influential in structuring the social studies curriculum. This is a dangerous procedure, as Dewey is interpreted so variously by different people. Also, it is usually objected that the "expanding-horizons" curriculum and the typical content of social studies is a product of the "so-cial efficiency" movement and not Dewey. It is clear that the social effi-ciency movement is a considerable vulgarization, and something of a perversion, of what Dewey meant by educating for social life. That move-ment's concern with social efficiency led some of its members, indeed, to be hostile to Mead's and Dewey's vision of social reconstruction. It may be noted in what follows, however, that the references to the con-tent of the social studies curriculum are supported in each case by quo-tations from Dewey. I could, of course, make my argument without ref-erence to Dewey, and so avoid the potential objection of "but that's not what Dewey meant." The disadvantage of this would be to ignore the clearest statements most commonly cited in support of an expanding-horizons curriculum, and also to ignore the very real, though complex, influence their accompanying arguments have had. That the kind of social studies curriculum I will criticize was made worse by the added influ-ences of the social efficiency movement seems to me beyond question. This is not, however, a historical study of causes but an analysis and criti-cism of the foundations of the social studies curriculum.

Within the gradual movement out from the local and immediate that one finds in the expanding-horizons curriculum, one apparent anomaly—a kind of hiccup in the smooth flow—is the typical study of the form of life of a North American aboriginal or First Nations society. The rationale for this within the expanding-horizons model is again given in Dewey's words. Such a study is a part of the gradual expansion toward understand-ing the complexity of students' present societies.

> Recourse to the primitive may furnish the fundamental elements of the present situation in immensely simplified form. It is like unraveling a cloth so complex and close to the eyes that its scheme cannot be seen, until the larger coarser features of the pattern appear and by seeing how these were solved in the earlier days of the human race, form some conception of the long road which has had to be traveled, and of the successive inventions by which the race has been brought forward in culture. (Dewey, 1916/1966, p. 215)

These are claims hardly anyone would echo or support today, yet the early social studies curriculum that is so vigorously defended by many has, as one of its supports, precisely these embarrassing arguments.

Throughout the social studies curriculum the students must always work from something within their immediate experience. Dewey (1916/1966) puts it: "What is here insisted upon is the necessity of an actual empirical situation as the initiating phase of thought" (p. 153). This prin-ciple is to apply not only to young children:

Even for older students, the social sciences would be less abstract and formal if they were dealt with less as sciences (less as formulated bodies of knowledge) and more in their direct subject-matter as that is found in the daily life of the social groups in which the student shares. (Dewey, 1916/1966, p. 201)

Given such an interpretation of the truism, it seems to follow easily that "the true starting point of history is always some present situation with its problems," and "local or home geography is the natural starting point" (Dewey, 1916/1966, pp. 214, 212).

A connected principle that informs the structure of the social studies curriculum is expressed by Dewey (1916/1966) as:

The knowledge which comes first to persons, and that remains most deeply ingrained, is knowledge of *how to do*; how to walk, talk, read, write, skate, ride a bicycle, and so on indefinitely. (p. 184; emphasis original)

Dewey (1916/1966), in drawing up what has been the theoretical blueprint for the social studies curriculum in North America—a blueprint whose general form and character, and rhetoric, have undergone only relatively superficial changes for more than half a century—claims that he has based it on what he calls the "psychological principle." That is, his curriculum plan derives not from some logical analysis of subject matter, but from an observation of how children actually learn. Thus in drawing up our social studies curriculum, we must expand from "actual empirical situations" (p. 153); we must establish a "progressive order, using the factors first acquired as means of gaining insight into what is more complicated" (p. 20); we must root all subject matter "in the daily life of the social groups in which the student shares" (p. 201); we must, "before teaching can safely enter upon conveying facts and ideas through the media of signs, provide genuine situations in which personal participation brings home the import of the material and the problems which it conveys," (p. 233). Finally, he assures us, "Recognition of the natural course of development. . . . always sets out with situations which involve learning by doing" (p. 184).

One effect of the usual interpretation of all this has been largely to banish history from the elementary social studies curriculum, and to provide only the sketchiest glance at "our nation's story." So, one reads as a common conclusion of social studies texts that "history itself as a content topic is inappropriate for very young children" (Sunal, 1990, p. 158). If one has to begin always from actual empirical situations it will be a long and difficult road to get to, say, Ancient Greece—unless, that is, one trivializes it to a look at how ancient Greek houses were different from and similar to our houses. But Sophocles, Thucydides, and Socrates didn't live and die to tell our children that.

We should then consider the typical interpretation of Dewey's "psychological principle," which has so profoundly influenced the form of the social studies curriculum, and see whether it is true. It is, of course, a truism that children must begin from what they know and build on that. But it is a very complex truism, early expounded in Plato's *Meno*. What has been lost between Plato and the modern interpretations of Dewey is a sense of the subtlety of the dilemma (see Petrie, 1982). What we see constantly in the typical social studies curriculum is the interpretation of what children know first and best in terms of the content of their experience. But what alternative is there?

Before children can walk or talk, before they can skate or ride a bicycle, they know love and hate, pleasure and pain, joy and fear, good and bad, power and powerlessness, and the rhythms of expectation and satisfaction, of hope and disappointment. They know love and hate, good and bad, better and more profoundly than they ever know even how to walk or ride a bicycle. Children who never learn to walk or talk or read or skate know love and fear, expectation and satisfaction, hope and disappointment.

What is at issue here is not whether children know better how to walk and ride a bicycle than they know love and hate, hope and disappointment. These represent quite different kinds of "knowledge," and attempting a comparison of them as kinds of knowledge even would be a bit odd. Two points are worth making here, however. First, the above suggests at least that there is an alternative way of interpreting the truism and that this alternative interpretation is sensible.

The second point is that if our concern in education is with understanding the world and experience and the growth of knowledge about these, our beginning seems more sensibly based on children's grasp of the most fundamental categories of thought whereby these are made meaningful, rather than on their ability to walk and skate. These latter, it might also be noted, are "knowledge" only in an extended sense of the word—we would more usually call them skills or abilities. We say we know how to skate, but such knowledge is subconscious. If we attempt to deal with it consciously, we begin to stumble and fall over. This again suggests a poor foundation for a process that is concerned with the development of conscious understanding of the world and experience. Well, one can obviously read too much or too little into Dewey's examples, and I'm guilty of a little of both here. What is clear, however, is the lack of any sense of the emotional and imaginative life of the child figuring in Dewey's arguments about what the child has available to expand understanding *from*.

The knowledge that comes first to persons and remains most deeply ingrained is not knowledge of "how to do"; it is the fundamental categories on which we learn increasingly to make sense of anything in the universe and in human experience. It does not follow, then, that "primary or initial subject matter always exists as a matter of an active doing, involving the use of the body and the handling of material" (Dewey, 1916/1966, p. 184). It does not follow, then, that the only access children can have to the world and wider human experience is through lines of gradually expanding content associations from their local environments and immediate experiences. Those environments and experiences provide not only restricted exposure to particular knowledge, they provide also fundamental categories for making sense of the world—and children can have direct meaningful access to anything that can be organized within those categories.

If one considers what most engages young children's minds, it is surely stories about monsters, witches, dragons, star-warriors, and princesses in distant times and places, rather than the subject matter, however actively engaged, of families, local environments, and communities. Indeed, we might note that the everyday things around us are the last things we come to appreciate intellectually. Our parents typically are the last people we come to know. As in the cliché, fish do not discover water until they are pulled from it. The young child's immediate surroundings, then, are too taken-for-granted to be meaningfully explored. It is, as T. S. Eliot noted, only at the end of all our exploring that we arrive where we started and know the place for the first time. It is, that is to say, a further mistake to assume that children do have access to their immediate surroundings and experience in any conceptually meaningful way. Those surroundings and experience give us concepts that we can use in exploring the world, but it is only at the end that we can hope to fit concepts and the content that gave them birth back together.

So children clearly do not have to be led from their everyday reality by a process of expanding horizons until they gain access to talking animals in bizarre places and strange times. It is clear that children have direct access to their curious imaginary realms. Indeed, they have much easier access to these than to the content of their everyday world when it is treated as "subject matter." Why should this be so? One reason is that fairy tales are organized on those fundamental moral and emotional categories that are the things children know first and best. Such tales embody struggles between good and bad, the brave and the cowardly; they give content to love and hate, fear and security.

My purpose here has been to show that the main organizing principle evident in the present social studies curriculum is based on a highly dubious interpretation of what children know best. That is, the logical form of the expanding-horizons curriculum seems to be based on a psychological error. Children do not know how to walk or skate better or earlier or more really than they know love and fear; and, anyway, observations about how well they know how to walk or skate are somewhat beside the educational point. In enunciating his psychological principle, then, Dewey articulates something that is far from the self-evident truth it has commonly been taken to be, and is anyway not the central observation to make about children's minds if one's focus of interest is their education.

Two other observations might be made about the elementary social studies curriculum. First, it seems intent on teaching children things they will learn anyway from their everyday experience of the world. If there are any 20-year-olds who do not understand the structure of neighborhoods, it is not because they were not taught it properly in grade one or two. Second, the social studies curriculum most eloquently expresses a contempt for children's intelligence.

It is almost as if adults assume that because children know so little they must also be stupid and unable to learn much. Consequently they are given as a central part of their elementary education a curriculum that is almost entirely vacuous and, where not vacuous, trivial.

Children, then, come to school already knowing good and bad, love and hate, power and oppression, joy and fear, and so on. They are—it is apparently a product of our evolutionary programming—eager to make sense of the world around them using these intellectual tools. In learning more about the world, these tools, or concepts, become more sophisticated and refined. But they are there when children arrive at school in simple yet powerful forms. Children can use them to understand Greek or African or Asian history as they use them to understand their own experiences of struggling for autonomy against oppression, of greed and generosity, of courage and cowardice, of chance happenings and causal sequences. And in using them to learn Greek or African or Asian history, they are also expanding and refining the tools or concepts they have available with which to make sense of the world. An elementary social studies curriculum that is largely filled with the superficial features of their local environments and immediate experience ignores the most powerful tools with which children can make sense of their world. Imaginatively grappling with the rich content of the world's history, which can be directly engaged by using these fundamental tools in learning, is simply passed over in the present social studies curriculum. It is no wonder that by grade six or seven these children have such difficulty in learning history. The tools by which they could make sense of it have been largely unused, and anyway, when history *is* presented it typically is not organized in terms of the fundamental concepts by which children could have access to it. What is lost in all this is the development of those intellectual tools that best enable children to make sense of human experience. The expanding-horizons social studies curriculum may thus be seen, paradoxically, as an instrument that helps to alienate children from their social experience. Bertrand Russell, after his first disastrous experiment in organizing a school, observed that the first task of education is to destroy the tyranny of the local and immediate over the child's imagination. The social studies curriculum (not TV), it might reasonably be argued, is the main instrument in North America for doing the opposite.

SOCIALIZING AND EDUCATING:
THE PAST VERSUS HISTORY

Social studies was invented in North America at a time when socialization was imperative, to generate that "essential similarity" among the children of the huddled masses coming from dozens of distinct European peasantries. One deliberate feature was to instill an image of American democracy quite at variance with the traditional social structures from which the immigrants came. Incidental to that was the undermining of the hold of those un-American cultures. It is perhaps unnecessarily dramatic, but not inappropriate, to see the social studies doing for the cultures of the immigrant peasantries of Europe what the U.S. cavalry was busy doing for the native cultures of this continent—*e pluribus unum*.

The structure of the social studies curriculum, focused on the immediate social experience of the student as the paradigm of the real and meaningful, carries its own profound message. History and geography, once harnessed within social studies, are made subservient to an ideology that elevates current American, or Canadian or Australian, experience into the ideal and paradigm form, and other times, places, and forms of life are relevant or meaningful to the degree that they share characteristics with it.

The term *social studies* began to appear in the early part of this century. It was associated with child-centered ideas about educating, which in turn were associated with interdisciplinary forms of curriculum organizing. If our focus is on "the needs of children" and how they make sense of things, we might conclude that disciplinary distinctions are largely insignificant. Thus any study of what John Dewey (1916/1966) calls "the associated life of man" (p. 211) should be considered all of a piece, not divided into separate disciplines taught in different ways at different times. "While geography emphasizes the physical side and history the social, these are only emphases in a common topic" (p. 211); they are simply "two phases of the same living whole" (p. 218). Thus history and geography, in becoming handmaids of social studies, were seen as radiating out from the student in temporal and spacial dimensions, providing wider contexts to enrich understanding of the student's immediate social experience.

Once in this yoke with social studies, history and geography increasingly lost their disciplinary autonomy and were made to serve as agents in the general socializing purpose of social studies. (Whether that socializing purpose was Dewey's socialist/reconstructivist kind or the more narrow "Americanization" program of the progressives at large, or the cruder social efficiency of the 1930s' reformers [Franklin, 1982] is not my concern here. In all cases, what was generally accepted was a slab of the curriculum, called social studies, given over to the socialization of students [see chapter 7 for an elaboration of this point].) When history becomes an agent of socializing, it begins to develop a different aim from that which distinguishes history as an academic discipline. The aim of history as a discipline is to come to understand the past in its own terms and, in its uniqueness, as far as possible. However difficult, or indeed impossible, the ideal achievement of this aim, it is what the discipline of history is about. I obviously cannot give here (nor could I anywhere) an adequate account of the aims of the discipline of history. And clearly there is no single generally accepted account. From Nietszche's *Use and Abuse of History* (1874/1949) to M. I. Finley's *The Use and Abuse of History* (1975), we can see a variety of claims about the proper use of history. What is needed for my argument here, however, is only the simple distinction between the use of history to discover and understand what really happened (hardly an uncomplicated formulation) and the abuse of history, which makes it subservient to present interests and present concerns, which focuses all the past on the present, and which destroys the autonomy of past events.

Initiation of children and students into disciplined historical understanding, in however fragmentary and incomplete a way, and providing them with some taste of the pleasure that is proper to such understanding, is an educational task. It isn't easy, of course. But it is worthwhile. It is very important that we distinguish this aim, and the teaching activities that will bring children toward it, from the aim of socializing and its use of the past. In socializing, we do not aim to bring children to an understanding of the past for its own sake, but rather we use the past in order to focus on the present. The socializing criteria that determine what parts of the past we study and how we study them are present social conditions and the experience of students.

A successful program of socialization will lead to its products' sharing attitudes and values, and images of their nation. Socializing uses of the past tend to concentrate on providing what Michael Oakeshott (1971) calls "a glimpse of the current myth of the history of the nation" (p. 63). This does not mean that it tells lies. "Myth" does not necessarily imply falsehood, but is used here rather in the sense of *that which organizes our affective responses* (Egan, 1973, 1978).

So, when one considers the implication of the expanding horizons, the assertion is plainly that the point of human history and human experience is our present. That is, our present is seen not as a mass of cultural contingencies, but as the end and purpose of history. History was invented in our culture with the breakdown of myth. The psychological effect of history was to generate a sense of a past that was different from the present. It thereby created a concept of a future that could also be different from the present. It generated the conditions of more rapid social change, the conceptual capacity to plan for a different future, and the psychological capacity to deal with changing social circumstances. In all these features it was quite different from the mythic consciousness that preceded it. Social study's use of history is, ironically, more akin to the mythic than it is to the historical. It encourages a sense of the superior value of our present and consequently undermines the capacity to deal with changing social circumstances.

Such a use of the past, then, is not concerned simply with building a picture of what happened, but is concerned with involving us in the picture—it is *our* picture—and with orienting our feelings about the elements that make up the picture. In teaching about the Declaration of Independence to children in America, for example, one does not seek to present such knowledge "for its own sake." It is a potent part of the American socializing story. It is not enough that children learn about the events and the characters. Clearly they are to approve of the events and identify with certain sentiments and characters. The socializing purpose would not be met if most American children regretted the Declaration of Independence and saw it is a tragic break from Great Britain, a break that destroyed the potential for a benevolent Pax Britannica to generate light and order throughout the world. One need only read accounts of the "fight for independence" in American textbooks and of "the breakaway of the American colonies" in English textbooks to see vividly what is meant by orienting students' affective responses to the events. Except in gross cases, neither account is *false*, but they are very different. There is no point either in arguing which is more or less true. The story being told to English and American children is a different one, making sense of different present circumstances. The event of "American Independence"/"the breakaway of the American colonies" has different affective meanings determined by its place in different stories. The Briton who observes "Pity about the breakaway of the American colonies" can hardly expect the American—in whose national story the event has a quite different place—to agree that it is a "pity" that the United States is still not governed from Westminster.

This socializing use of the past, this telling of a national story, is different from the study of history. It is not different in that it is false or simplistic whereas history is true and complex—there can be as many errors and false-hoods and simplifications in historical narratives as in an account of a nation's story. It is different in its purpose and methods and in the way the mind works in learning or discovering the one or the other—though it might be noted that the telling of the national story more easily falls into falsehood. If the prime purpose is to "body forth" the current myth of the nation's history, it will often be possible to present the myth more powerfully and dramatically by leaving out bits here, inventing bits there, exaggerating the villainy or heroism of this character or that nation. That this form of falsification is far from uncommon in widely used textbooks in Amercian schools is well documented (see, for example, Fitzgerald, 1979).

However carefully we present "our story," we are selecting according to a principle that heightens the significance and inevitability of the present. This is a much more subtle perversion of history than outright falsification. If we focus everything toward the present, significance is determined by how far any event can be shown to have contributed to present conditions. Thus huge chunks of the past are condemned to "irrelevance" by this criterion. Yet, of the variety of things that make up the present, much is trivial, random, and insignificant in any more general account of human history. What happens in presenting our story, in using the past to focus on our present, is to exaggerate the present and the value of present institutions. Our story, or metanarrative, represents the whole significant history of the world as having the purpose of bringing about the present conditions that we experience. This does *not* encourage—one aim of social studies—critical reflection on the present; rather, it encourages a sense of awe and respect before the conditions and institutions that the massive drama of history has brought about. It heightens their sacredness; it gives them a sense of inevitability, of necessity (or alternatively, if this pious aim is not achieved—as seems so often the case—students are left with a sense of alienation from this story, which they cannot fit their experience into). That is, this reduction of history to serve current social aims—especially when those aims are determined by the main powerful institutions of the society—serves a conservative ideological purpose, in which any commitment to accuracy is decidedly secondary.

The disciplined study of history is different from this primarily in that it does not seek to tell a story that is focused on the present. Nor does it seek to tell "our" story. The past is not seen as a drama in which we associate with one side against another; we do not focus especially on *our* ancestors, *our* religious faction, *our* nation, or on *our* heroes and heroines. In the study of history we are concerned with what happened. The struggle of humanity, the causal roles of blind chance and iron necessity, are everywhere evident. We look to history not for practical lessons, but for human understanding: It is an expansion of our experience. We can learn from it discipline in making sense of human experience generally and in making sense of our own experience, but not in the sense sought by social studies. In contrast with social studies, where the students' experience is the focus of attention and where the students' opinions are elicited and valued, in the study of history students' opinions are irrelevant; what they think about the past does not matter. What matters is what happened, what someone else's opinion was, what other people thought. It helps us to treat our own experience with something like the attempts at objectivity we learn to bring to others'. Social studies tends toward narcissism; history takes the students' attention away from themselves.

A study of, say, the Declaration of Independence that seeks to start from students' experience with the purpose of explaining present social experience will *tend* to reduce the thoughts and reasons of its agents to those of students' experience. Now obviously the results of typical social studies exercises aimed at making the Declaration of Independence and the making of a constitution meaningful ("Imagine you have been shipwrecked on a desert island and there's no hope of rescue; you've got to write your own constitution, your set of rules for running your society. Break up into small groups and brainstorm it") need not be always complete reductionism for all students everywhere. But the present-oriented purpose of socializing that determines relevance from present conditions and experience tends constantly toward reductionism, toward provincializing the alien and different, toward homogenizing the exotic and the strange.

The aim of a historical study of the Declaration of Independence would be to expand students' experience by means of the thoughts and reasons of the historical agents. The focus of teaching would be on making the alienness and difference of those thoughts and reasons comprehensible to modern students. Now obviously one cannot completely get inside the thoughts of others and of course there will always be some ethnocentric and present-centric reductionism involved. But the hard discipline of history is centrally about overcoming as far as possible for each person the reduction of past experience to present experience and about the expansion of present experience and understanding into those alien worlds and lives that preceded ours. A dominant criterion in the selection of content for social studies is relevance to the present experience of students, and such a criterion carries little or no defense against the reductionism whose most effective enemy is the study of history.

Trying to suggest the distinction in this abstract way may seem to imply that history is an austere, hard, and sterile discipline, appropriate only for high IQ mini-researchers. The educational benefit history can offer is, I think, accessible to all children; it is a study that is properly full of vividness, drama, real heroes and heroines, and endless engagement.

A further conclusion from this argument is that typical statements of aims for social studies tend toward contradiction. The aim to focus on students' immediate social experience is in conflict with the aim to teach them to be critical thinkers about their society. If one wants to teach a measure of objectivity and an ability to think critically about events and institutions, one should focus on teaching academic history. If one wants a compliant citizenry who accept the institutions and conditions around them as somewhat sacred, as greater and finer than any that exist elsewhere, as the product and purpose of the historical drama, then one should continue the socializing use of the past, which is at present a central feature of social studies in North America.

RELEVANCY TO DEMOCRACY

If all the worlds past, present, and future jostle for a place in our social studies curriculum, how are we to determine which bits to include and which to exclude? Will a study of the circumstances leading to the Declaration of Independence more likely carry us toward achieving our aims than a study of the Knights Templar during the Crusades or piracy in the South China Sea during the Ming dynasty? If such a decision is usually made easily, we must have a criterion derived from our aims that allows us to select bits of the world past and to omit others. This criterion seems clearly derived from the general purpose of helping students become competent citizens by understanding the major discernible influences that have formed the society of which they are a part. This generally means that more recent and local history is given greater prominence, because it can be seen to have most influenced the present forms of social and material life. So the further back in time we go, and the more distant in place we go, from the student, the less "relevant" detailed historical events become.

CONCLUSION

The present expanding-horizons form of the social studies curriculum seems to have become a fixed element of the public schools' curriculum. No significant alternatives have threatened to replace it, particularly in the elementary years, until the recent neoconservative attempts to replace its "tot sociology" (Ravitch, 1987) with some history. The combined, and rarely challenged, assumptions that using the past to focus on present social experience and that moving gradually out from the child's immediate social experience are secure pedagogical foundations for making thoughtful citizens allows the expanding-horizons myth-inducing social studies curriculum to persist. What energy one sees within the study of social studies is largely spent on matters of pedagogical techniques. Thus we have a library shelf of books on using techniques of, for example, inquiry or case-study or discovery procedures. The surprise of these is that they, too, seem nothing that would have struck the reader of *Democracy and Education* (Dewey, 1916/1966) as novel. Perhaps, indeed, novelty is not their point; rather, they may be seen as the persisting attempt to put Dewey's ideas into practice. Any apparently well-founded criticism of progressivist practice is usually passed off as scoring not against Dewey but against an excess of misguided followers or a misunderstanding of Dewey. While one may acknowledge that Dewey's ideas have never properly been put into practice, one may do so only in the sense that one can say the same about Plato, Rousseau, and everyone else. What seems, after more than half a century, to be *practicable* has found form in the social studies curriculum as nowhere else, and the results—whoever is responsible—are less than inspiring.

When the thing we call a myth becomes conscious, we can call it an ideology. I have used the term *myth* above because the ideological aims of the typical social studies curriculum seem to be largely unconscious to the promoters of that curriculum. It is curious that there should be so much concern about techniques for making good citizens and so little concern about the implicit ideology inherent in the social studies curriculum. If we are promoting and perpetuating a myth of the history of the nation in our program of socialization, we should surely be careful and self-critical in how we go about it. A look at the literature about social studies suggests an alarming innocence about the ideological implications of the typical social studies curriculum. In a pluralistic society, one can hardly believe that there is ideological unanimity, yet what is one to conclude from the virtual silence on this topic among social studies professors and teachers? Certainly there are some curriculum theorists who are drawing attention to the ideological implications of the curriculum as a whole and of the present organization of the schools (e.g., Michael Apple, 1979). Social studies in particular would seem likely to repay study from this perspective.

In totalitarian societies, "historians" or rather expositors of the myths (or, if conscious, ideology) of the nation were considered important and kept under careful control. One did not find critical historians working in state institutions in totalitarian societies (Geyl, 1961). The academic discipline of critical history has the aim of focusing on the past to understand what happened, not of focusing on the present to influence what happens.

It may be disturbing to conclude that the socializing use of the past, which is becoming dominant in schools, is more like the use made of the past in totalitarian societies than it is like the use made by the academic historians of one's own nation.

The conclusions I have reached tend to be branded elitist. The notion that children should be initiated into disciplined forms of inquiry and understanding by the study of remote, "irrelevant" knowledge rather than by becoming familiar with the immediate social issues around them has been branded, by Dewey most insistently, a betrayal of North American societies. My argument is that the betrayal has been wrought by Dewey's style of socializing social studies, and it is a betrayal both of education and of democratic values. "Elitism" is making the best form of education available to only a few. The democratic ideal of education is to make the best form of education available to all. The democratic ideal is not achieved, and elitism is not defeated, by making the best form of education available to almost nobody.

Dewey intended the social studies curriculum to be a reaction against the elitist, useless, ornamental, schooling of the privileged few. Social studies was to be the heart of the democratic curriculum. From the point of view of my argument, the remarkable influence of John Dewey at a critical point in the development of North American educational systems has been, and continues to be, tragic. It is a blow from which North American primary and secondary educational institutions still show little sign of recovering. Dewey is still held in enormous and even growing reverence by people who value his timely observations about the importance of sensitively attending to children's ways of making sense of things, and who cannot distinguish this good advice from the confused and contradictory curriculum recommendations he made. The practical follies of progressivism are laid at others' doors, and it is often claimed that Dewey's ideas have never been put into practice. What these ideas are supposed to be varies enormously depending on the interpreter. The flabby generalities that fill the pages of his educational writings are tolerant of almost any interpretation. The occasional piece of "fine" rhetoric is held up as the justifying text for whatever program the interpreter happens to be proposing. Dewey's influence, it seems to me, came at a time when American energy was turning to build the world's greatest educational system and to realizing the radical democratic dream of making the best education available to every child. One can hardly blame Dewey alone for subverting this ideal near the inception of the attempt to put it into practice, but *Democracy and Education* best expresses the blueprint for the kind of curriculum that has turned North American schools into not especially effective socializing institutions.

CHAPTER 10

Metaphors in Collision: Objectives, Assembly Lines, and Stories

I was not going to include this essay because it deals with topics, such as "behavioral objectives," that are no longer current in educational discourse. But in recent discussions with students and recently accredited teachers, I discovered that nearly all of them in their professional preparation programs were taught to plan their teaching using versions of the "objectives" models the essay criticizes. Some of the terms used had changed from the height of the behavioral objectives movement in the early 1970s, but the metaphors and analogies that are discussed here still seem to dominate thinking about how to plan teaching. One struggles to slam nails into coffins only to find that the coffins have no base and the ghoul is cavorting around in fresh clothes and makeup. So here it is, a new attempt to put a nail or two in the base as well. I feel uncomfortable in noting that the only reference to Elliot Eisner's work in what follows is a slightly critical comment on his use of "expressive objectives." In retrospect, his critique of the "objectives movement" and his incessant pointing to its inadequacies was significantly responsible for bringing it into disrepute. If I was nailing a late nail in the coffin, Eisner had slammed in the first half-dozen. (I should note, too, that he read this manuscript—prior to my writing these introductions—and wrote the generous introduction without any comment on what is clearly a negligent treatment of his contribution. It will be clear that in my attempts to construct the pro and con arguments in this essay, I have drawn heavily on Eisner's ideas.) This essay first appeared in 1988 in Curriculum Inquiry, 18(1), 63–86. *I am grateful to the editor and publisher for permission to reprint it here.*

INTRODUCTION

There is a growing and increasingly influential literature, and supporting empirical research, that stresses the constructivist nature of human sense-making. In learning, it is becoming increasingly clear, we do not mirror the world in concepts nor "internalize" preexisting knowledge. Rather, we constantly construct and recreate images of the world and of experience, and undergirding these images—holding them together, as it were—seem to be forms akin to those that shape narratives and stories,

147

forms that shift on metaphors and analogies even as we try to tie them to the kinds of formal logical structures we can grasp more explicitly.

This literature seems to imply challenges to a number of the most general assumptions that have dominated much educational theorizing and research during this century. Rather than try to give a sketch of the range of these implied challenges, I will explore a particular challenge and pursue the alternative perspective offered. Rather than remain only at the level of rhetoric, pursuing the arguments to and fro, I will try to follow the implications of the arguments in the direction of technique, to see whether and how the alternative perspective can yield alternative practices to those presently dominant.

Choosing a particular topic to focus on is not easy as the constructivist challenge is all-pervasive; it invades even the language that has become standardized within the somewhat positivistic traditions of educational research. We are constantly invited to focus differently on the commonest topics of educational discourse. The positivistic tradition has, for example, made central to educational discourse a somewhat restricted and precise conception of "learning." A huge amount of research has been done on this topic, which has helped to "operationally" define and restrict it. In the constructivist view this conception of learning tends to be dissolved in the more comprehensive notion of sense-making. "Making sense" involves not only what was encompassed in "learning," but draws us to focus on the individual's constructive activity, which in turn invites us to consider those elements prominent in our construction of sense, such as narrative, metaphor, analogy, and so on. Some sensitivity to the language, then, must accompany us into whatever topic is chosen.

For this exploration of some implications drawn from the constructivist view I will focus on the topic of planning for teaching. I will discuss a constructivist alternative within the context of the currently dominant planning techniques that seem to be most widely recommended in teacher preparation programs. What seems commonly stressed and most highly developed within these techniques is the use of "objectives," and the manner of finding and stating these, and so I will broach a constructivist alternative to these in particular. Because my concern is the competing practices that follow from different perspectives and from the use of different metaphors and analogies, I will try to bring to the fore some of the suppressed metaphors and analogies that seem to underpin the currently dominant planning procedures. This is where the "assembly lines" come in. Perhaps some readers might find the analogy drawn between the derivatives of the Ralph Tyler's model (1949) and the assembly line too crude, and suggestive of straw-manning. It is a connection observed and developed before (Callahan, 1962), and one quite evident—running about vigorously in flesh and blood—in discussions of "teacher effectiveness," "accountability," and a range of other topics. The assembly-line analogy, then, may suggest a distortion of the planning techniques recommended by Tyler and others, but the distortion is not mine. It is a distortion evident in the textbooks and the practices that have moved from the complexity and richness of Tyler's model to the cruder forms so common and so evident all about us. My point throughout is not that the analogy with assembly lines is consciously drawn on, but rather that subconsciously it serves as a kind of template for thinking about specific ways of planning teaching.

The alternative analogy from which I want to explore planning for teaching is the story form. While there is a large literature about the value of fictional stories in education, the studies of narrative and metaphor on which I will draw suggest that there is also an important sense in which the story form provides a fundamental sense-making context. The fictional story is only one of the uses of the story form, and it is one that I will not be concerned with here. Rather, I want to draw on those elements of the story form that give structure, coherence, and meaning to *whatever* content is "plotted" or organized in the appropriate way. This underlying story form, then, can be as useful in making sense of physics and mathematics and history as of the more traditional content of fictional stories. I will discuss this sense of "story form" later.

I will begin, then, by briefly discussing the "objectives movement." I realize this is rather a stale topic in educational discourse. The staleness comes, I think, in part at least from the difficulty of getting the competing arguments sufficiently clear that they can be resolved by analysis or empirically. In part, also, as I will suggest later, the staleness is due to the opponents of the objectives movement offering only arguments and no alternative planning procedures, certainly none with the technical neatness of some of the derivatives from Tyler's (1949) model. I will try to explore the analogical basis of the objectives movement and its main planning technique and also review the main arguments that have been mounted against the movement. I will then propose an alternative constructivist technique derived from the story-form analogy.

THE "OBJECTIVES MOVEMENT": DOMINANCE AND DISSENT

One of the commonest components in teacher preparation programs and courses on curriculum development is a framework for planning that begins with the identification and statement of objectives. The use of objectives statements has grown from an occasional and irregular procedure around mid-century to a relatively precise and uniform technique throughout the English-speaking world. This development is seen by some as one of the crucial marks of progress in the curriculum field; it is a part of what the Tanners (Tanner & Tanner, 1980, ch. 3) describe as "The Emergence of a Paradigm for the Curriculum Field."

While one can identify a number of precursors to Ralph Tyler's (1949) framework for curriculum planning, his short book is generally recognized as the key document in persuasively introducing a clear scheme for planning. He makes the sensible argument that rational planning is hindered unless one's objectives are clearly articulated. The statement of precise objectives is the crucial step in his procedure: "Educational objectives become the criteria by which materials are selected, content is outlined, instructional procedures are developed and tests and examinations are prepared" (p. 3).

A significant group of educationalists have measured progress in the study of education in terms of the increasingly tight technical precision and control achieved in the deployment of objectives in planning and organizing curricula and teaching: "In our view this development is one of the most important educational advances of the 1900s and signals a very significant attack upon the problems of education" (Popham & Baker, 1979, p. 20). This group has proposed that the appropriate precision for objectives statements is to have the objectives describe the behavioral outcomes of learning: "The more explicit the instructor can be regarding the statement of instructional objectives, the better. The only kind of specificity that really helps in improving teacher behavior empirically is the specification of goals in terms of student behavior change" (Popham, 1973, p. 13).

Teaching is, of course, an intentional activity. If "objective" is used to mean only "intention," then claims for the importance of having objectives in planning teaching or curricula is not particularly dramatic. Some of the drama has resulted from claims about the desirability of making one's objectives explicit in a particular form as a key part of a particular procedure. Other educationalists have resisted the behavioral objectives movement not only on theoretical but also on empirical grounds. Surveys of studies comparing objectives-governed teaching with that of regular classes have not generally supported the strong claims for what will result from their use. The positive results achieved in industry by use of "management by objectives" procedures (Steers & Porter, 1974) have not been reflected in education. Duchastel and Merrill's (1973) conclusion from reviewing such studies, echoed by Melton's (1978) survey, is inconclusive. Many case studies indicated positive effects of objectives on student learning but in a significant number of cases no significant effects at all could be discerned. This is not what we would expect from one of the most important educational advances of the 1900s.

Regardless of the empirical state-of-play, which seems unlikely to come conclusively to the aid of one side or the other, various forms of the Tyler (1949) framework have become standard parts of the curriculum of teacher preparation courses and of courses on methods of teaching and instructional design. The Tanners (1980) are surely right to see this framework as a central nub, giving focus and form to a great deal of curriculum research and theorizing. The advance of the objectives model in one of its many forms has gone forward on what seems like the irrefutable basis of common sense: If you aren't clear about your objectives, you don't know how to proceed, and can't tell when or whether you have achieved whatever you had in mind when you started. Our objectives are statements of our ends, and provide thereby criteria that enable us to select the best means to those ends.

The influence of this commonsense view has become very widespread. Paul Hirst (1974), for example, claims this general procedure is essential for rational curriculum planning: "We must first formulate our objectives clearly, in realistic and operational terms, and then, in the light of these, move on to the questions of content and method" (p. 7). A hint of the force of this general view may be seen in Eisner's (1969) argument for substituting "expressive objectives" for "behavioral objectives" as more appropriate in education:

> An expressive objective describes an educational encounter. It identifies a situation in which children are to work, a problem with which they are to cope, a task in which they are to engage; but it does not specify what from their encounter, situation, problem, or task they are to learn. . . . An expressive objective is evocative rather than prescriptive (pp. 15–16)

Eisner chooses to call "objectives" what are patently something else. Clearly this is in large part a sensible rhetorical strategy, but it eloquently gives witness to the pervasiveness of the common view that rational planning must begin with stating objectives.

Not, of course—educational studies being what they are—that this dominant view has won its status as an almost unquestioned assumption without dissenting voices. Kliebard (1975) has criticized Tyler's "rationale" keenly, concluding that one might sensibly wonder "whether the long-standing insistence by curriculum theorists that the first step in making a curriculum be the specification of objectives has any merit whatsoever," and rather regretfully observing that its attraction is clear and powerful to "those who conceive of the curriculum as a complex machinery for transforming the crude raw material that children bring with them to school into a finished and useful product" (p. 81).

To many dissenters it is this clear appeal that is the proper source of suspicion about Tyler's (1949) framework and its various descendants. Its elegant clarity and simplicity seems fine in textbooks, but fits the complexities of educational practice at the cost of deforming education into a too-simple process. Some of the objections, such as the claim that problems commonly arise from sticking too rigidly to prespecified objectives, or that children can easily mimic behavioral goals without achieving true understanding, or that such objectives deny the developing autonomy and freedom of the student, are in the end unconvincing because they rely in turn on a simplistic interpretation of the framework—a response well-developed by Tanner and Tanner (1980, ch. 3).

What is lacking is any persuasive alternative conception. Stenhouse (1975) has articulated an image of the teacher not "in the role of the creator or man with a mission" (already we feel a little wary at this caricature) but as an "investigator" whose plans are to be "conceived as a probe through which to explore and test hypotheses and not as a recommendation to be adopted" (p. 125). "To attach the value-laden tag, *objectives*, to some of our hypotheses is an odd and usually unproductive scientific procedure" (Stenhouse, 1970, p. 80). The basic metaphor he develops is that of the teacher or curriculum developer as dealing with a practical research task in contrast with that of the teacher as determiner of a technological process.

Stenhouse (1975) and Richard Pring (1973) have argued that we should start, not with statements of objectives, but by clarifying and seeking agreement on value positions or basic principles. When we have articulated these, we can infer flexibly what activities are most appropriate for teachers and students at any point. We can change our minds about activities, try different materials, use different instructional methods, remaining constantly responsive to the ongoing, freely developing, complex life of the classroom, but guided not by objectives but by clearly understood principles. While the "feel" of such proposals contrasts strongly with the systematic organization of Tyler's (1949) proposal and even more so with the technologizing developments of that proposal, it remains possible to argue that beginning with such values and principles is not necessarily so different from objectives statements.

The more influential, though generally silent, dissent from the objectives models comes from teachers. It has frequently been observed, with either satisfaction or exasperation, that many teachers ignore such frameworks when they do their planning. Their planning tends most commonly to be initiated from particular practical concerns or problems or from available materials, not from objectives. They are more likely to begin from a question about how best to get some particular curriculum-prescribed content across, given the particular resources they have and the conditions of their classroom at a particular time of year, than to begin by stating objectives.

What we have, then, is a situation in which objectives-dominated frameworks are central to curriculum development and planning for teaching. Discomfort with their ubiquity has led to numerous arguments against such frameworks, but none of these arguments has proved generally persuasive. Part of the problem is that the conception of "objective" and the procedures recommended vary considerably. The "soft" end of the continuum interprets "objective" as little stronger than "intention," and acknowledges a variety of ways of stating objectives as appropriate. At the "hard" end of the continuum, "objective" is interpreted strictly in behavioral or performance terms, and the procedures for planning are similarly rigorously insisted on. The rhetorical problem for dissenters from the general orthodoxy is that even the hardest interpretation draws on the commonsense notion that you need to know what you are doing before you set about something.

Tyler's (1949) framework and its descendants are built on an analogy that has had a compelling force, particularly in North America. I want to explore this analogy briefly. It is that of the assembly line (Callahan, 1962). The objectives movement has had much of its success not so much because its frameworks adequately deal with the realities of educational practice, as because the power of the assembly-line analogy has made it easy to conceptualize education in terms of it. That is, the claim that Tyler's framework simplifies dangerously and deforms the educational process cannot carry any weight against those who conceive of education in terms of that framework. Analogies are not right or wrong, just more or less adequate. One cannot argue against an analogy very easily. What one can do, to disturb it, is try to explicate its sources and point to significant differences between the source and the application of the analogy. The problem here is that one merely runs over a set of abstract arguments that have limited power to disturb the analogy. We use analogies to think with; it is not so easy to think about what we think with.

What I will do in addition to considering the limitations of objectives frameworks is to sketch an alternative. As the objectives frameworks are derived in significant part, I will argue, from the assembly line, the alternative I will sketch is derived from the story. Planning teaching, in this alternative framework, can be considered analogous to telling good stories rather than attaining objectives. I will argue that the story framework can capture more of the proper character of education than does the objectives framework.

CONFRONTING AN ANALOGY

Technology and Analogy

Rational thinking is a late and rare achievement in human history. Matching words and concepts with the nature of things requires constant effort, and tends to collapse easily into the more relaxed, less taxing and less disciplined, logic of myth. Even after the systematizing of various principles of rationality in ancient Greece, the structure of mythic speculation provided a kind of template for rational reflection. So the mythic cosmos ruled by gods of air, earth, fire, and water retained a grip on early rational cosmologies and provided the basis for medical research (Cornford, 1907). As long as physicians thought in terms of, or by means of, a theory of humors, the function of the heart, with its constant thumping, was difficult to work out. The function of the heart became clear—perhaps we might even say "became knowable"—after the invention of the pump. Jonathan Miller (1978) argues strongly that the pump did not just provide clues to the functioning of the heart, but rather that until its invention we had nothing adequate to think *with* about the heart. Our technology provides analogies that we can use to reflect back on ourselves. We can see this process even more vividly at work in our attempts to make sense of the functioning of that even more mysterious organ within us—our brain.

Seeing the brain in terms of complex clockwork was never very persuasive because, when cut up, the brain evidently lacked anything even vaguely resembling clockwork. Even so, this did not prevent the brain from being seen in terms that echoed the most sophisticated state of earlier technology. Increasing knowledge of physiology provided another fertile source of analogies. Seeing the functioning of the brain in terms of the functioning of muscles played a clear role in the formulation of faculty psychology. (It is nicely ironic that the textbook accounts of a progressive psychology represent faculty psychology as one of the few convincingly dead and superseded doctrines while we witness its resuscitation by Chomsky [1972], Fodor [1983], Gardner [1983], and others.)

With the invention of the telephone and then the telephone exchange, allied with the earlier discovery of electrical impulses in the brain, a powerful new analogy for the brain's functioning appeared. The operation of an electrical impulse going from a source at the end of one line to a central processing exchange, and shooting off to ring a bell at the end of another line, can easily be seen as analogous to the finger touching a pin, the impulse shooting up to the brain, which exchanges the signal to other signals, which results in muscles moving the finger away from the pin. If one looks at human behavior in the raw, if that were possible, it is odd to see the response to a pin-prick in a finger as a paradigm of the brain's functioning. Yet this has been so common an image, I suspect, because of the persuasive force of the—usually hidden and unconscious—analogy with the telephone exchange. It is perhaps unfair to suggest that behaviorism owes more to the technology of the telephone system than it does to observation of human behavior. That is, the hidden analogy enabled human behavior to be seen in terms of a relatively easily grasped technological process. Behaviorism has succumbed, apparently, not to any of the arguments that have been mounted against it—these have not changed much in half a century—but rather to the more persuasive analogies derived from the most sophisticated modern computers. The newer analogies encouraged us to think of the brain as a computer, and the mind as a program it is running. The simpler technological analogues that underlie behaviorism did not allow any place for thinking about, say, consciousness. It thus became a part of the doctrine of behaviorism that there was nothing much to be thought about consciousness. The task of psychology is to make sense of mental phenomena and so, in the long run, an analogy that prevents us from thinking productively about evident features of the phenomenon will lose out to an analogy that at least puts them on the agenda. Consciousness, for example, is one of the things we are interested in, so an analogy that promises to give us some tools with which to think about it is going to be attractive. The analogies derived from the most sophisticated, and even projected, computers is—this time quite overtly—at the heart of the developing cognitive-science view of the brain.

Analogies are merely analogies. They are not to be judged right or wrong, true or false. The question to be posed about an analogy is how *adequate* it is for making sense of whatever it is being used to make sense of. The pump proved to be a good analogy for the functioning of the heart; it was adequate to allow people to develop a more accurate picture, which then allowed them to see the heart in more productive ways. Neither clockwork models nor telephone exchanges have proved adequate analogies for making sense of more than minor functions of the brain. And computers and programs as analogies for the functioning of the brain and mind are increasingly recognized as inadequate. Attention is focused on how far the accounts given actually reflect our sense of what we want in describing or explaining the brain, and on the valuable critical work of people like John Searle (1984), who point out ways in which the computer analogy suppresses absolutely crucial features of the human brain.

The purpose of this little ramble is twofold. First, it is useful to bear in mind the pervasiveness of metaphors and analogies in our thinking, and, second, it is important occasionally to try to be explicit about and reflect on the adequacy of any analogies we may be using.

The Assembly-line Analogy

One of the most successful technological developments of the early part of this century was the assembly line. To take advantage of this efficient system of production, it is necessary first to plan in precise detail one's objective, then one arranges the materials to be used in appropriate places along the line, then one deploys the various skills necessary to fit the materials together, and then one has an evaluation process to make sure that what emerges is what was planned.

The Tyler (1949) framework for curriculum design and its various derivatives dealing with planning for teaching—with distinct steps for objectives, content, methods, and evaluation—are not susceptible to being seen in terms of the structure of an assembly line simply by coincidence. The language of the assembly line appeared in influential educational texts quite early in the century. Franklin Bobbitt's (1918) was one of the more insistent voices that tried, with considerable success, to persuade Americans to apply to education principles that were so successful in industry: "Education is a shaping process as much as the manufacture of steel rails" (p. 11). He pointed out that "it is possible to set up definite standards for the various educational products. The ability to add at a speed of 65 combinations a minute, with an accuracy of 94 per cent is as definite a specification as can be set up for any aspect of a steel plant" (p. 15).

The assembly-line analogy is not usually so explicit today, but its persisting influence is seen when we hear people talk of "process" and "product" in education, when we hear education compared to an applied science like engineering, when teaching is represented as a technology, and when we see planning frameworks that differ from the assembly-line model only in details of their wording. Sometimes the analogy draws from more modern technological procedures, but the basic analogy underlying the objectives-dominated planning schemes is that of the assembly line.

There are two main strategies pursued by those who consider an analogy to be inadequate. The first is to point insistently at precisely those aspects of the phenomena it deals with least adequately, and the second is to offer a quite different analogy that deals not only with those phenomena covered by its competitor but also with those its competitor deals least adequately with. I will try both of these in turn, trying to show an inadequacy of objectives-dominated planning procedures in education.

PROPOSING AN ALTERNATIVE

Insistent Pointing

This is a set of overlapping arguments to the effect that education is not the kind of thing the objectives-dominated procedures can deal adequately with. They are arguments of the "pointing-at" type. They say, look, here is a crucial feature of education your model fails to deal with adequately. Let me briefly rehearse a few of these overlapping arguments and see where they take us.

1. One cannot precisely state objectives in education because each individual child is different, and what each will get from any unit or lesson or curriculum will vary profoundly depending on abilities, backgrounds, intentions, and so forth. Indeed, an odd feature of education is that the more educated people become, the more different they become from each other. Education seems concerned with elaborating and developing diversity and individual differences. For example, at a basic level of literacy, the writing styles of most people are rather similar—dominated by the particular conventions of their time and place. At the highest levels of literacy, writing styles are much more distinctive. We can recognize excellent writers by their individual style. What we can see in this example is a reflection of a crucial feature of education—that it aims toward diversity and individual differences. A planning model that requires precise prespecification of objectives will tend constantly in a direction opposite to what is educationally desirable. It tends toward convergence in what is essentially a divergent process.

Comment: Those who consider the objectives schemes adequate will be able to reply that if diversity is desired, then one can build this into one's objectives. The more one knows and can specify about this kind of diversity, the more it can become a matter for precise objectives statements. In addition, or alternatively, they might note that the objectives can sketch out necessary elements that all are to achieve, and scope can be left for individual developments based on this common knowledge, skill, or understanding. Those who think the objectives schemes inadequate will repeat that there are not common elements for all, but that the nature of education is such that a planning scheme requiring such objectives is constantly tending to reduce and deform education. Diversity cannot be specified in principle, and diversity is not something that is built on some "common core."

There does not seem much room here for decisively showing to those who conceive of education in terms of an objectives scheme that it fails adequately to deal with diversity. The problem is that those committed to objectives schemes tend also to be committed to a conception of education that sees later diversity emerging from some "common core."

2. The point of education is not the achievement of some objective but is rather a quality of engagement with the world. The achievement of particular knowledge may be of no educational significance at all. Whitehead (1929) has eloquently stressed the uselessness of being merely well informed, of having accumulated endless "inert" knowledge. Knowing certain things and being able to do certain things *may* be educationally trivial. Education has to do with a quality of one's engagement with knowledge and so with the attaining of depth of understanding. In R. S. Peters' (1965) phrase, it is not a feverish preparation for some end but a matter of traveling with a different view. If a sense of wonder is achieved at some aspect of a topic, one does not push on to achieve one's stated objectives. That is to destroy, not advance, education. It is the quality of engagement with any aspect of knowledge or the world that is the educational point. John Dewey (1928) noted that if the educator "can organize his qualitative processes and results into some connected intellectual form he is really advancing scientific method much more than if, ignoring what is actually most important, he devotes his energies to such unimportant by-products as may now be measured" (p. 200).

Comment: The same point as was made above is always available to the objectives planner: If that engagement is the educational point, then you must write that in clearly as your objective. The reply that it is commonly not predictable cuts no ice because one can formulate one's objectives to allow for a focus on such things when they occur. That is on the accommodating side. A less accommodating response is to observe that if such "qualities" cannot be predicted, nor apparently can be described with any clarity, then they also cannot be evaluated and cannot meaningfully be prescribed in one's objectives. But this, of course, is the precise point of the objection, argue those who consider the objectives schemes to be inadequate to deal with education. The nature of education is such that it has these distressing characteristics; a scheme that cannot deal with them is inadequate to education. It reduces and deforms education to force what looks like aspects of it—learning knowledge and skills—into an inappropriate mold. Again, the problem here is that both sides mean something different by "education," or see education in terms of different analogies.

3. The objectives-dominated framework sees education as having what has been called a "means-end" character. The planning process then is one of specifying ends and determining the means that will achieve those ends. Tyler (1949) is explicit about this, as is Paul Hirst (1974). Curriculum planning necessarily involves stating objectives, claims Hirst, and his analysis draws out the "essentially means-ends character" of the process (p. 7). The critic of this view points to John Dewey's (1929) insistence on the "integrity and continuity" (p. 72) of the educational process, such that its aims are derived from ongoing situations, not externally specified in advance. R. S. Peters (1965) has argued that "'education' picks out no particular process; it implies criteria which processes must satisfy" (p. 37), and so the procedures we use in education are not conceivable as merely means to ends, they are themselves to be selected according to the same criteria we use in selecting our ends—they are, that is, tied together in a way quite different from the selection of whatever means will most efficiently achieve independently chosen ends in an industrial production process. This reflects Pring's (1973) point mentioned earlier about a set of principles guiding our curriculum and teaching decisions at every point. In such circumstances we do not need, and cannot have, distinct objectives that are separately specified, and to which our means are then subject.

Comment: I think, on the whole, that this argument is generally taken as gobbledygook by proponents of objectives-dominated schemes. If one conceives of education in terms of a means/ends "paradigm," then presenting an alternative, subtly but profoundly different, just meets with simple incomprehension. Insistence on the alternative tends to run up the kind of frustration that arises when someone can only see the image as a duck and cannot see it as a rabbit. (This is not itself a good analogy, of course, because it suggests the duck and rabbit are indeed sharing a single image that is seen differently. The conflict between conceptions of education involves also what phenomena actually are part of the "image.")

4. The objectives-dominated schemes see the parts of the process as constituents of the end in a sense not essentially different from the components on the assembly line being gradually fitted together to constitute the final product; or at least, the underlying analogy and the practice of objectives statements assume such a view. A further set of arguments against the use of objectives-dominated schemes tries to indicate ways in which they imply a conception of education that is at odds with a more proper conception. Let us consider two examples of this kind of argument. The parts that are to be fitted together along the assembly line produce something at the end that is nothing other than those parts in a new configuration. The task for the opponent of the assembly-line analogy is to show how this feature of the assembly line is crucially different from the case in education.

4.1. If we are making an automobile on our assembly line, there comes a point for fitting the steering wheel. Steering wheels do not look like motor cars; a visitor from another galaxy or ancient Rome would not be able to infer the shape of an automobile from the steering wheel, or a hub cap, or rear window, or seat-belt lock, or any other part. The relationship between parts and whole is evident only when they all come together. An automobile door by itself is not much of a contributor to our ability to get around. Indeed, toting an automobile door around would be something of a hindrance to our locomotion. Fitted to the rest of an automobile, however, it is a contributor to the overall comfortable functioning of the machine. Education, on the other hand, is not made up of components that become education only when they are fitted together in the end. The relationship of parts to whole in education is rather more like that in a hologram than in an assembly line, to search for a competing, more adequate analogy. If we break the plate containing the interference pattern of a hologram into pieces, each piece when illuminated shows the image of the whole, though increasingly blurred the smaller the piece. A "part" of education has a character more like that of a piece of a hologram than a piece that is to be fitted to an automobile.

4.2. The human mind is not like an assembly line; it does not act as the passive, containing backdrop to accumulating products. The pieces of an automobile remain exactly the same as they were before being fitted into place. The human mind—searching for another analogy—is more like a stomach; it consumes and transforms knowledge. Knowledge does not accumulate into structures, as in a textbook. It coalesces into meanings, which will be different for each mind.

Comment: The response to these arguments from proponents of objectives-dominated schemes tends to be that they are interesting but not particularly relevant. Use of objectives in planning does not commit one to seeing the human mind as an assembly line, nor to the idea that the mind does not transform knowledge. Such planning procedures simply commit one to being as clear and precise as possible in stating objectives— and this may include specifying transformations of knowledge in whatever ways we understand such processes (and if we do not understand them, they can hardly be any part of our objectives). Similarly, the hologram analogy is interesting, but hardly a convincing underminer of the use of objectives in planning. To whatever degree the hologram analogy points at an understood sense of how knowledge is educationally potent, then we can include this in our objectives. To the degree that it remains vague, it cannot be a meaningful part of anyone's planning or teaching.

5. The best move in such arguments is always to try to turn the strongest part of the opponents' argument back on them. The sociology of knowledge attack on traditional educational philosophy looked like a runaway winner until its argument was turned against itself. (If all claims to truth are socially conditioned, then the claim that all claims to truth are socially conditioned is itself socially conditioned and so need not be accepted as true.) The similar move in this case is not quite so neat, but, echoing some of the arguments above, is to ask whether the proponent of planning-by-objectives in education can precisely define education, or even precisely define the overall aims of a particular curriculum area. If one cannot precisely define education, how can one know that one's precisely defined objectives are a part of it? The degree of precision required in objectives-dominated schemes is inappropriate to education. As Aristotle first pointed out, rationality requires that we be only as precise as a field will allow. It is then irrational to demand in educational planning a degree of precision that is in excess of what is appropriate to the field. The degree of precision that is appropriate to a field is what determines sensible discourse within that field. It is not a regrettable fact that education is not more precise. Precision is a virtue only when it is appropriately related to appropriate tasks. The finest precision in education comes from recognizing the appropriate form and level of sensible discourse. It is in this sense that calls for greater precision in planning by objectives reflect imprecise thinking about education.

So what sense does it make to demand precise objectives if we cannot be precise about what the objectives are objectives of? It is like demanding absolute precision in the direction of the next step taken while being unsure about where one is headed. We may logically demand, then, that anyone requiring a certain kind of precision in the statement of short-term objectives in education should be able to state in equal precision the nature and aims of education in general. If that cannot be done precisely, it is irrational to demand a different level of precision in stating objectives within education.

Comment: I think this is taken usually as an argument for obfuscation. Clearly learning some history, arithmetic, geography, and so forth, is a part of the educational process. The concern of proponents of objectives-dominated planning is that greater efficiency be introduced into achieving these. Without such planning procedures, teaching tends to be haphazard and often chaotic. All that is being asked for, and provided for, is a little more control and care in planning the curriculum and teaching. All this talk of perverting, deforming, undermining education seems ludicrously out of place, and not a little irritating. People aiming to bring some more scientific precision to education do not like being cast in the role of Genghis Khan and his civilization-razing hordes—if you'll forgive the analogy. The problem here is that the argument tends to be ignored by proponents of objectives frameworks. What makes learning particular historical facts educational? If we cannot answer that precisely, how can we write precise objectives for a particular history lesson and feel confident that those are educational objectives? That does seem a reasonable question. Part of the problem is that so much of the content of the curriculum is assumed uncomplicatedly to be a part of education, as though education were an uncomplicated thing, easily identified. Opponents of objectives schemes tend to be primarily concerned with what might be the *substance* of objectives, whereas proponents of the schemes tend to focus on their *form*. If education lies in qualities of engagement with knowledge, rather than with knowledge itself, then perhaps we need to reflect on the ways in which we state objectives for such an enterprise.

Well, this is an attempt to summarize the main objections to the planning-by-objectives schemes. The final argument is not that we can have no idea what education is, but *is* about degrees and kinds of precision that it is legitimate to ask for within a complex enterprise like education. A lot of the difficulty is tied up with other common analogies, particularly that of the journey. Education is not a journey in a particular direction, it is not an industrial or manufacturing process, it is not a jigsaw puzzle of facts to be fitted together in the right places; it is complicatedly what it is. All of these analogies can help us think about it. Problems arise when we begin to let the analogy take over the thing itself—when we lose our hold on the complex reality and let it be replaced in part or whole by the analogy.

Let me turn now from pointing at what seem to be problems with objectives schemes and offer an alternative analogically based procedure for planning teaching. This one derives from the story form.

Another Analogy: The Story

Why should we look to the story as a source of ideas about educational planning? There are a couple of superficial reasons. First, the story has been one of the main media for initiating children into the adult world of knowledge and understanding in most places and times. Through myth and story-shaped ritual, or myth and ritual intertwined, the young have been inducted into full membership of their culture. Clearly our educational needs are significantly different from those of myth-using cultures, but the near universality of the story form as the conveyor of the most important truths about the world and experience should provide at least a superficial tug on our attention. Second, we can observe the power of stories to convey information and understanding in a curiously compelling and engaging form. *Robinson Crusoe*, as Rousseau (1762/1911) has argued in some detail, teaches a great deal while describing the castaway's adventures. Much the same can be said of the *Star Wars* films. Every teacher knows the engaging power of a vivid anecdote or story, but we have been less attentive to the possibilities of abstracting from stories elements that can be more generally useful in educational planning. There appears to be, on the face of it, a reason to explore such a possibility.

One might note, in addition, that the role of the story or the shaping narrative is becoming increasingly recognized in all subject areas, even in the sciences, which had once seen themselves as positivistically immune from subjective shaping. This increasing recognition is part of our growing sense of the contribution of the organizing mind to the construction of meaning in any field, or perhaps of the patterns the mind imposes or requires to make the world and experience meaningful.

There have been various attempts to characterize the essential features of stories, from those who try to list specific narrative devices to those who see stories as external reflections of structural properties of the mind. As Chomsky (1972) proposes a Language Acquisition Device (L.A.D.)—a special sensitivity and structural predisposition to make sense of language—so some would see, perhaps as a transformation of this L.A.D., that we must also have a Story Acquisition Device. Our sensitivity to the story form is sufficiently remarkable (Ames, 1966; Applebee, 1978) for some to suggest a mental predisposition to organize events, intentions, characters—the stuff of social activity—into particular purpose-driven causal patterns. The story is the crystalization of this predisposition; it is the narrative form that most precisely reflects the predisposition to make sense of the world and of experience in affectively engaging ways. Stories have beginnings and ends, unlike "reality." The beginning sets forces, usually binary, into play. These are driven by comprehensible purposes, by plausible sequences of causality, until in the end we know how to feel about the entities—the characters, their behavior, the events—that make up the story. The kind of meaning proper to stories is affective; it engages us by drawing us into the sequence of events. It draws us in by reflecting precisely a pattern by which we seem predisposed to make sense of the world. My purpose is to try to use features of this pattern in order to make curriculum content more engaging and meaningful to children.

If we begin to explore the realm of education as in some sense analogous to the story form, we will see it in unfamiliar but perhaps interesting perspectives. The content of the curriculum as a whole will no longer be seen as a set of subject matters or forms of knowledge to be taught, but as a set of great stories to be told. Planning lessons or units of study, similarly, will be seen not in terms of objectives to be attained but as good stories to be told.

Let us take one of these a little further and see whether the superficial plausibility of the story analogy can translate into something of practical use that is *adequate* to our typical educational purposes. Let us consider, for the sake of example, the planning of lessons. The task is to look at the way stories work and see whether we can borrow some of their engaging communicative power and incorporate it into a framework for planning that provides an alternative to that devised by Tyler (1949) and developed by others since. My aim will be to provide a framework that is similar in kind to that devised by Tyler, but different in structure. It will embody principles derived from the story rather than principles derived from the assembly line.

One evident feature of stories is that significantly different kinds appeal at different ages. Some of the main structural characteristics of the kind of story that appeals to typical 6-year-olds are different from those that underlie the kind of story that appeals to 16-year-olds. We might, then, expect the planning framework suitable for 6-year-olds' lessons to be different from that suitable for planning for 16-year-olds. For present purposes let us focus on 6-year-olds. No doubt different analyses of stories, or concentration on different features of stories, might yield a number of possible frameworks for planning teaching. Here is one possibility. Rather than establishing each element piece by piece, I will present the framework first and briefly discuss the rationale for it afterward.

Elaborating the Alternative

1. *Identifying importance:*
   What is most important about this topic? What is affectively engaging in it?
2. *Finding binary opposites:*
   What powerful binary opposites best catch the importance of the topic?
3. *Organizing content into story form:*
   3.1 What content most dramatically expresses the binary opposites, in order to provide access to the topic?
   3.2 What content best articulates the topic into a developing story form?
4. *Conclusion:*
   What is the best way of resolving the dramatic conflict inherent in the binary opposites? What degree of mediation of those opposites is it appropriate to seek?
5. *Evaluation:*
   How can one know whether the topic has been understood, its importance grasped, and the content learned?

(A proper exposition of this framework would require much lengthier treatment than is possible here, along with numerous examples from different curriculum areas. I provide these elsewhere [Egan, 1988, 1989], but want here only to establish that the story form can provide us with an analogy for planning teaching that is at least as adequate as that of the assembly line. At least, this suggests ways to enlarge our repertoire of planning tools.)

Perhaps I should stress again that I am in no way interested in the incorporation of fictional stories into teaching regular curriculum content.

I am not advocating the fictionalizing of curriculum material, or replacing regular content with fictional stories about it. I am concerned with principles derived from the story form that can be used to organize regular curriculum content into more accessible and engaging forms.

When preparing to tell a story, we do not begin by formulating objectives. The story is not a means to some end. The elements of the story together constitute a complex of feelings, images, and events, and establish a particular quality and meaning for them—what I have elsewhere called an "affective meaning" (Egan, 1978). Our concern is somewhat different from the fictional storyteller's, however. We begin by asking what is important about our topic. We will ask of it much the same question newspaper editors ask reporters when they say "What is the story on this?" It is a question that asks why anyone should care about this topic, and requires the answer in a vivid form. It is not so much a question of why children should find it engaging, as a more general question about what is engaging about it for the planner or teacher. If the teacher can identify nothing that is affectively engaging about the topic, it is hard to see how he or she will be able to imbue it with the quality that can make it educationally worthwhile for children. Identifying importance will require imagination in the teacher, but the teacher's imaginative act should lead to engaging the imagination of the children later.

For a lesson on communities for a second-grade social studies class, one might identify importance in terms of the human struggle for security against fear. That is one of the important, affectively engaging, features inherent in this topic. (One could, of course, identify others: This first item does not require that we identify *the* importance of a topic, only *something* important about it.) This important feature will thereafter serve as our touchstone of relevance for any content we include to "body it forth." It serves rather like Richard Pring's (1973) organizing principle over our lesson.

This security/fear theme is not an objective. We are not going to teach about security and fear. One reason we are not going to teach about them is that children already know them profoundly. Rather, we will use these fundamental abstract concepts in order to make meaningful the content about communities that will be organized in terms of them. Another reason why what is identified as important is different from an objective, in the normal use of that term in the educational literature I have been referring to, is that the sense of educational importance identified is not an end-point to be achieved by means of the content. Rather it is the principle that guides the teacher's recognition that the skills, knowledge, experiences that constitute the lesson embody the appropriate quality. It is the principle that enables the teacher to decide part way through the lesson, for example, to focus in detail on a particular activity and ignore others because that particular activity is powerfully evoking the appropriate engagement: It serves more like a holographic interference pattern than a two-dimensional plan that requires all the pieces to be put in place.

The binary opposites are in there because they enable the student to gain a clear initial grasp on the topic, as I argue in more detail in Chapter 2.

Answering 3.1 gives us a starting point for the lesson. It requires considering the topic overall to find whatever can most vividly embody, or "body forth," the main structural elements. If it is a lesson on North American Indians, and we have selected survival/destruction as our binary opposites, we will select an incident that most vividly shows the constant struggle for survival against a powerful threat of destruction. (Plains Indians would take about three day's food on a hunting trip. It is the third day and they have not come across game. Such an incident can be dramatized with appropriate detail as a starting incident.)

The binary opposites, which have been chosen because they can show something important about the topic, provide the criteria for the selection and ordering of the remaining content of the lesson. As with any good story, our underlying structure will ensure that all the content will further the development of the topic coherently. As deviation from the underlying structure plot weakens a fictional story and threatens to dissipate meaning, so inclusion of content other than that which furthers the theme picked out by our choice of binary opposites will tend to confuse children, lose their interest, and dissipate meaning. Our chosen binary opposites provide clear criteria for building a coherent lesson. (Some other lesson may examine the same topic in light of different binary opposites that can focus attention on different content.)

In concluding the lesson, answering item 4, it will be clear that the binary opposites have provided a clarity of organization to the topic that might now be elaborated, or mediated. For example, if we have organized a lesson about the Vikings on a civilization/barbarism structure, in which Alfred the Great represents civilizing, building energies and the Vikings are seen largely as barbarian destroyers, then our conclusion may focus on the remarkable constructive achievements of the Vikings, and on their courage and energy.

The final section focuses us again on what was educationally important about the lesson. It encourages us to evaluate what matters educationally, and to be wary of just considering superficial indices of incidentals.

What is sketched briefly here is a framework for planning a lesson that—to put it at its least ambitious—can work. That is, one can sit down and plan a lesson by answering the questions in the framework, and, having done so, one will have an outline or a plot that can guide the teaching of the lesson. On the face of it there are no reasons to think that this framework leaves out some crucial element that should be a part of educational planning, and it is not unreasonable to expect it to be at least as engaging, as coherent, and as accessible as any likely to result from use of the objectives-dominated frameworks. By this perhaps startling claim, I mean only that, on the face of it, the story-form framework does not obviously lead the planner to omit something of educational, and practical, importance. And in addition, simply on the face of it, principles of coherence and accessibility are brought to the fore, as are some structural features that make stories engaging. Clearly the implicit claims here are not simply analytic, and will properly be subject to empirical testing. More to the immediate point, it is a framework that nowhere requires the stating of objectives. Its sense of direction and coherence is determined not by means/ends planning, but by making clear what is educationally important about the topic and letting that guide more detailed selection and organization of content in terms that will be accessible and meaningful to the child. The point of this alternative framework is not simply to get away from objectives-stating but, because of how conceiving education in terms of sets of objectives directs teaching, to focus precisely on the substance of teaching and the quality of educational engagements.

CONCLUSION

Is this fuss about nothing much? Is identifying importance, for example, in no significant way different from stating objectives? I think the differences are profound and educationally important, but somewhat hidden by the looseness and varied use of the term *objectives*. My argument is not that one can plan teaching or curricula in a way that obviates the sensible use of objectives about a lesson that results from any planning framework or model. As teaching is an intentional activity, one can always point to some intended feature of teaching and talk about it as an objective. Rather, my argument is about the adequacy of talking about educational planning in one way or another, and the implications that go with talking and thinking about it in one way rather than another. At present in the typical teacher preparation program, much more time and energy go into instruction in the use of objectives schemes for planning than into reflection on the nature of education. It will commonly follow, then, that the former will inform the latter; that is, the conception of education inherent in the assembly line–derived framework will shape students' conception of education—rather than vice-versa, as it should be. Starting our planning by stating precisely the end-conditions of an educational event raises a number of problems pointed at above. Most insistently we have

to ask how it can make sense to demand greater precision *within* education than, even the proponents of such procedures acknowledge, can be
given *about* education. How can we state clearer objectives for its components than we can for the overall process? It really won't do to go on as
though logical absurdity doesn't matter.

Identifying importance is a matter of trying to be clear about what can
make a topic educationally significant, about what can imbue the topic
with the appropriate quality. From this we choose structuring principles
that help us to recognize at what points we are in danger of merely conveying inert information. None of this provides us with a guide that is more
precise and sure than our conception of education itself. What it does is
keep our conception of education alert and constantly to the fore in the
process of planning and teaching.

The less "hard" or less restricted sense of "objectives," and the use of
some variant on the Tyler (1949) framework, cannot obviously be shown
to be wrong or not useful. Clearly a framework that enables a teacher to
systematically organize a lesson or unit cannot be discarded. What one
might reasonably regret is the dominance by a single framework, or variants on it, especially when that framework is so bound up with industrial
processes. The logic of machines meshes poorly with the logic of human
affairs—the logic of stories, I think, meshes rather better.

The temptation in proffering an alternative framework to that which
is dominant is to argue that it should be considered as a replacement—a
temptation to which I have clearly yielded. Pulling back from the agonis-
tic stance, I should conclude by observing that my argument is aimed primarily at those interpretations of Tyler's (1949) framework that demand
as a starting point of planning teaching a kind of precision in stating objectives that is inappropriate to education. (It may be appropriate to tasks
like fixing radios or, indeed, building automobiles.) I hope this alternative
will be considered, initially at least, in the spirit in which it is offered: as
an attempt to develop an alternative framework for planning teaching that
draws principles analogically from a quite different source than does the
dominant framework. I have described it in the context of, and in contrast to, the dominant Tyler framework in order to clarify some of the reasons that justify even bothering to try to articulate an alternative.

CHAPTER 11

The Analytic and the
Arbitrary in Educational Research

I wrote this essay with the intention of stopping empirical research as it is currently conducted in education. To my amazement, this did not immediately happen. I was impressed by Jan Smedslund's critique of research in social psychology, and simply applied his argument to education. His claim is that most empirical research in psychology is really pseudo-empirical, and a product of conceptual confusions. I thought that some of the events surrounding this essay were instructive about how difficult it is to establish grounds for communicating with fellow-educators who worked with, I suppose, different presuppositions from mine.

I first read a draft to a group of educational psychologists locally. I took a few examples of research more or less at random and tried to show, following Smedslund, that the researchers had confused genuinely empirical issues, which were not generalizable, with analytic elements that established necessary connections between the subjects of the research, and so they had produced what looked like, but weren't, empirical findings that could be generalized. My colleagues claimed that my argument worked only because I had carefully chosen examples of bad research that exemplified the confusion I was demonstrating. I argued that the confusion was true of almost any empirical generalization based on psychological research, and challenged them to give me an example of a piece of research that would be immune to the critique. They came up with the example I use in this chapter of the "finding" that ordered lists are more readily remembered than random lists. After the essay appeared, I was accused of carefully selecting my example to show my case!

Smedslund chose at random Bandura's "self-efficacy" research, showing that what was generalizable from it could be decomposed into analytic connections. Bandura wrote a response to this that seemed to me, with my presuppositions, to show little comprehension of Smedslund's argument. When I next raised the issue with educational psychology colleagues I was told that Smedslund's argument had been decisively dismissed by Bandura and didn't merit any further attention.

I may, of course, be missing some obvious flaw in the chapter that follows, but, when I examine typical pieces of new educational research, Smedslund's insight seems to me to leave most research results devastated. Perhaps the problem—from my point of view—is that the kind of thinking Smedslund calls for is not a part of the training of educational researchers. None of us is good at accommodating arguments that cut away the foundations of what we have based our careers on, but I do think it is worth trying to be hospitable to fundamental criticisms now and then. While Smedslund's analytic and arbitrary confusion may not be so absolutely devastating as he, and I, have thought, some sensitivity to the common flaw it points to could save us from a lot of bad research.

The essay first appeared in the Canadian Journal of Education, *Vol. 13, No. 1, 1988, pp. 69–82, and I am grateful to its editor and publisher for permission to reprint the essay here.*

INTRODUCTION

Doing research on human subjects in complex settings with the aim of improving something so problematic and value-laden as education presents the researcher with a daunting range of conceptual difficulties. The educational researcher cannot turn with any confidence to a body of educational theory for help. What is available from that direction is, rather, disputes about what an educational theory might look like, with no evident examples of such a thing on the ground to guide thinking and research (Hirst, 1966, 1972, 1983; Nagel, 1969; O'Connor, 1957, 1972). The help offered by psychological theories about such apparently educationally relevant phenomena as, for example, "learning" is not without problems of its own. On the one hand, we have doubts expressed about the basic security of such theories (Gauld & Shotter, 1977; Louch, 1966; MacKenzie, 1977), as in one of Wittgenstein's (1963) more notorious observations:

> The confusion and barrenness of psychology is not to be explained by calling it a "young science"; its state is not comparable with that of physics, for instance, in its beginnings. (Rather with that of certain branches of mathematics. Set theory.) For in psychology there are experimental methods and *conceptual confusion.* The existence of the experimental method makes us think we have the means of solving the problems which trouble us; though problem and method pass one another by. (p. 232)

And, on the other hand, we have doubts expressed about the applicability to education of research based on psychological theories. It is argued, for example, that the concept of learning embodied in psychological theories is significantly unlike any concept of learning that is proper to education (Oakeshott, 1967; Petrie, 1982). Then we have also a series of problems about moving from research findings to educational practice (Egan, 1983).

Most of these conceptual difficulties have been well rehearsed in recent years. In general they begin from the observation that the "dominant paradigm" in educational research uses methods derived from research into natural phenomena. Dispute centers on the ways in which human behavior is like or unlike other natural phenomena; or, rather, on the degree to which human behavior is a cultural phenomenon, bound up with intentions and meanings, and so resistant to being adequately dealt with by the dominant paradigm. There is a sort of *impasse* in current disputes, at least until the objectors can show the researchers that there is something about the regularities of human behavior that prevent the fruitful application of the methodologies from the physical science paradigm, or until the researchers actually come up with a relatively secure generalization or theory about human behavior that looks anything like those common in the physical sciences.

One of the crucial inconveniences of human behavior for the easy applicability of a methodology designed to deal with questions about natural phenomena is that human behavior does not come in discrete units. The dominant research methodology in educational psychology is used to establish empirical relationships between observable behaviors. A set of problems surrounds how we conceptualize and label human behaviors. Educational psychology, and psychology in general, relies heavily on concepts and labels—such as learning, motivation, development, and so forth—that are complex and interconnected in subtle ways. Similarly, even the simplest labels for behaviors—lift, throw, open, kick, and so forth—are applicable only within networks of intentions and meanings. One problem that follows from this observation is that of ensuring that the behaviors between which we wish to establish empirical connections are not already covertly tied through the labels we assign to them. Jan Smedslund (1978a, 1978b, 1979) has argued that the empirical connections established by much psychological research are already made by conceptual ties, and so the connections established are "pseudo-empirical." If his argument is sound, it would appear, on the face of it, to present yet another difficulty for the dominant paradigm of educational research. Smedslund argues that often what appear to be empirical findings in psychology are a product of confusing what he calls analytic and arbitrary components in the research design. If he is correct, a great deal of educational psychology research will have to be considered pseudo-empirical. The implications of his observations for the future of psychological research, and empirical research in education, are far reaching, and merit some discussion.

THE ANALYTIC AND THE ARBITRARY

By the analytic, Smedslund (1979) means things that are true as a matter of logical necessity, or by definition, or by tautology: in the Kantian sense in which the concept of the predicate is contained, although covertly, in the concept of the subject, and a denial of the statement in which they are contained would involve a contradiction. Thus "all unmarried men in Vancouver are bachelors" is true as a matter of logical necessity or by definition. We could treat the question "Are all unmarried men in Vancouver bachelors?" as an empirical question. We could design a tight survey, run it with great care, and analyze the results by the most sophisticated statistical methods. We could then announce that we had empirically established that 100% of the bachelors in Vancouver are unmarried. And, by such a procedure, we would indeed have established the truth of the proposition empirically. The empirical research is, of course, unnecessary, and we need feel no caution generalizing our results to Chicago or Paris. The connection between bachelors and unmarried men is established by analysis or definition. Smedslund's argument concerning a great deal of research in psychology is that the concepts dealt with very commonly contain a covert analytic element, an element that is made more difficult to see by their containing an admixture of arbitrary components as well.

The question, then, is whether commonly in educational psychological studies the experimenter confuses an analytic element and an arbitrary element. The analytic element guarantees connections between the two things whose relationship is being studied. The arbitrary element is genuinely empirical, but is not generalizable beyond the circumstances and subjects of the experiment. By confusing the two, educational psychologists routinely produce pseudo-empirical results, which they accept as straightforwardly empirical findings with some generalizing power.

Let us first try to clarify the kind of covert analytic component that may be found in educational research that draws on psychology as its "parent discipline." A number of people have noted the tautological nature of Thorndike's formulation of the "law of effect" (e.g., Louch, 1966)—that people tend to repeat behaviors that have pleasurable consequences. What is established here is a supposedly empirical connection between the tendency to repeat behaviors and the warranted expectation of pleasurable consequences. But rather like the previous example, there is an analytic tie between the two. Choosing to repeat a behavior, if one can, and expecting pleasurable consequences are not independent things. What we mean by choosing to repeat a behavior is tied up in the expectation of pleasurable consequences. If we ran experiments that showed cases of people not choosing to repeat behaviors they expect to be pleasurable, we would have to conclude that there was something wrong with the way we were identifying what was pleasurable for them. We identify a repeated behavior that is freely chosen, by the chooser expecting pleasurable consequences. Indeed, one might say that expecting pleasurable consequences could serve as part of a definition of what is meant by choosing to repeat a behavior.

Similarly, it has been pointed out before (e.g., Louch, 1966) that if we consider the list of propositions that Hilgard (1956), claimed psychologists have established with some degree of certainty, we will find other examples of this kind. His first proposition is that "brighter people can learn things less bright ones cannot learn" (p. 486). In this case, he is claiming that careful psychological research has established a secure empirical connection between brightness and ability to learn. But, again, the two are analytically tied. What we mean by brightness involves ability to learn more than is normal. It is a matter of definition, not empirical study. (It may be argued that empirical research has given precision to the degrees of brightness and what is learnable, but this will be countered below in the discussion of the arbitrary component.)

Hilgard's (1956) second proposition is that "a motivated learner acquires what he learns more readily than one who is not motivated" (p. 486). Here again what is meant by motivation is analytically tied to what is meant by learning more readily. One cannot identify the motivated learner independently of behaviors that exemplify more ready learning.

These propositions do not establish empirical relationships between distinct things. Rather, they articulate partial definitions of the first term: For example, a motivated learner is one who learns more readily, and who does *x* and who does *y*; a bright person is one who learns more, and does *x*, and does *y*; a bachelor is one who is unmarried, and who is a male. The point about these "findings" is not that they are obvious, or commonsense, or trivial. The psychologist could properly respond to such a point by observing that science often is involved in securely establishing things that seem obvious or trivial, but that once securely established scientifically, such findings can prove crucial steps to powerful theories with great explanatory power. The point here is more challenging. It is that such findings are not empirical findings at all; what are being presented as the results of empirical research are "findings" that are in part matters of logical necessity or analytic truths.

And the arbitrary component? All of the experiments that supported Hilgard's (1956) propositions did not yield identical results. Some bright children learned some things better than others, and on different days might have scored somewhat differently. The causes of these individual differences between subjects on tests and between the performance of subjects on different days are enormously varied. If an experiment involves learning random seven-digit numbers, and one of the numbers is that of your telephone, you will obviously remember it better than any of the others. Such contaminations of experimental results due to arbitrary factors is compensated for by, among other things, having sufficiently large groups of subjects. A large part of the methodology of educational research involves techniques of controlling for such arbitrary contaminants.

Let us imagine a research program that seeks to establish an empirical connection between ease of learning and degree of organization in lists. (I take this example because after rehearsing this argument with a group of educational psychologist colleagues, this was chosen by them as a clear case of an empirically established generalization). A useful product of such research might be information about how to organize lists so that they might most readily be learned. After some initial experiments, one might conclude as a first generalization that ordered lists are learned more easily than random lists. The first thing we need to observe about this conclusion is that it is another of those pseudo-empirical findings. The analytic component involves the necessary connection between order and learning. A detailed definition of learning would imply or involve notions of order—the structure of the human mind, important for what can be learned and how, and what is conceived of and recognized as ordered are not distinct things. Order, meaning, and learning are analytically tied. If people in our experiment learned random lists more readily, we would scan the lists for an hitherto unsuspected order. What we *mean* by ordered, then, is analytically connected with what we can more readily recognize and learn.

To return to the earlier example: If one of the elements learned readily was a random seven-digit number, we might wonder what unsuspected order or meaning it had for that subject. On discovering that it was the subject's telephone number, we would be satisfied. But a great deal of the irregularity in experimental results is due to such arbitrary elements. Usually they are not as simple or dramatic as in this example. What one cannot do with these arbitrary elements is generalize from them. The fact that subject x learned a random seven-digit number readily does not allow us to generalize either about that subject's ability to learn random seven-digit numbers or about anyone else's ability to learn them, or to learn that particular number.

So in the case of this simple experiment about learning lists, we have an analytic tie that guarantees that we will establish a strong positive correlation between orderedness in the lists and ease of learning. We have also, however, an arbitrary element that guarantees that what will count as ordered for one subject will vary in indeterminate ways from what counts as ordered for another. By confusing the two, by not distinguishing the analytic component from the arbitrary component, we treat the results of our study as an empirically established connection, which we may then seek to generalize.

The analytic component, however, generalizes absolutely. The arbitrary component cannot be generalized at all. We do not need an experiment to establish the analytic component. And the arbitrary component is immune to control.

IMPLICATIONS OF THE ARGUMENT

What range of educational research is affected by this argument? It would seem to affect all empirical research that aims at theory building and even establishing empirical generalizations. Let us consider Smedslund's (1979) general argument, then return with it to one further example. He implies that the language of educational psychological research uses concepts among which there exists a network of analytic connections. This empirical research needs to draw on theories articulated in terms of these concepts, yet is itself unable to generate such theories. Where, then, are the theories to come from?

In Smedslund's (1979) account, the crucial mistake in psychology has been its adoption of the physical sciences model. His concern is not so much the adoption of the methodology, but rather the attempt to build similar kinds of generalizations, theories, and laws by means of the methodology. In his view, psychology might better see itself as a discipline more like geometry than physics. As he puts it:

> The conceptual framework of psychology, as embodied in ordinary language, is anterior to and structures our everyday dealings with people, and also our scientific interpretations of data and our theorizing, in the same way as, e.g., the conceptual framework of geometry is anterior to and structures our dealings with space. There may, therefore, exist a parallel between the task confronting contemporary psychology and the task that confronted the Greek scientists in antiquity, beginning with Thales. . . . In both cases, what is required is an analytic effort to explicate and systematize the intuitively and unreflectively known conceptual framework used in everyday life. The validity of the outcome is to be proved logically rather than empirically. (pp. 1, 2)

This is a rather radical proposal. It seems to suggest that theory generating in psychology, and educational psychology, become attached to epistemology. What might such theories look like? Smedslund (1976) gives some examples, of what he calls "common-sense theorems" or "ordinary language theorems." Consider the following:

1. If a person performs an act, he both can do it and tries to do it. Conversely, if he does not perform an act, he either cannot do it, but tries; or can do it, but does not try; or neither can do it nor tries to do it.
2. If a person wants x and gets x, he will get some satisfaction from this. If a person gets no satisfaction from getting x then it is not x that he wants.
3. If a person wants x and knows that act A will lead to his getting x and he can do A and no other want or knowledge interferes, then the person will do A.
4. If a person wants x and does A and gets x and believes that A always leads to x, then the next time he wants x he will again do A. (p. 3)

These "theorems" seem to be universally valid. Perhaps they could be tightened up a bit, but as they stand they describe relationships that must hold among things like "wanting," "acting," "satisfaction," and so on. One might compose an indefinite set of such sentences that describe similar relationships among other terms. They are relationships that would always be supported by empirical tests, but the empirical tests would not establish their truth. They are analytic truths, and it would be a conceptual confusion to try to establish them empirically, just as it would be to establish a geometrical theorem empirically. They are sketches of some of the simpler logical relationships that exist in our natural language among certain terms common in some branches of psychology. The above theorems, for example, cover the "law of effect," and go beyond it in scope.

Smedslund (1979) has demonstrated how what are taken as straightforward empirical research programs in psychology conclude with findings that are directly derivable from sets of such commonsense theorems. They are confused, however, by being mixed with a set of arbitrary components. He has demonstrated this on an article on social psychology, selected "blind" on the basis of criteria that would establish it as significant among researchers in the area. Also, he has shown that all of the supposedly empirically established conclusions supporting Bandura's "Self-efficacy: Towards a Unifying Theory of Behavioral Change" can be derived from 36 "commonsense theorems."

As geometry carries us beyond our intuitive grasp of special relationships, so a formal discipline of psychology might be expected to carry us beyond our intuitive grasp of the relationships within and among such general concepts as learning, motivation, development, and so on. As geometry provides a set of useful theoretical axioms on which the builder and navigator can rely, so may the formal psychologist establish a set of psychological axioms on which the educator, and the educational researcher, can rely. What seems to remain for empirical research is the establishment of limited and local findings, applicable to particular subjects, at particular times, in particular circumstances.

Now this conclusion might seem only to echo a major trend in educational research of the last couple of decades. We have seen somewhat similar conclusions in the disillusionment of, for example, the Aptitude-Treatment-Interaction (A.-T.-I.) research program stimulated by Cronbach, (1957, 1975), leading to Snow's (1977) conclusion that while the search for general theory in such areas is perhaps impossible, we may still hope to establish A.-T.-Is. with local applicability. Also, the disillusionment with Piaget's general theories has followed the realization that much of their plausibility derived from mixing what we can call analytic and arbitrary elements: Acquisitions that are empirically established as occurring in a particular sequence turn out on analysis to be such that the later acquisitions logically presuppose earlier ones (see, e.g., Brainerd, 1978; Hamlyn, 1978; Phillips & Kelly, 1975) and a close examination of the data shows ad hoc contrivances to deal with the considerable arbitrariness (Brainerd, 1973, 1977). So perhaps Smedslund's (1979) argument may, after all, appear only a dramatic way of reaching conclusions that are embedded in much present educational research practice. Many researchers see their task as elucidating particular problems, clarifying trends, exposing particular regularities in specific contexts, and so on, not establishing general theories or even particularly powerful empirical generalizations. I think Smedslund's argument threatens to cut deeper. Another example might at this point help us to explore his argument further.

OBJECTIVES AND PERFORMANCES

For an example I wanted to consider an educational prescription based on some empirical research. I thought a place to find such things relatively unselfconsciously stated was in a textbook on curriculum, and so I more or less randomly flicked through one that I had at hand until I hit what seemed like a straightforward empirical matter. In David Pratt's *Curriculum: Design and Development* (1980) I found a section on aims with the subheading "Empirical Evidence." The evidence is in support of the claim that setting clear and precise goals is likely to enhance students' learning.

Pratt (1980) begins by citing Mace's "classic, although rudimentary study" (p. 142) of 1935. A group of students working on computation problems were given a specific daily standard to surpass. This group performed better over a 10-day period than did a group who were simply instructed to "do their best to improve." Pratt then cites a set of more re-

cent studies that support and extend Mace's finding, including a set that
has led to the expansion in industrial settings of "management by objectives." He further cites Duchastel and Merrill's 1973 survey of studies using
objectives and Melton's 1978 survey of such studies. Both of these surveys indicate the usual inconsistencies that result when similar studies are
conducted in slightly different ways with different subjects in different
settings. But by looking for general trends among them it is possible to
conclude that the use of objectives in many cases seems to improve students' performance.

What are we to make of this empirical evidence, however, if we look
at it through Smedslund's (1979) lens? Mace's (1935) study, however
rudimentary, surely shows an empirical connection between specific goal
setting and performance. Figure 11.1 is a graph that shows his results.
Group A was instructed to surpass a specific standard prescribed for each
day (10 subjects); Group B was instructed to do their best to improve and
given no specific standard (10 subjects) (Mace, 1935, p. 21). (The Alternative Group A line has been added, and should be ignored initially).

Where would we look for analytic connections in a case like this? As
a first sortie, we might consider the connections between being set goals

FIGURE 11.1   Goal Setting and Performance

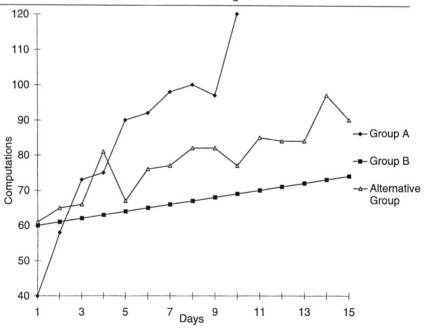

and having a sufficient motive to achieve the goals set. We recognize casually that there are degrees of energy that are normally elicited by various kinds of challenge or incentive, and that people normally expend energy appropriate to the challenge they face. What is considered an appropriate amount of energy is normally the minimum required to achieve the goal set. What would we say if someone expended greater energy than is required to achieve a set goal? We would say that there is some additional challenge operating, of a kind to be explained by that individual's history or cultural context.

We might begin to convert such an initial sortie into commonsense theorems:

If P is challenged to perform T in S, and P can perform T in S and the challenge evokes sufficient motivation to perform T in S, and no other circumstances intervene, P will perform T in S.

If P is challenged to perform $T + n$ in S, but the challenge evokes sufficient motivation to perform only T in S, and no other circumstances intervene, P will perform T in S. (If P performed $T + n$ in S, it would mean that the challenge evoked sufficient motivation to perform $T + n$ in S, or that some other circumstance intervened to provide the extra motivation.)

Let us return to Mace's (1935) findings with these proto-commonsense theorems, or tautologies, or analytic truths. They begin to sketch some necessary connections between challenge, motivation, and performance. These are not empirical matters; they are matters that turn on what the terms mean. They point us to consider what motivation is evoked by the challenges in Mace's experiment. In general it can be concluded that providing a precise challenge evokes motivation to perform what one is challenged by, if one can perform it and the circumstances are such that one is sufficiently motivated to perform it. The two groups in Mace's study differ in the challenge that is posed to them and the motivation the challenges evoke. Group B, we may say, is being challenged to perform $T + n$ while being given sufficient motive only to perform T.

While lacking Mace's raw data, we can assume that it is possible, even likely, that the worst-performing subject in group A performed less well than the best-performing subject in group B. That is, what challenge evokes what degree of motivation in what subject is a matter to be explained in terms of individual histories, cultural backgrounds, neuroses, and so forth. The best-performing subject in group B, let us say, performed $T + n$. In this case we will search for an explanation in terms of the peculiarities of this subject; we will, that is, look in this subject's personal history for the intervening circumstance that provides the added motivation to perform more than is motivated by the challenge itself. This is the realm of the arbitrary.

The averaging out of the scores for the two groups suggests a positive correlation has been established empirically between the setting of goals and performance. In such cases the arbitrary element is likely to be very large: That is, what counts as an adequate motive to perform particular tasks in particular circumstances will vary considerably for different people. The averaged-out results, however, sketch roughly the confusion of the analytic tie between challenge, motivation, and performance and the array of arbitrary elements. The genuinely empirical part has been disguised by the averaging procedure. What is genuinely empirical is precisely the product of the arbitrary differences in performance that result from the individual differences in the way particular challenges evoke different degrees of motivation and these produce different performances. What can be explored empirically is just what challenges most, or least, motivate what individuals in what circumstances to perform in what ways. What cannot be explored empirically is whether setting a challenge in appropriate circumstances will evoke the motivation to perform a task. What is perceived as generalizable from Mace's (1935) results is what is a product of the analytic component. The arbitrary component—what challenges motivate what individuals in what circumstances—is not generalizable; it yields data about those individuals in those circumstances only.

It might seem that the studies cited by Duchastel and Merrill (1973) and by Melton (1978) are indeed finding what particular kinds of challenge evoke what degrees of motivation in particular subjects in particular circumstances, and that their research designs are implicitly built on an axiom such as is sketched above. And perhaps Mace (1935) too presupposed such an axiom and his study performs the empirical task of showing that the challenge involved in setting precise objectives is more productive than the challenge involved in the exhortation to do your best to improve. From such studies one may hope to discover empirically what particular kinds of challenge motivate most people to perform best. The problem with Mace's and the other studies is that they have not in fact excluded the analytic component from their research designs. What would we make of Mace's study if we reversed the performances of the two groups in the results? We could have produced precisely such a result if we provide group A with a gradually improving standard that is, over the period, lower than that performed by group B (alternative group A standard). Would we then say that we had discovered that exhorting subjects to do their best to improve produced better performances than setting progressively higher standards for them to achieve? We would say only that in the particular circumstances, the exhortation to improve presented a more stimulating challenge than did the specific standard prescribed. What Mace's study allows us to say is that in certain circumstances setting precise objectives can enable us to stimulate better performances than does the vague exhortation. What we cannot generalize from this and the other studies is that setting precise objectives will stimulate better performances than will giving vague exhortations. Insofar as particular precise objectives represent $T + n$ and vague exhortations represent T, then this generalization follows from our commonsense theorems. The problem with the research studies we have is that they do not deal simply with empirical questions, but they mix in also some form of the question about whether presenting a challenge to achieve $T + n$ in circumstances where subjects are able to perform $T + n$ and are sufficiently motivated to perform $T + n$ will stimulate better performances than a challenge to perform T in similar circumstances. The generally positive results are due to the presence of the analytic component and the enormous diversity is due to the morass of arbitrary elements involved.

CONCLUSION

This very rationalist enterprise proposed by Smedslund pushes "armchair" inquiry back into realms once thought securely claimed by empiricism. The plausibility of Smedslund's notion of psychology-as-geometry rather than psychology-as-physics will in part turn on the production of many more detailed analyses such as those he and his colleagues have carried out. The challenge following this article—$T + n$—is to convert the sketches concerning learning and organized lists and objectives and performance into sets of precisely formulated commonsense theorems. The challenge seems sufficient to motivate someone to perform the task in some circumstances, but sufficient to this chapter the challenge it started with—in this case merely T.

From Smedslund's perspective, psychologists and educational psychologists have been, as it were, doing geometry the hard way—as an empirical study with imprecise and unreliable measuring instruments. It is time to begin doing it Euclid's way—working out the necessary relationships among our phenomena and establishing a set of axioms that can then be applied to the diversity of the world. The future of educational research, in such a program, would see a dramatic convergence of the skills of the philosopher and those of the empirical researcher.

References

Ames, L. B. (1966). Children's stories. *Genetical Psychological Monographs, 73,* 337–396.

Apple, M. (1979). *Ideology and the curriculum.* London: Routledge and Kegan Paul.

Applebee, A. N. (1978). *The child's concept of story.* Chicago: University of Chicago Press.

Arblaster, A. (1975). Socialism and the idea of science. In B. Parekh (Ed.), *The concept of socialism* (pp. 134–153). London: Croom Helm.

Armstrong, M., Connolly, A., & Saville, K. (1994). *Journeys of discovery.* Melbourne: Oxford University Press.

Ashton, P. T. (1975). Cross-cultural Piagetian research: An experimental perspective. *Harvard Educational Review, 45,* 475–506.

Bartlett, F. (1932). *Remembering, a study in experimental and social psychology.* New York: Cambridge University Press.

Berger, P. L., & Kellner, H. (1979). Marriage and the construction of reality. In H. P. Dreitzel (Ed.), *Recent sociology, No. 2* (pp. 49–73). New York: Macmillan.

Bettelheim, B. (1976). *The uses of enchantment.* New York: Knopf.

Blumenberg, H. (1985). *Work on myth.* Cambridge, MA: MIT Press.

Boas, F. (1911). *The mind of primitive man.* New York: Macmillan.

Bobbitt, F. (1918). *The curriculum.* Boston: Houghton-Mifflin.

Brainerd, C. J. (1973). Neo-Piagetian training experiments revisited: Is there any support for the cognitive developmental stage hypothesis? *Cognition, 2,* 349–370.

Brainerd, C. J. (1977). Cognitive development and concept learning: An interpretive review. *Psychological Bulletin, 84*(5), 919–939.

Brainerd, C. J. (1978). Learning research and Piagetian theory. In L. S. Siegel and C. J. Brainerd (Eds.), *Alternatives to Piaget: Critical essays on the theory* (pp. 69–109). New York: Academic Press.

Bransford, J. D., & Johnson, M. V. (1972). Contextual prerequisites for understanding: Some investigations of comprehension and recall. *Journal of Verbal Learning and Verbal Behavior, 11,* 717–721.

Bransford, J. D., & McCarrell, N. S. (1975). A sketch of a cognitive approach to comprehension: Some thoughts about understanding what it means to comprehend. In P. N. Johnson-Laird & P. C. Wason (Eds.), *Thinking: Readings in cognitive science* (pp. 377–399). Cambridge: Cambridge University Press.

Bruner, J. (1986). *Actual minds, possible worlds.* Cambridge, MA.: Harvard University Press.

Buck-Morss, S. (1982). Socio-economic bias in Piaget's theory and its implications for cross-cultural studies. In S. Modgil & C. Modgil (Eds.), *Jean Piaget: Consensus and controversy* (pp. 261–272). New York: Praeger.

Burke, P. (1985). *Vico.* New York: Oxford University Press.

Butler, M. (1981). *Romantics, rebels, and reactionaries.* Oxford, England: Oxford University Press.

Callahan, R. (1962). *Education and the cult of efficiency.* Chicago: University of Chicago Press.

Cassirer, E. (1946). *Language and myth* (S. K. Langer, Trans.). New York: Harper.

Chomsky, N. (1972). *Language and mind.* New York: Harcourt Brace Jovanovich.

Cole, M., & Scribner, S. (1974). *Culture and thought: A psychological introduction.* New York: Wiley.

Coleridge, S. T. (1817). *Biographia literaria, or, biographical sketches of my literary life and opinions.* New York: Kirk and Mercein.

Cooper, D. E. (1986). *Metaphor.* Oxford, England: Blackwell.

Cornford, F. M. (1907). *Thucydides mythistoricus.* London: Edward Arnold.

Cronbach, L. J. (1957). The two disciplines of scientific psychology. *American Psychologist, 12,* 11.

Cronbach, L. J. (1975). Beyond the two disciplines of scientific psychology. *American Psychologist, 30,* 2.

Cullingford, C. (1985). *Parents, teachers and schools.* London: Robert Royce.

Cullingford, C. (1986). "I suppose learning your tables could help you get a job"— Children's views about the purpose of schools. *Education 3–13, 14*(2), 41–46.

Darling, J., & Van de Pijpekamp, M. (1994). "Rousseau on the education, domination and violation of women. *British Journal of Educational Studies, 42*(2), 115–132.

Dewey, J. (1928). Progressive education and the science of education. *Progressive Education, 5* (July–September).

Dewey, J. (1929). *The source of a science of education.* New York: Liveright.

Dewey, J. (1956). *The child and the curriculum/The school and society.* Chicago: University of Chicago Press.

Dewey, J. (1963). *Experience and education.* New York: Collier Books.

Dewey, J. (1966). *Democracy and education.* New York: Free Press. (Original work published 1916)

Dodds, E. R. (1951). *The Greeks and the irrational.* Berkeley and Los Angeles: University of California Press.

Donald, M. (1991). *Origins of the modern mind.* Cambridge, MA: Harvard University Press.

Donaldson, M. (1978). *Children's minds.* London: Croom Helm.

Douglas, M. (1966). *Purity and danger.* London: Routledge & Kegan Paul.

Dray, W. H. (1964). *Philosophy of history.* Englewood Cliffs, N. J.: Prentice-Hall.

Duchastel, P. C., & Merrill, P. F. (1973). The effects of behavioral objectives on learning: A review of empirical studies. *Review of Educational Research, 43,* 53–68.

Durkheim, E. (1915). *The elementary forms of the religious life.* London: Allen & Unwin.

Durkheim, E. (1956). *Education and sociology* (S. D. Fox, Ed. and Trans.). New York: Free Press.

Durkheim, E. (1965). *The elementary forms of the religious life* (J. W. Swain, Trans.). New York: Free Press.

Egan, K. (1973). Mythical and historical reference to the past. *Clio, 2,* 3.

Egan, K. (1978). What is a plot? *New Literary History, 9,* 3.

Egan, K. (1982). What does Piaget's theory describe? *Teachers College Record, 84*(2), 453–476.

Egan, K. (1983). *Education and psychology: Plato, Piaget and scientific psychology.* New York: Teachers College Press.

Egan, K. (1988). *Primary understanding.* New York: Routledge.

Egan, K. (1989). *Teaching as story-telling.* Chicago: University of Chicago Press.

Egan, K. (1990). *Romantic understanding: The development of rationality and imagination, ages 8–15.* New York: Routledge.

Egan, K. (1992). *Imagination in teaching and learning.* Chicago: University of Chicago Press.

Egan, K. (1997). *The educated mind: How cognitive tools shape our understanding.* Chicago: University of Chicago Press.

Egan, K., & Nadaner, D. (Eds.). (1986). *Imagination and education.* New York: Teachers College Press.

Eisner, E. W. (1969). Instructional and expressive educational objectives: Their formulation and use in curriculum. In W. J. Popham, E. W. Eisner, H. J. Sullivan, & L. L. Tyler (Eds.), *Instructional objectives* (AERA Monograph Series on Curriculum Evaluation. No. 3). Chicago: Rand McNally.

Eisner, E. W. (1979). *The educational imagination.* New York: Macmillan.

Eisner, E. W. (1993). Forms of understanding and the future of educational research. *Educational Researcher, 22*(7), 5–11.

Eliade, M. (1959). *Cosmos and history.* New York: Harper & Row.

Elkind, D. (1981). *Child development and education: A Piagetian perspective.* New York: Oxford University Press.

Ellis, A. K. (1986). *Teaching and learning elementary social studies.* Boston: Allyn and Bacon.

Evans-Pritchard, E. E. (1937). *Witchcraft, oracles and magic among the Azande.* New York: Oxford University Press.

Finley, M. I. (1975). *The use and abuse of history.* New York: Viking.

Finnegan, R. (1970). *Oral literature in Africa.* New York: Oxford University Press.

Finnegan, R. (1977). *Oral Poetry: Its nature, signficance, and social context.* Cambridge, England: Cambridge University Press.

Fitzgerald, F. (1979). *America revised.* Boston: Little, Brown.

Flavell, J. H. (1984). Discussion. In R. J. Sternberg (Ed.), *Mechanisms of cognitive development* (pp. 187–209). New York: Freeman.

Fodor, J. (1985). Fodor's guide to mental representations: The intelligent auntie's vademecum. *Mind, 94,* 76–100.

Fodor, J. (1996, November 28). It's the thought that counts. *London Review of Books,* 22–23.

Fodor, J. A. (1983). *The modularity of mind*. Cambridge, MA: MIT Press.

Frankena, W. K. (1965). *Philosophy of education*. New York: Macmillan.

Frankfort, H. A. (1961). *Ancient Egyptian religion*. New York: Harper.

Frankfort, H. A., Wilson, J. A., & Jacobsen, T. (1949). *Before philosophy*. Harmondsworth, England: Pelican.

Franklin, B. M. (1982). The social efficiency movement reconsidered: Curriculum change in Minneapolis, 1917–1950. *Curriculum Inquiry, 12*(1), 9–33.

Frazer, J. G. (1900). *The golden bough* (2nd ed.). London: Macmillan.

Gardner, H. (1983). *Frames of mind*. New York: Basic Books.

Gardner, H. (1985). *The mind's new science*. New York: Basic Books.

Gardner, H., Kircher, M., Winner, E., & Perkins, D. (1975). Children's metaphoric productions and preference. *Journal of Child Language, 2,* 125–141.

Gardner, H., & Winner, E. (1979). The development of metaphoric competence: Implications for humanistic disciplines. In S. Sacks (Ed.), *On metaphor*. Chicago: University of Chicago Press.

Gauld, A., & Shotter, J. (1977). *Human action and its psychological investigation*. London: Routledge & Kegan Paul.

Geertz, C. (1973). *The interpretation of cultures*. New York: Basic Books.

Geyl, Pieter. (1961). Soviet historians make their bow. In *Encounters in history* (pp. 341–351). Cleveland, Ohio: Meridian,

Goodman, P. (1962). *Compulsory miseducation and the community of scholars*. New York: Vintage.

Goodman, P. (1970). *New reformation*. New York: Random House.

Goody, J. (1977). *The domestication of the savage mind*. New York: Cambridge University Press.

Goody, J. (1986). *The logic of writing and the organization of society*. New York: Cambridge University Press.

Goody, J. (1987). *The interface between the written and the oral*. New York: Cambridge University Press.

Goody, J., & Watt, I. (1968). The consequences of literacy. In J. Goody (Ed.), *Literacy in traditional societies* (pp. 304–345). New York: Cambridge University Press.

Gould, S. J. (1977). *Ontogeny and phylogeny*. Cambridge, MA: Harvard University Press.

Gould, S. J. (1996). *Full house: The spread of excellence from Plato to Darwin*. New York: Harmony.

Griffin, J. (1980). *Homer*. New York: Oxford University Press.

Hall, G. S. (1904). *Adolescence: Its psychology and its relations to physiology, anthropology, sociology, sex, crime, religion, and education* (*vol. 2*). New York: D. Appleton.

Hamlyn, D. W. (1978). *Experience and the growth of understanding*. London: Routledge & Kegan Paul.

Hardy, B. (1968). Towards a poetics of fiction: An approach through narrative. *Novel, 2,* 5–14.

Havelock, E. (1963). *Preface to Plato*. Cambridge, MA: Harvard University Press.

Havelock, E. A. (1976). *Origins of Western literacy*. Toronto: Ontario Institute for Studies in Education.

Havelock, E. A. (1986). *The muse learns to write*. New Haven: Yale University Press.

Hayek, F. A. (1970). The primacy of the abstract. In A. Koestler & J. R. Smythies (Eds.), *Beyond reductionism* (pp. 216–228). New York: Macmillan.

Heath, S. B. (1983). *Ways with words.* Cambridge: Cambridge University Press.

Hilgard, E. R. (1956). *Theories of learning.* New York: Appleton-Century Crofts.

Hirsch, E. D. (1987). *Cultural literacy.* Boston: Houghton-Mifflin.

Hirst, P. (1966). Philosophy and educational theory. In I. Scheffler (Ed.), *Philosophy and Education* (pp. 78–95). Boston: Allyn & Bacon.

Hirst, P. (1972). Response to O'Connor: The nature of educational theory. *Proceedings of the Philosophy of Education Society of Great Britain, Vol. 6, No. 1* (pp. 110–118). Oxford: Blackwell.

Hirst, P. (1974). *Knowledge and the curriculum.* London: Routledge & Kegan Paul.

Hirst, P. (1983). Educational theory. In P. Hirst (Ed.), *Educational theory and its foundation disciplines* (pp. 3–29). London: Routledge & Kegan Paul.

Hollis, M., & Lukes, S. (Eds.). (1982). *Rationality and relativism.* Cambridge, MA: MIT Press.

Horton, R. (1970). African traditional thought and Western science. In B. Wilson (Ed.), *Rationality* (pp. 131–171). Oxford: Blackwell.

Horton, R. (1982). Tradition and modernity revisited. In M. Hollis & S. Lukes (Eds.), *Rationality and relativism* (pp. 201–260). Cambridge, MA: MIT Press.

Huizinga, J. (1949). *Homo ludens.* London: Routledge & Kegan Paul.

Illich, I. (1993). *Hugh of St. Victor.* Cambridge: Cambridge University Press.

Inhelder, B., & Piaget, J. (1969). *The early growth of logic in the child.* New York: Norton.

Jarolimek, J. (1982). *Social studies in elementary education* (6th ed.). New York: Macmillan.

Jenkyns, R. (1980). *The Victorians and ancient Greece.* Cambridge, MA: Harvard University Press.

Kelly, A. V. (1977). *The curriculum: Theory and practice.* London: Harper and Row.

Keynes, J. M. (1936). General theory of employment, interest and money. London: Macmillan.

Kirk, G. S. (1965). *Homer and the epic.* New York: Cambridge University Press.

Kliebard, H. M. (1975). Reappraisal: The Tyler rationale. In W. Pinar (Ed.), *Curriculum theorizing* (pp. 70–83). Berkeley, CA: McCutchan.

Kliebard, H. M. (1986). *The struggle for the American curriculum: 1893–1958.* Boston: Routledge & Kegan Paul.

Knapp, M., & Knapp, H. (1976). *One potato, two potato.* New York: Norton.

Kozol, J. (1967). *Death at an early age.* Boston: Houghton Mifflin.

Leach, E. (1967). Genesis as myth. In J. Middleton (Ed.), *Myth and cosmos* (pp. 1–13). New York: Natural History Press.

Lévi-Bruhl, L. (1985). *How natives think* (L. A. Clare, Trans.; C. S. Littleton, Intro.). Princeton: Princeton University Press. (Original work published 1910)

Lévi-Strauss, C. (1962). *Totemism.* New York: Merlin.

Lévi-Strauss, C. (1966a). *The savage mind.* Chicago: University of Chicago Press.

Lévi-Strauss, C. (1966b, December 22). The culinary triangle. *New Society*, 937–940.

Lévi-Strauss, C. (1967). The structural study of myth. In *Structural anthropology* (pp. 202–228). New York: Anchor Books.

Lévi-Strauss, C. (1969). *The raw and the cooked.* New York: Harper and Row.

Lévi-Strauss, C. (1978). *Myth and meaning.* Toronto: University of Toronto Press.

Lord, A. B. (1964). *The singer of tales.* Cambridge, MA: Harvard University Press.

Louch, A. R. (1966). *Exploration and human action.* Berkeley: University of California Press.

Luria, A. R. (1976). *Cognitive development: Its cultural and social foundations.* Cambridge, MA: Harvard University Press.

Luria, A. R. (1979). *The making of mind.* Cambridge, MA: Harvard University Press.

Mace, C. A. (1935). *Incentives: Some experimental studies* (Report No. 72). London: Industrial Health Research Board.

MacIntyre, A. (1981). *After virtue.* Notre Dame, IN: University of Notre Dame Press.

MacKenzie, B. D. (1977). *Behaviorism and the limits of scientific method.* London: Routledge & Kegan Paul.

Malinowski, B. (1922). *Argonauts of the western Pacific.* London: Routledge & Kegan Paul.

Malinowski, B. (1954). *Magic, science and religion.* New York: Anchor.

Melton, R. F. (1978). Resolution of conflicting claims concerning the effects of behavioral objectives on student learning. *Review of Educational Research, 48,* 291–302.

Milburn, G. (1984). On discipline stripping: Difficulties in the application of humanistic metaphors to educational phenomena. *Canadian Journal of Education, 9*(4), 361–375.

Miller, J. (1978). *The body in question.* New York: Random House.

Morss, J. R. (1990). *The biologizing of childhood: Developmental psychology and the Darwinian myth.* Hove, East Sussex: Erlbaum.

Nagel, E. (1969). Philosophy of science and educational theory. *Studies in Philosophy and Education, 7,* 143–157.

National Council for the Social Studies. (1984). Essentials of the social studies. *Social Education, 52*(1), 9–12.

Neitzsche, F. (1949). *The use and abuse of history.* New York: Bobbs-Merrill. (Original work published 1874)

Oakeshott, M. (1962). *Rationalism in politics and other essays.* London: Methuen.

Oakeshott, M. (1967). Learning and teaching. In R. S. Peters (Ed.), *The concept of education* (pp. 156–176). London: Routledge & Kegan Paul.

Oakeshott, M. (1971). Education: The engagement and its frustration. *Proceedings of the Philosophy of Education Society of Great Britain, Vol. 5, No. 1* (pp. 43–76). Oxford: Blackwell.

Oakeshott, M. (1991). *The voice of liberal learning.* New Haven, CT: Yale University Press.

O'Connor, D. J. (1957). *An introduction to the philosophy of education.* London: Routledge & Kegan Paul.

O'Connor, D. J. (1972). The nature of educational theory. *Proceedings of the Philosophy of Education Society of Great Britain, Vol. 6 No. 1* (pp. 97–109). Oxford: Blackwell.

Olson, D., & Torrance, N. (Eds.). (1991). *Literacy and orality.* Cambridge: Cambridge University Press.

Olson, D. R. (1977). Oral and written language and the cognitive processes of children. *Journal of Communications, 17*(3), 10–26.

Olson, D. R. (1986). Learning to mean what you say: Towards a psychology of literacy. In S. de Castell, A. Luke, & K. Egan (Eds.), *Literacy, society and schooling* (pp. 145–158). New York: Cambridge University Press.

Olson, D. R. (1994). *The world on paper.* Cambridge: Cambridge University Press.

Ong, W. J. (1982). *Orality and literacy.* London: Methuen.

Ong, W. J. (1971). *Rhetoric, romance, and technology.* Ithaca: Cornell University Press.

Ong, W. J. (1977). *Interfaces of the world.* Ithaca: Cornell University Press.

Ong, W. J. (1986). Writing is a technology that transforms thought. In G. Baumann (Ed.), *The written word: Literacy in transition* (pp. 23–50). Oxford: Clarenden Press.

Opie, I., & Opie, P. (1959). *The lore and language of schoolchildren.* New York: Oxford University Press.

Opie, I., & Opie, P. (1969). *Children's games in street and playground.* New York: Oxford University Press.

Opie, I., & Opie, P. (1985). *The singing game.* New York: Oxford University Press.

Paley, V. G. (1981). *Wally's stories.* Cambridge, MA: Harvard University Press.

Paley, V. G. (1984). *Boys and girls: Superheroes in the doll corner.* Chicago: University of Chicago Press.

Paley, V. G. (1990). *The boy who would be a helicopter.* Cambridge, MA: Harvard University Press.

Parry, M. (1928). *L'Epithé tradionelle dans Homére.* Paris: Société Editrice les Belles Lettres.

Parry, M. (1971). *The making of Homeric verse: The collected papers of Milman Parry* (A. Parry, Ed.). Oxford: Clarendon Press.

Peabody, B. (1975). *The winged word.* Albany: State University of New York Press.

Peters, R. S. (1965). *Ethics and education.* London: Allen and Unwin.

Petrie, Hugh G. (1982). *The dilemma of learning and inquiry.* Chicago: University of Chicago Press.

Phillips, D. C., & Kelly, M. E. (1975). Hierarchical theories of development in education and Psychology. *Harvard Educational Review, 45*(3), 354.

Piaget, J., & Inhelder, B. (1956). *The child's conception of space.* London: Routledge & Kegan Paul.

Pitcher, E. G., & Prelinger, E. (1963). *Children tell stories: An analysis of fantasy.* New York: International Universities Press.

Plato. (1892). *The dialogues of Plato* (B. Jowett, Trans.). London: Macmillan.

Plato. *The republic of Plato* (F. M. Cornford, Ed.). (1941). New York: Oxford University Press.

Popham, W. J. (1973). *Criterion-referenced instruction.* Belmont, CA: Fearon.

Popham, W. J., & Baker, E. L. (1979). *Systematic instruction.* Englewood Cliffs, NJ: Prentice-Hall.

Postman, N. (1982). *The disappearance of childhood.* New York: Delacorte Press.

Postman, N., & Weingartner, C. (1969). *Teaching as a subversive activity.* New York: Delacorte Press.

Pratt, D. (1980). *Curriculum: Design and development.* New York: Harcourt Brace Jovanovich.

Pring, R. (1973). Objectives and innovation: The irrelevance of theory. *London Educational Review, 2*, 46–54.

Putnam, H. (1981). *Reason, truth and history.* New York: Cambridge University Press.

Ravitch, D. (1983). *The troubled crusade.* New York: Basic Books.

Ravitch, D. (1987). Tot sociology or what happened to history in the grade schools. *American Scholar, 56*, 343–353.

Ravitch, D., & Finn, C. E. (1987). *What do our 17-year-olds know?* New York: Harper and Row.

Rorty, R. (1979). *Philosophy and the mirror of nature.* Princeton: Princeton University Press.

Roszak, T. (1969). *The making of a counter-culture.* New York: Doubleday.

Rousseau, J. J. (1911). *Émile* (B. Foxley, Trans.). London: Dent. (Original work published 1762)

Rumelhart, D. E. (1975). Notes on a schema for stories. In D. G. Bobrow & A. M. Collins (Eds.), *Representation and understanding* (pp. 211–236). New York: Academic Press.

Scribner, S., & Cole, M. (1981). *The psychology of literacy.* Cambridge: Cambridge University Press.

Searle, J. (1984). *Minds, brains and science.* Cambridge, MA: Harvard University Press.

Siegler, R. S. (1991). *Children's thinking* (2nd ed.). Englewood Cliffs, NJ: Prentice-Hall.

Simon, B. (1978). *Mind and madness in ancient Greece: The classical roots of modern psychiatry.* Ithaca: Cornell University Press.

Smedslund, J. (1976). *A re-examination of the role of theory in psychology.* Paper presented at the 21st International Congress of Psychology.

Smedslund, J. (1978a). Bandura's theory of self-efficacy: A set of common-sense theorems. *Scandinavian Journal of Psychology, 20.*

Smedslund, J. (1978b). Some psychological theories are not empirical: Reply to Bandura. *Scandinavian Journal of Psychology, 19.*

Smedslund, J. (1979). Between the analytic and the arbitrary: A case study of psychological research. *Scandinavian Journal of Psychology, 20.*

Snow, R. (1977). Individual differences and instructional theory. *Educational Researcher, 6,* 10.

Spence, J. E. (1984). *The memory palace of Matteo Ricci.* New York: Viking Penguin.

Spencer, H. (1861). *Education: Intellectual, moral and physical.* London: G. Manwaring.

Spencer, H. (1969). *Herbert Spencer* (A. Low-Beer, Ed.). London: Collier-Macmillan.

Steers, R. M., & Porter, L. W. (1974). The role of task-goal attributes in employee performance. *Psychological Bulletin, 81,* 434–452.

Stenhouse, L. (1970). The humanities curriculum project. *Journal of Curriculum Studies, 1,* 26–33.

Stenhouse, L. (1975). *An introduction to curriculum research and development.* London: Heinemann.

Street, B. (1984). *Literacy in theory and practice.* Cambridge: Cambridge University Press.

Sunal, C. S. (1990). *Early childhood social studies.* Columbus, OH: Merrill.

Sutton-Smith, B. (1981). *The folk stories of children.* Philadelphia: University of Pennsylvania Press.

Sutton-Smith, B. (1988). In search of the imagination. In K. Egan & D. Nadaner (Eds.), *Imagination and education* (pp. 3–29). New York: Teachers College Press.

Tanner, D., & Tanner, L. N. (1980). *Curriculum development: Theory into practice.* New York: Macmillan.

Taylor, C. (1982). Rationality. In M. Hollis & S. Lukes (Eds.), *Rationality and relativism* (pp. 87–105). Cambridge, MA: MIT Press.

Todorov, T. (1982). *Theories of the symbol* (C. Porter, Trans.). Ithaca: Cornell University Press.

Turner, F. M. (1981). *The Greek heritage in Victorian Britain.* New Haven: Yale University Press.

Tyler, R. W. (1949). *Basic principles of curriculum and instruction.* Chicago: University of Chicago Press.

Vernant, J. (1983). *Myth and thought among the Greeks.* London: Routledge & Kegan Paul.

Vico, G. (1970). *The new science* (T. G. Bergin & M. H. Fisch, Trans.). Ithaca: Cornell University Press. (Original work published 1744)

Van Groningen, B. A. (1953). *In the grip of the past.* Leiden, The Netherlands: E. J. Brill.

Vygotsky, L. (1978). *Mind in society: The development of higher psychological processes* (M. Cole et al., Eds.). Cambridge, MA: Harvard University Press.

Walker, D. F. (1975). Straining to lift ourselves. *Curriculum Theory Network, 5*(1).

Warner, J. H. (1940). The basis of J.-J. Rousseau's contemporaneous reputation in England. *Modern Language Notes, 55,* 270–280.

Warnock, M. (1976). *Imagination.* London: Faber.

Wells, Gordon. (1987). *The meaning makers.* London: Hodder and Staughton.

Wertsch, J. V. (1985). *Vygotsky and the social formation of mind.* Cambridge, MA: Harvard University Press.

White, A. R. (1990). The language of imagination. Oxford: Blackwell.

Whitehead, A. N. (1929). *The aims of education.* London: Macmillan.

Wilson, B. R. (1970). *Rationality.* Oxford: Blackwell.

Winner, E. (1988). *The point of words: Children's understanding of metaphor and irony.* Cambridge, MA: Harvard University Press.

Wittgenstein, L. (1963). *Philosophical investigations* (G. E. M. Anscombe, Trans.). Oxford: Blackwell.

Wolf, F. A. (1884). *Prolegomena ad Homerum.* Berlin: Halle. (Original work published 1795)

Wood, M. (1985). *In search of the Trojan War.* London: BBC.

Young, M. (1971). *Knowledge and control: New directions for the sociology of education.* London: Collier-Macmillan.

Young, M. (1977). Curriculum change: Limits and possibilities. In M. Young & G. Whitty (Eds.), *Society, state, and schooling* (pp. 236–252). Lewes, Sussex: The Falmer Press.

Index

About the Author

Kieran Egan was born in Ireland in 1942. He was brought up and educated in England. He read History (Hons.) at the University of London, graduating with a B.A. in 1966. He worked for a year as a Research fellow at the Institute for Comparative Studies in Kingston-upon-Thames and then moved to the U.S.A. to begin a Ph.D. in Philosophy of Education at Stanford University. He worked concurrently as a consultant to the I.B.M. Corp. on adaptation of a programming method, called Structural Communication, to new computing systems. He completed his Ph.D. at Cornell University in 1972. His first job was at Simon Fraser University in British Columbia, where he has remained ever since. He is the author of a dozen or so books, and editor or co-editor of a few more. He is author of around one hundred articles. In 1991 he received the Grawemeyer Award in Education. In 1993 he was elected as the first person in Education to the Royal Society of Canada. Various of his books have been translated into more than half a dozen European and Asian languages. His most recent book is *The Educated Mind: How cognitive tools shape our understanding* (Chicago: University of Chicago Press).